Jack Bush

Jack Bush

Contributing Editor Karen Wilkin

Hudson Hills Press
New York

We wish to acknowledge the special role and assistance of Aaron Milrad in the publication of this book.

First American Edition

© Text: 'Introduction,' David P. Silcox; 'Jack Bush,' Clement Greenberg; 'Jack Bush: The Development of a Canadian Painter,' Dennis Reid; 'Breakthrough: Jack Bush and Painters Eleven,' Barrie Hale; 'Jack Bush in Retrospect,' Kenworth W. Moffett; 'A Dealer's Memoir,' David Mirvish; 'Jack Bush in the 1970s,' Charles W. Millard; 'The Red Barn: The Search for a Formal Language,' Duncan Macmillan; 'Triumph over Adversity,' Ken Carpenter; 'Where did the time go?' Phyllis Tuchman; 'The Legacy,' Terry Fenton; 'Jack Bush and European Modernism,' John Elderfield; 'Jack Bush: His Imagery,' Karen Wilkin

© Illustrations: Estate of Jack Bush, 1984

Published in Canada by McClelland and Stewart in association with Merritt Editions Limited.

Published in the United States by Hudson Hills Press, Inc., Suite 301, 220 Fifth Avenue, New York, NY 10001.
Editor and Publisher: Paul Anbinder

Distributed in the United States by Viking Penguin Inc.

Cataloguing in Publication Data
Main entry under title:
Jack Bush

Includes index.

I. Bush, Jack, 1909-77 2. Painters– Canada– Biography.
I. Bush, Jack, 1909–   II. Wilkin, Karen.

ND249.B8J32 1984   759.11

Library of Congress Catalogue Card Number 84-81368
ISBN 0-933920-12-1
Manufactured in Hong Kong

In Memory of Jack Bush

Contents

Preface

THIS BOOK WOULD NOT EXIST WITHOUT THE CO-OPERA-tion and support of many people. I would like to thank all of the contributors for their enthusiastic response to the original proposal, and am deeply indebted to the Trustees of the Jack Bush Estate and to Mabel Bush for their invaluable support. In addition, I would like to acknowledge the generosity of Jennifer Cosgriff, Lois and Georges de Menil, Susan and Marcel Elefant, Nahum Gelber, Clement Greenberg, Graham Gund, Goldie and Harold Konopny, William Lakey, Lavalin Inc., Ruth Mitchell, A.J. Pyrch, Steinberg's Inc., Doug Udell, Elizabeth and Bogislav von Wentzel, and Westburne Industrial Enterprises.

I am grateful, too, to David Mirvish, André Emmerich Gallery, New York, Waddington Galleries, London, and Waddington and Shiell Galleries, Toronto, for making photographs available. The assistance of the Art Gallery of Ontario is appreciated and I am personally obliged to the Canada Council and to Trent University for assistance with the research phase of this publication.

Clement Greenberg's essay, 'Jack Bush,' appeared first in the catalogue of an exhibition at Robert Elkon Gallery, New York, in 1980. Barrie Hale's essay, 'Jack Bush and Painters Eleven,' is adapted from a work-in-progress, *Out of the Park: Modernist Painting in Toronto, 1950-1980*, and is reprinted with the author's permission.

NOTE: Colour illustrations are in strict chronological order, but the positioning of black and white illustrations has been more flexible. They have frequently been inserted with relation to textual references.

K.W.

Introduction

DAVID P. SILCOX

GOOD ART IS DURABLE. THOSE WHO HAVE CONTRIBUTED to this book would agree that Jack Bush's paintings surely will endure. Yet Jack Bush as a man is equally worthy of celebration and, now that death has completed his life, we can begin to describe this particularly attractive and honourable person. Bush was so widely admired that sometimes I wonder how many of his friends might wish to exchange his works for his presence if they could. I think that I might, and the references to Bush's special personality in the diverse essays that follow make me think that others might too.

Bush seemed, when you met him, like someone you had always known and liked. I met him first at his Park Gallery exhibition in 1959 while I was working at Hart House at the University of Toronto. Over the next few years we met sporadically, generally in company with Ken Lochhead, Robert Murray, Anthony Caro, or at the David Mirvish Gallery. In 1968 I got to know Bush well when I invited him to be a jury member for the Canada Council. For nearly a month we worked, travelled, and ate together as we crossed the country to see and to assess the work of young artists. After that we met more often to talk and to look at paintings. And I accepted when he asked me to help care for his paintings after he died.

As we set off on our Council trip, Bush told me, with a mixture of pride, anxiety, and relief, that I had invited him at the moment he had lost courage and thrown away his crumpled letter of resignation from the commercial art house he was working for. After we spoke, he retrieved the letter, smoothed it out, and sent it off. Whether this anecdote was strictly true or not, Bush gave me credit for weaning him from what had become, by that time in his life, onerous work.

I suspect that Bush was going to devote himself full-time to painting anyway, but he always spread credit around liberally. Clement Greenberg, with whom I serve as a trustee, also says Bush gave him more credit than was properly his due. Bush was generous in his acknowledgment of artists, young or old, living or dead, whom he admired, and was eager for their recognition. He wanted more attention to be paid to Maxwell Bates (1906-1980) whom we visited on the Council trip, and in his characteristic expression, using baseball similes and metaphors, he thought of David Milne (1882-1953) as 'a major leaguer, one of the home-run hitters.'

Perhaps this generosity was his subtle way of recruiting supporters, but I believe it was simply his generous nature and his innocent goodwill. Bush saw himself as an instrument of forces or impulses over which he had no control – a fate, in the guise of friends, artists, critics, dealers, or whomever, was forever pushing him and his work into the right place at the right time. Bush made me believe our trip was a turning point, but in any case the next ten, and last, years of Bush's life were to be the best of his painting years.

As an assessor of young talent, Bush was both a champion and a disappointment. I had expected him to deal incisively and efficiently with the supplicants, but by asking questions instead of pronouncing verdicts, he turned decisions back to his two colleagues, the Montreal painter Marcel Barbeau and the Vancouver curator Doris Shadbolt. When they decided or haggled to a compromise, Bush would simply agree, in nearly all cases. He seemed to shy away from making judgments and to find it difficult, if not impossible, to say no. Often he excused himself by saying that he was 'only on the making end' of art and had no responsibilities or capability for the administrative aspects of it. His pronouncements, when they did come, were ambiguous, summary, and trite: 'Boy!' 'Okay by me,' 'Swell!' 'Looks good!' or 'Sounds good to me.'

ABOVE Bush's studio at 1 Eastview Crescent, January 1977

Despite his genuine reluctance to decide someone else's future, Bush had a hovering, avuncular concern that never allowed matters to wander too far off course. During visits to studios you could count on Bush to talk to the artist intimately, confidentially, and, I supposed, inspiringly. While he never spoke against any applicant, those for whom he sensed an affinity he argued for persuasively and was insistent without being dogmatic. His taste and interest ranged much farther than I had anticipated and he rounded up distant strays like a superb sheep-dog. In terms of talent, Bush was ready to take the long shot, the highest risk. He seemed to know which oysters had the little piece of grit that might become a pearl.

Without tangling himself in the bureaucratic sorting, Bush turned the trip into an artistic and patriotic mission. He cared about the condition of art in Canada, and he seemed to make young artists his special concern. He saw himself as a useful model or example for them. Having emerged on the far side of hardship and a lifetime of searching, he knew, I think, the value to a burgeoning artist of someone who had travelled the path already. Perhaps he remembered what he had found helpful, and sensed too that tradition is passed from person to person as much as from painting to painting. He embodied the image of someone who had kept an eye steadily on his aesthetic goals all his life, despite the difficulty of making a living, and had remained lively, engaged, optimistic, and hard-working throughout. Bush thought the future of art in Canada had been, was, and would be in good hands. The night he received the Order of Canada, the country's highest recognition, was one of the proudest of Bush's life.

By the end of our journey together, Bush had revealed himself to me as a man of unexpected contradictions. The foremost of these complexities was something I had not run into before: an artist of major accomplishments who seemed not to have much capacity for intellectual discourse. Frankly, I had no idea what to make of this then. Some artists reveal their knowledge in academic terms, in their familiarity with art history; some in scientific or philosophical curiosity; others in various forms of activity not necessarily related to their art. Somehow they demonstrate a certain mental agility and capacity. But Bush was, rather, like a drummer who simply had a perfect sense of rhythm or a singer with perfect pitch. His gifts as an artist seemed separate within him. Although Bush was not ignorant, he sometimes gave the impression of being so and he had a disarming way of confessing or admitting his limitations, though he did so without embarrassment. Perhaps he expected the rest of the world to view him as he viewed it: with a benevolence verging on the indiscriminate. Anyone who knew him well could confirm that his

dictum of saying nothing unless he could say something good was seldom breached. Bush could be irritatingly optimistic.

Besides his art, Bush did have an area where his real mental depth and range were evident and that was music, primarily jazz. In music too, I realized later, his knowledge was not only extensive but his receptiveness was unusually sensitive. He was an accomplished jazz pianist. In music, as in his art, Bush claimed that his comprehension was entirely intuitive. The details of his knowledge and passion could only occasionally be glimpsed through the scrim of generalities he normally held up. For me, it helps to think of Bush's art in terms of analogies to music. One strange thing Bush told me was that sometimes he would play jazz records while he fiddled with colour patterns or combinations on his television set. He had bought a colour television as soon as they were available and positively exulted in the acidic pastels he could summon from his dials. Like Scriabin or Baudelaire, Bush had some compulsion to associate colours and sounds.

Bush's personality only fuelled speculations about the contradictions he embodied. He was the consummate gentleman, nattily dressed, hair never out of place, a sort of matinée-idol look about him, smiling, pleasant, gregarious. Like a chameleon, he easily took on the colouration of those around him, never giving offense, yet never being anyone other than himself. His paintings, however, often did give offense. They could be jolting, crude, or jarring and as different from the man as one could imagine. As Clement Greenberg points out, they had an awkward and uneasy quality, and it was generally this attribute that Bush particularly liked. Bush's easy-going, tolerant, innocent, and self-effacing manner was remarked upon by all his associates, sometimes as a disparaging observation of his failure to adopt a bohemian style or an egocentric stance appropriate to a painter. Appearances to the contrary, however, Bush was an energetic, stubborn, shrewd, and ambitious man. Behind the proper, smiling, tradition-loving artist crouched a fairly radical artist whose originality was irrepressible. The greater the artist, according to George Bernard Shaw, the greater the contradictions.

In retrospect, Bush's sympathy for young artists gives rise to another contradiction: Bush probably had a wider and deeper influence on the generation of painters now in their thirties than any other Canadian artist, an impact similar to that of Paul-Emile Borduas in Quebec in the 1940s. Yet not one of the painters who acknowledges his influence paints like Bush or looks like a little Bush. Bush's influence, as Terry Fenton's essay makes clear, was one of inspiration, purpose, and determination.

Bush's life was a stereotype, in many respects, of the

suburban man. He had a steady job, raised an average-sized family, went to church regularly, lived in a suburban home with the usual suburban furnishings and interests: holidays in the lake district, occasional trips to Europe, and the routine of shopping, chores, visits to friends. The exception was that for most of his life Bush was a Sunday painter. Sequestered away in his house, in a small room about ten by twelve feet, Bush lived another life as an important painter. Paintings were rolled for storage, and displayed by unrolling them on the living-room floor. Some paintings received their horizontal and vertical arrows there, indicating they looked fine from either the kitchen side or the hall side. In later years the amenities of the Mirvish Gallery or the ample space of Bush's studio gave infinitely better conditions for viewing, but somehow the crowded, partial view afforded in his living-room had more magic and excitement for me.

These fundamental contradictions shine out through the essays which constitute this book. Clement Greenberg draws attention to Bush's courtly demeanour and the persistent awkwardness which his paintings had on first viewing, an aspect of his work which seems less obvious today. Greenberg also observes that Bush's work, like David Smith's, keeps getting better with familiarity and time. Duncan Macmillan's essay, 'The Red Barn,' carefully documents Bush's evolution from representation to abstraction. Karen Wilkin shows how constant and consistent Bush's imagery remained throughout his entire career. John Elderfield explores Bush's relation to European painting, a profound and crucial matter on which Bush himself could be frustratingly vague. Bush's first visit to Europe was in 1962 and he remained a quintessential 'North American' painter but, as Elderfield points out, the 'primal conventions' of Bush's work were established in his study of Matisse, Monet, Klee, Miró, and other Europeans. Certainly one can recognize in Bush the strong sense of descent, of being part of, of handing on and extending the great and noble heritage that encompasses both the twentieth century's European masters and the Canadian tradition which he also served loyally. Kenworth Moffett's essay on Bush's later years touches on some of these matters from a different perspective.

Barrie Hale and Dennis Reid deal with two different aspects of Bush's professional career as a painter in Canada. There has been a tendency to look only at Bush's work of 1959 and after, yet any comprehensive view of either the man or the artist has to include these early years. That they shaped his attitudes, techniques, and ultimate ambitions is certain. Hale points out that Bush was a vigorous force well before Painters Eleven was formed in 1954, although how much Bush received from and gave to his colleagues in that group is still a provocative topic. Reid traces Bush from his education, through the formative early years as a commercial artist, to the post-Second World War period, and points out the various and likely influences Bush was subject to from the Group of Seven, the Canadian Group of Painters, and individual artists such as Charles Comfort, Lawren Harris, and Jock Macdonald.

Jack Bush the man emerges clearly and vividly in the essays and reminiscences about him. Terry Fenton deals with Bush's influence on younger artists and notes the difficulty in separating Bush's art from his personality. Yet there is no doubt that what Bush did as a painter was felt by artists in Canada, the United States, and England as well as in other European countries. The personal recollections of David Mirvish, Bush's Canadian dealer for eleven years, and those of his friends and colleagues – William Winter, a painter and Bush's partner in commercial art for many years, K.M. (Kate) Graham, Robert Murray, Allan Walters, Walter Moos, Aaron Milrad, Robert Elkon, and Martha Baer – are fascinating portraits of a man who obviously left a lasting impression. Everyone who knew Jack Bush emphasizes his easy, kindly disposition towards others.

Yet Bush had his difficulties too. He was a heavy smoker and a heavy drinker most of his life. It would be dishonest to say that his drinking had no effect on his mind when it was obvious to those close to him that, toward the end of his life at least, it did. The clerks at the liquor store on Avenue Road near his home all knew him by name and he knew theirs. With my Presbyterian background I had contempt for what seemed to me to be lack of will and I once made the mistake of interfering with Bush's decision to have a martini after a week or more on the wagon. We were at his watering-hole near his studio when he told me, politely but firmly, that the problem he had was certainly serious, but that it was his problem, not mine. And there were times in Bush's life when his optimism and his nonchalance were severely challenged. Ken Carpenter draws our attention to paintings of the later 40s and early 50s which show Bush wrestling with profound anxieties and disturbances.

With so many varied perspectives and remembrances of a life itself so varied, this book will serve as a useful and lasting introduction to Jack Bush and his work. The *catalogue raisonné* which Karen Wilkin is now embarked upon will eventually provide detailed notations on Bush's work over his nearly fifty active years. Inspired by what is offered here, perhaps someone will undertake a full biography and delve more thoroughly into Bush's childhood years, into other aspects of his career, and into his relations with such artists as Kenneth Noland, Kenneth Lochhead, Jules Olitski, Frank Stella, Lawrence Poons, Michael Steiner, and Anthony Caro.

If I wanted to find a metaphor for Bush as I think of him now I might use one of his own last paintings, *Mood Indigo*. When I submerge myself in its sonorous perfection, I am led to ask whether, had he lived longer, Bush could have excelled or equalled his last great phase of painting. It is, of course, a moot question. But Charles Millard, in his essay on Bush's late work, draws the picture many of us have of Bush, maturing late and increasing steadily in assurance, richness, and simplicity until it seemed he had almost no place left to turn. In Millard's words, the 'extraordinary grace' of the last works reminds him of Olitski or of Miró with their complexity and simpleness, their sense of purpose yet accidental quality, their quiet sophistication yet ordinary lack of pretension, and their careful structure yet effortless appearance. The fullness of the painting and the fullness of the man seemed to coalesce in the short time before his death, a wonderful legacy for him to leave for us all.

DAVID P. SILCOX is assistant deputy minister, Department of Communications, Canada. He is the co-author of a critical study of the painter Tom Thomson, *The Silence and the Storm*.

Jack Bush

CLEMENT GREENBERG

BUSH DIDN'T HAVE THE *PANACHE* OF AN ARTIST. THIS could deceive people, which was highly ironical, for if there was ever an artist who put the whole of himself into his art it was Jack Bush. Not all superior artists reflect the superiority of their art in their persons or characters. Bush did. He was a complete, an integral gentleman, with the gentleness of a gentleman. And also the cheerfulness that goes, as I think, with gentleness. I see all this in his art, and a lot more: his honesty and diffidence, and, yes, his fearlessness.

He wasn't afraid to look awkward, in any context, if he felt he had to. It belonged to Bush's character to suppress his accomplishedness. As Terry Fenton has seen, he would let his drawing come out seeming more than subtly clumsy – sometimes in the interests of colour, sometimes not. An English painter-critic, seeing his first Bushes, could say that he was amateurish. More than a few people not unendowed with taste have had trouble with his pictures because they didn't seem to 'sit' right. Yet Bush could draw, and 'place,' and design, like an angel. I'll grant that he could overdo this apparent awkwardness. He could be puckish, almost perverse, with it. There was also his playfulness. He put into his pictures such things as travel souvenirs, flags, road signs, emblems, knowing well enough that they weren't supposed to belong in canonically abstract art. As Terry Fenton, again, has seen, he took the risk of looking eccentric. He didn't give a damn.

Bush reminded me once of a generalization I'd made about how facility and accomplishedness could trap an artist. As if that had influenced him. Well, he liked to exaggerate my role with respect to his art, out of sheer generosity. But his blithe rejection of facility, of smoothness, of anything at his easy command, was altogether of his own doing. His affinity for anything he sensed as

challenging was native. Without making a point of it, he was a highly ambitious artist. At bottom he was phenomenally sure of himself; that was why he could afford to be diffident, in approaching art as in approaching people.

Why did he mature so late? I don't know the whole answer. There was the place and the time. There were the circumstances. To the end he led a very responsible and respectable life. He had maybe to outgrow self-abnegation. Somehow, with his hopeful, optimistic nature, he must have known that his time would come and that he could afford to wait. This would have belonged to his deep self-confidence.

That apparent awkwardness of his made Bush one of the most eye-testing artists of our time, along with Hans Hofmann, Adolph Gottlieb, and David Smith. All four were, and still are, touchstones: if you can't see how good the first three are you can't really see abstract painting well enough; if you can't see how good Smith is you can't see abstract sculpture well enough. As it seems to me, neither Hofmann nor Gottlieb was as unworried as Bush was by the obstacles to appreciation their art presented. (This isn't to make a value comparison.)

It wasn't always the look of awkwardness that unsettled – or over-settled – a Bush painting. As in both Gottlieb's and Hofmann's cases, it was just as often an old-fashioned concern for the filling in and balancing out of the rectangle. (What amounts to negative evidence of this is the absolute success of the few Bushes done in triangular format.) That concern belonged to a generation of painters freshly schooled by Cubism. That schooling haunted all three (and still haunts younger painters like Lichtenstein, Rauschenberg, and Held; Smith, in leaving painting for sculpture, exorcized as it were the anxieties left by his Cubist schooling). And yet this concern for the rectangle, while it could make for a kind of lumpiness and awkward-looking constriction, could also endow a picture with a certain weight, a full-bodied presence that re-deemed everything else. It made colour more *there*, and it was colour that in the upshot made all three of these great painters.

Colour. Bush's lust for colour was, when he first went into abstraction, checked by the example of New York Abstract Expressionism. Only after the mid 50s, when he

YELLOW ON BLUE acrylic on canvas, October 1971
78½" x 32½" (199.4 x 81.9 cm)
Jack Bush Heritage Corporation Inc.

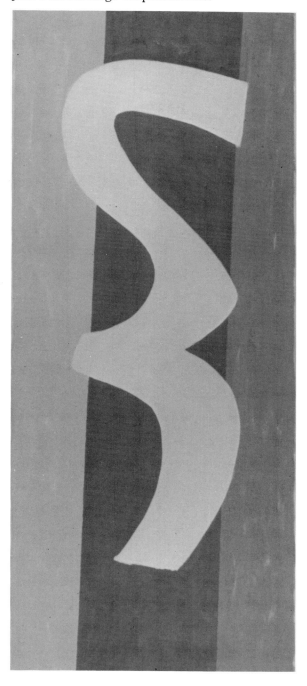

began referring to his own watercolours, did he start to indulge that lust, at first only discreetly, but in what were already wonderful pictures. He learned from Louis and especially Noland about the possibilities of a ground of cotton canvas left unprimed and unsized. After a while he exhausted these possibilities for himself, and went on. With Noland, like him and not like him, he became a supreme colourist. When it comes to putting one colour next to another, Noland and Bush are alone in this time, and maybe in any other. The juxtaposition of colours is different from the suffusion, the blending and flooding of them. I'm talking here about distinct, discrete hues in their adjacency. Not that one way is inherently better than the other, not at all. Only that the latter way is rarer, at least in Western art.

Bush was a master of saturated colour too, and of warm colour. Again, neither saturation nor warmth of colour is intrinsically better than unsaturation or coolness of colour. It's Bush's particular personal prowess that showed a master of saturation and warmth. (Here too Noland – whose influence Bush acknowledged – is the only one who competes.) As we get further and further away from the time at which the pictures were made, colour takes over more and more in the experiencing of Bush's art, trans-cending the awkwardness of drawing and layout, making it more and more beside the point. I can't think of any recent art in which I've witnessed quite such fruitful aging. Monet's 'Lily Pad' murals are the nearest precedent I can think of in my own experience. David Smith's sculpture is the only contemporary parallel.

Of so many Bushes, as of so many Smiths, it can be said that they never again look as bad – if they did look bad – as on first sight. They keep getting better and better, and looking newer too. Re-acquaintance with more than a few Bush pictures, as with more than a few Smith sculptures, makes me wonder about the failures of eye that let me find fault on the first acquaintance. This speaks for originality, and also for what I have to say is character.

Bush, like Smith, happened to be at the top of his powers when he died. His art was getting still stronger, as the very last paintings show. He was also getting happier (which I can't say Smith was). This has nothing to do, necessarily, with art, but ever so much with Bush, the man. All in all (as with Pollock) I prized the man more than the art. Which doesn't in the least imply a value judgment of the art.

CLEMENT GREENBERG is one of the most distinguished critics of twentieth-century art. *Art and Culture* is the best known of his many publications.

Jack Bush: The Development of a Canadian Painter

DENNIS REID

IT IS A MATTER OF RECORD IN THE EXHIBITION CATA-logues that Jack Bush's career as a painter grew slowly but steadily from the mid 30s until early in 1948, when he suddenly stopped exhibiting. About two years later he began to show again with various official Canadian artists' associations, and was soon displaying his work with the frequency he had attained in 1947. Bush kept up this steady pace with each of the organizations through to the early 60s, then in 1964 he abruptly resigned from them all. By then he had established commercial relations with dealers in New York and London as well as Toronto. Increasing sales from his now regular one-man shows finally in 1968 gave him the security he felt he needed to put aside the commercial illustration and advertising design business with which he had earned his living since graduating from high school in Montreal some forty-two years before.

Bush, the third of four children, was born in 'the Beaches' area of east-end Toronto on 20 March 1909. His family moved to London, Ontario, in 1911, for six years, then to Montreal, where Bush received the bulk of his education and where he grew up. William Charles Bush, his father, was manager of the Montreal branch of one of Toronto's largest commercial printing and design firms, Rapid Grip Co, later known as Rapid, Grip & Batten, and when Jack graduated from Westhill High School in 1926 he was put to work as an apprentice in his father's office. Though this might reflect a sense of family tradition, it represented as well the general furtherance of his education. At the same time, in fact, Jack enrolled in regular evening classes with the Scottish portrait painter and muralist, Adam Sherriff Scott (1887-1980). The following

school year (1927-8) Bush switched to the evening classes sponsored in Montreal by the Royal Canadian Academy of Arts. These classes were concerned chiefly with drawing from the figure and were conducted by the French-born and Italian-trained academic portraitist, teacher, and painting-restorer, Edmond Dyonnet (1859-1964), the secretary of the RCA, who, even in the late 20s, was widely known as a man of conservative opinions, violently opposed to modern trends in art. Bush doubtless received a sound training in technical matters during these early days in Montreal, but there was little in the experience to stimulate his imagination about art. The few paintings and drawings that have survived from the period bear out this judgment.

Bush returned to Toronto and a better-paying job at the head office of Rapid, Grip & Batten in 1929. Again he enrolled in evening classes. Toronto had a long tradition of sketching clubs for commercial artists, informal organizations for evenings of drawing from the model and for field-sketching excursions on the weekends. By the end of the 20s the evening classes at the Ontario College of Art had filled this role, and it was there that Bush enrolled. He later described it as, in part, a social activity shared with a number of young commercial artists, 'three or four nights a week, drawing from the figure, with two reasons in mind: one, to improve my ability as an illustrator and designer, and the other, for the sake of drawing and painting itself.'[1] He kept this routine for more than ten years, and the ambience of the Ontario College of Art defined his interests as an artist throughout the 30s.

When Bush arrived in Toronto, the Group of Seven – which had held its first exhibition in 1920 – dominated the artistic life of the city. All of the seven but Varley lived in Toronto. J.E.H. MacDonald had just been appointed principal of OCA (in November 1929), and Arthur Lismer had just left the college, after ten years teaching there, to

ABOVE Bush with *Village Procession*, March 1946, on receiving the Rolph, Clarke, Stone purchase award, 74th Spring Exhibition of the Ontario Society of Artists, Art Gallery of Ontario

TEXT CONTINUED ON PAGE 13

CHILDREN PLAYING oil on canvas board, 1934
8¾" x 10⅞" (22.1 x 27.6 cm)
Art Gallery of Ontario, purchase with assistance from Wintario, 1979
Toronto, Ontario

VILLAGE PROCESSION oil on masonite, 1946
24" x 30⅛" (61 x 76.5 cm)
Art Gallery of Ontario, gift from the Georgia Weldon Estate, 1965
Toronto, Ontario

ROAD TO ORILLIA watercolour, 1949
16¾" x 22¾" (42.6 x 57.8 cm)
Alcan Smelters and Chemicals Ltd
Montreal, Quebec

RED SKY, WHITE SUNS watercolour, 1952
13¾" x 17⅞" (35.0 x 44.7 cm)
Jack Bush Heritage Corporation Inc.

head up the education program at the Art Gallery of Toronto. The more-or-less annual exhibitions of the Group were still being held at the Gallery, and Bush would have seen two of them, in April 1930 and December 1931. Although the Group began to break up following MacDonald's death in November 1932 and Harris' departure for the United States two years later, the 'National School' marked Bush's early years in Toronto. 'The Group of Seven, of course, were the top boys,' he recalled many years later. 'I still can't get over the habit that we got into, which was to go out into the field to make sketches Saturday and Sunday, with a little pad, just like A.Y. Jackson, with a little painting kit and all the rest of it. We would also go on two trips a year, one in the spring and one in the fall, to the North country, Haliburton or Belfountain or some such place and come home with a batch of twenty sketches that we had painted up there.'[2]

There is no evidence that Bush had direct contact with any of the Group in the early years of the Depression. His principal instructors at OCA were Frederick S. Challener (1869-1959) – an Englishman largely London-raised, although settled in Toronto by 1883, who had a considerable reputation as a muralist and portrait painter, but who would have reinforced the lessons Bush received earlier in Montreal from Scott and Dyonnet – and a younger man, John Alfsen (1902-1971). Alfsen, a portraitist, was born in Long Rapids, Michigan, but had lived in Toronto from the age of thirteen. He began teaching life drawing and painting at OCA in 1929, following a stint at the Art Students League in New York and travel and studies in France, Belgium, and Italy. Alfsen was not an innovative artist, but with him Bush had for the first time a teacher who might stretch his thinking about painting. As the 30s progressed, there is some evidence in his oil sketches and small canvases that Bush was working to extract more force from his colour while at the same time defining form with greater clarity. We see this particularly in the 1933 *Mabel in a Blue Polka Dot Dress* (page 13), a portrait of Mabel Mills Teakle of Montreal, a childhood friend Bush was then courting. They were married the following September.

Despite Bush's lack of contact with members of the Group of Seven, their presence was felt in Toronto, and numerous landscape sketches from 1929 through the mid 30s attest to the grip that the Group held on his imagination during his early twenties. *York Downs, Toronto* of 1929 is typical, composed as it is of roughly blocked-in colour areas, with the broad brushwork describing only major forms. It is tied to the work of Jackson, Lawren Harris, and MacDonald, in particular, in that it displays the saturated colour often used by those painters during the 20s and avoids anecdotal detail, pursuing the dominant mood of the place that is its subject. *Children Playing* (page 9) of 1934 reveals how even in his urban scenes Bush turned to the Group, in this case Harris and his sketches of some ten years before done in 'The Ward,' a region of older modest houses in the neighbourhood of OCA and the Art Gallery of Toronto.

Throughout his early twenties in Depression-era Toronto, Bush's studies at OCA never amounted to more than a few hours a week, and his field sketching consisted of only a week or two a year. His days were taken up entirely with his work at Rapid, Grip & Batten, and although some of the Group of Seven had been employed there before the First World War, by the 30s their influence within that firm and on commercial art generally in Canada was already a matter of history. A number of younger artists were making their reputation in the commercial studios of the city by then, and it was to them that Bush turned for direction and inspiration. One of the most prominent of this younger generation was Charles Comfort.

MABEL IN A BLUE POLKA DOT DRESS oil on canvas, 1933
27⅛" x 20" (68.9 x 50.8 cm)
Jack Bush Heritage Corporation Inc.

Comfort was born near Edinburgh, Scotland, in 1900, but was brought to Canada at the age of twelve and settled in Winnipeg. He began work in a commercial art studio as an apprentice the following year, and during the evenings studied art as best he could in Winnipeg. He managed a year off to attend the Art Students League in New York, 1922-3, and two years later moved to Toronto. In 1929, the year Bush returned to Toronto, Comfort also was hired by Rapid, Grip. He stayed on for two years before setting up a small, independent design studio with two friends. Then in 1935 Comfort became director of mural painting at OCA, where Bush enjoyed the benefit of his teaching in some of the evening classes.

Comfort exhibited widely, was a respected portraitist, and was commissioned to develop the decorative figurative murals for the new Toronto Stock Exchange in 1936-7, marking him as one of the more promising younger Canadian artists of the day. That he was among the most sought-after of Canadian illustrators and commercial designers during the 30s would only have added to his stature in Bush's eyes. The painting *Mabel in a Blue Polka Dot Dress* in fact owes something of its directness, and certainly its fresh, clear, and broadly applied colour, to such well-known Comfort watercolour portraits as the *Young Canadian* (a portrait of the painter Carl Schaefer done in 1932) or his huge *Portrait of Professor Felix Walter* (1933).[3] Even Bush's landscape oil sketches of the mid to late 30s, with their broad, simple forms, their bright, clean colour, and their decorative compositional designs, are closer to Comfort's landscapes than the Group of Seven precedents they both ultimately depend upon. Indeed, it is not too much to say that Charles Comfort was the major influence on the development of Bush's art during the 30s. Although there were numerous painters working at design, and designers who also worked at painting, Comfort was the exemplary model of the type, and in that respect he can be described as the principal influence in Bush's career decisions as well.

Bush slipped slowly into the expected Toronto pattern. He exhibited first with the Ontario Society of Artists in March 1936, and with the Royal Canadian Academy in November. (He had first exhibited with the RCA in 1930 – a work entitled *La vieille maison* – but not since.) The following year he exhibited with the Canadian Society of Painters in Water Colour, although nowhere else. In 1938 he had works accepted by the juries for both the OSA and CSPWC, and showed in a special advertising art section of the RCA. By 1939 he had pretty well settled into the comfortable routine of annual art society shows. He was elected to the membership of both the OSA and CSPWC in 1942, was elected vice-president and treasurer of the latter

body in 1943 (he served three years), and president in 1945. The following year he served as vice-president and treasurer of the OSA, and was elected to the position of associate of the Royal Canadian Academy. He was by the end of the Second World War, at the age of thirty-six, as thoroughly a part of the Canadian art establishment as it was then possible to be.

Bush's domestic life also progressed as might be expected. After his marriage to Mabel Teakle in 1934, his first son was born in 1935, followed by a second in 1938, and a third in 1942. In 1941 he left Rapid, Grip & Batten, and entered into partnership with two other commercial artists, much as Charles Comfort had a few years before. The small firm rented space in the same building Comfort and his partners had inhabited between 1932 and 1936 at 9 Adelaide Street East. Bush's partners were William Winter (b 1909) and Leslie Wookey (1906-1973).

Wookey, Bush & Winter, as the firm was known, soon developed a reputation for clean, quick, effective work; their advertisement announced 'Design and Illustration for Discriminating Art Directors.' Bush's specialty was illustration, and he worked in a number of styles, though in greatest demand were his coloured, sentimental-realist figure paintings, similar to (although not quite as ingratiating as) the pictures of the well-known American magazine illustrator, Norman Rockwell. Bush's paintings did not seem to suffer by the practice of such commercial work; in fact, his reputation grew apace equally in the two distinct areas.

At times during the early years of the war Bush exhibited watercolours, such as *Circus #2* (1939, page 14)

CIRCUS #2 watercolour, 1939
22½" x 27⅜" (57.2 x 69.5 cm)
Jack Bush Heritage Corporation Inc.

or *Testing Army Trucks – Camp Borden* (1943), which, in their development of a narrative theme through the depiction of detailed incident, in style, and certainly in handling, approach his commercial illustrations. Yet in their broad, rhythmic compositions, full of drama and heroic swagger, as indeed in their emphasis upon narrative incident or anecdote, they could suggest the influence of such current 'American Scene' painters as Thomas Hart Benton, John Steuart Curry, and Grant Wood. These American Regionalists attracted the attention of a number of Canadian artists during the later 30s, and Charles Comfort in particular saw in their work a possible alternative to those twin tyrannies of landscape and nationalism imposed by the Group of Seven.

Modified though it might be by a detached, cool stylishness, the national landscape at the outbreak of war still exercised an unrelenting hold upon the bulk of the painters of Toronto, Comfort and Bush included. Bush's small oil sketches and watercolours, brought back from regular field-trips to the hinterlands of Toronto – works like *Looking Toward Toronto, Caledon* (1938) or *Bruce Beach #1* (1939, page 15) – attest to this fidelity. As smoothly accomplished as they are in design and as pleasing, even distinctive, in colour, they display no ambition to reach beyond the general level of performance chronicled in the annual exhibitions of the OSA. *Lonely Road*, Bush's major canvas of 1938, shown in March with the OSA, reveals a fulsome pleasure in design and an arbitrary, although attractive, use of colour. Such comfortable competency relates it directly to the contemporary landscapes of Comfort or of A.J. Casson (b 1898), a later addition to the Group of Seven who in 1940 was president of the OSA, and, like Comfort, a leading commercial

BRUCE BEACH #1 watercolour, 1939
11³⁄₈" x 15⁷⁄₈" (28.9 x 40.4 cm)
Jack Bush Heritage Corporation Inc.

designer as well as a prominent painter. Bush was entirely content with such company, accepting the given themes and subjects, pleased to be working clearly defined, albeit narrow limits, aspiring to a quality of finish and presentation.

By the end of the war in 1945 it was clear that Bush was one of the accomplished painters of the community, a distinction signalled by his election to the presidency of the CSPWC that year, and to associate status in the RCA and vice-presidency of the OSA the following year. His work was beginning to display specific personal traits. Although hindsight reveals a characteristic taste for certain colours and textures almost from the beginning of his career, by the mid 40s such elements begin to dominate. Field sketches like *Shacks, Lumbermill, Utterson,* and *Village Funeral,* both of 1945, show his familiar high-keyed yet saturated, just-off-primary colours: mustard, dusty-pink, light blue, with blue-greens and browns, always accented with flashes of brilliant white and contrasting black shadows. The texture of the brush work – often laid down with the ground independently of colour – gives sweeping movement to the composition, and the forms bend and twist in tense sympathy. There is a clarity and openness to such work that relates it still to Comfort, but the mood is sombre and the subjects more complex, more richly observed, than we would expect from that artist. Bush was finding his own voice.

That he was approaching a personal idiom was recognized at the time, and he was accorded a number of small exhibitions with painters of similar background with whom he shared concerns. The first was at the Women's Art Association on Hazelton Avenue in 1944 where he was linked with R. York Wilson (b 1907). Then in 1945 Bush and one of his business partners, William Winter, showed at Hart House in the University of Toronto. His first public one-man show came in 1946, at Trinity College, also on the campus of the university, and then in February 1947 he joined with Winter again for an exhibition at Adelaide House in Oshawa, a small city on Lake Ontario east of Toronto. No catalogues or check-lists of these exhibitions appear to have survived, but we know from a newspaper review of the Oshawa show that the viewer made no distinction between the work of Bush and Winter, 'two Toronto artists now reaching their prime.' The paintings are described as masculine in subject, 'strong, powerful, dramatic conceptions ... demanding things with something to say and something to give.'[4]

The year before, in March 1946, Bush had won the Rolph, Clarke, Stone award at the OSA exhibition for best picture with *Village Procession* (page 10), a painting based on his oil sketch of 1945, *Village Funeral*. In May 1947 his major contribution to that year's OSA show, *Yesterday*, was featured on the cover of *Saturday Night* magazine, accompanied by a poem of Harold Caverhill's that had been inspired by the painting. The following year he was praised in a profile article in the *London Free Press*.[5] Later in 1948 he was elected to membership with the successors to the Group of Seven, the Canadian Group of Painters, although, curiously, he failed to submit work for exhibition with the CGP that year, or with the OSA, the CSPWC, or the CGP the following year. Such a prolonged absence from the shows must have caused a stir among Bush's colleagues. Certainly his next public appearance did, in a one-man show at the new Gavin Henderson Galleries on Yonge Street in October 1949.

The exhibition, 'New Paintings by Jack H. Bush,' was calculated to make a strong impact. A small catalogue was published in which it was claimed that these 'provocative new paintings' were 'the first of Mr Bush's work to be exhibited in over two years.' Although this was somewhat of an exaggeration (Bush had shown last with the OSA in March 1948, nineteen months earlier), it did serve to emphasize the extent of his break with the past. The critics were impressed. Pearl McCarthy in the *Globe and Mail* made much of this metamorphosis: 'Jack Bush was recognized as a clever, liberal artist before he sank himself into this period of intensive, personal work. The results eminently justify the period, being on a higher level than any of his former work. He has been painting where there were canyons, and this vast subject matter gave him scope for the use of colour as an integral part of form, as well as for the romantic imagination which has always marked his pictures. While the new paintings tend toward the abstract, the canyons and mysterious figures will thrill even those usually afraid of the abstract. Contemplation, plus more profound use of form, make this Bush exhibition important.'[6]

Rose MacDonald, writing for *The Telegram*, also stressed the dramatic turn to new subjects and new forms, the result, she suggested, of some inner struggle: 'Mr Bush has not been showing his work for some time, though he had hitherto taken an outstanding place among the younger men painting in Canada. Nothing that he has done previously quite prepares one for the powerfully impactive character of these paintings in which the artist seems to be concerned with a mighty spiritual conflict, a sort of Jacob-wrestling-with-the-Angel mood.'[7] To reinforce her point, MacDonald described her reading of a few of the pictures, including *The Long Night* of 1948: 'Very strange, difficult to understand, nevertheless ... extraordinarily moving in the composition of faceless figures posed in attitudes of sorrow, and seeking of bitterness, and perhaps

of pity ..' She observed that an underlying religious theme at times became explicit, as in *Agony*, in which 'the artist has sought and found new and powerful terms in which to express the agony of the crucifixion.' 'But he is not always so sombre as all this would indicate,' she continued, and, in support, described *Floating Spirit* (circa 1948, page 163) as 'a beautifully imaginative work ... which has a wonderful buoyancy expressed in the brush-work and in the ethereal blue and in the use of white.' And in a series of studies for the *Flute Player*, MacDonald saw a source for some of the formal concerns evident in this new work. These studies, 'like a number of the Bush paintings, distinctly indicate Picasso influence, as a quite fascinating exercise in figure painting simplified to extremity and in treating problems of light.'

Certainly by 1949 Bush was aware of Picasso. Lenore Crawford in her 1948 profile in the *London Free Press* stated categorically that 'because he is a young man his influences are naturally Steinbeck novels, Benny Goodman's clarinet, Picasso's strong work.' (She thought Bush had been 'born slightly more than 30 years ago.' He was thirty-nine.) Looking at some of these paintings now, it is not of Picasso one thinks – except perhaps in studies of large figures – but of those people who continued the narrative tradition in American painting after the Regionalists, and particularly Ben Shahn. However, the issue at the time was not a question of sources, but of the fact of change itself. Bush, it would appear from the catalogue statement, wished to signal some fundamental break with his work of the previous twenty years. The critics acknowledged his change and, taking their lead from the catalogue statement, stressed that it had resulted from deep questioning and investigations undertaken during the two years that Bush had withheld work from the society shows. Was there in fact a radical change?

If we examine the works exhibited following *Village Procession*, we see that there is a steady evolution of form as well as a move into new subjects. *Across the Valley*, a watercolour Bush showed with the CSPWC in January 1947, introduces with its sharp angularities and spare colour washes a brittle, tense quality that we have not seen before. *Yesterday*, the oil painting that attracted attention when it was shown in the OSA exhibition of March 1947, is even more angular and, with its view of one open door through another, with all of the planes pitched slightly out of kilter, suggests the angst of early German expressionist films. His usual concern for texture in his oils softens the forms to some degree, and the colour is more characteristic than in *Across the Valley*, although dark and moody, much darker in mood even than the funereal *Village Procession* of the year before.

SPRING WILLOWS oil on masonite, nd
24" x 60' (61 x 151 cm)
Terry Bush, Toronto, Ontario

ARMORIES - TORONTO, 1939 oil on canvas, 1943 (from a 1939 sketch)
35⅝" x 39⅝" (90.5 x 100.7 cm)
Mendy Sharf, Toronto, Ontario

House of Doors (page 88), one of two watercolours he showed with the CSPWC in February 1948, suggests even more strongly a stage set. A small ponderous figure pushes open one of a jumbled array of doors, seemingly unaware of smoke billowing from a crack in a sloping wall. A mysterious long ladder rests behind another door. The dirty mustard, dusty pink, and clouded powder blue are Bush's familiar colours, but the image of fatalistic despair, to all appearances a metaphor for a state of mind, is new. We must not read such things too literally, however. One work Bush included in his 1949 one-man show, *Exploration*, he had exhibited before with the OSA in March 1948 as *Adventure*. It too suggests a modernistic stage set, with angular, architectonic forms crowding the foreground of a dark landscape of the mind. The colours are the hues of *House of Doors*, but the tone is lighter (although the landscape setting is ominous), with young boys scrambling over and around the slab-like blocks, one even climbing a long ladder, familiar from *House of Doors*.[8]

About 1947, then, Bush abandoned the painting of landscapes based on field sketches and moved slowly toward the expression, or at least the investigation, of deep feelings: confusion, fear, and despair. If we look at the full range of work exhibited in 1949, and particularly those pieces such as *The Long Night*, *Agony*, and *Floating Spirit* painted after he stopped exhibiting in 1948, we also see images of faith, hope, and resolution. Writing in his studio journal, Bush himself identified the reason for this significant turning in his work: 'Experimental work suggested by Dr. J. Allan Walters, and commenced in Sept. 1947. The idea being to paint freely the inner feelings and moods. Around March 1948 he further suggested starting from scratch on a blank canvas with no preconceived idea, and just let the thing develop in colour, form and content.'[9] Bush had begun to explore his 'inner feelings and moods' with works like *Yesterday* before Dr Walters' suggestion, but it was only with therapy on a regular basis that he began to work toward resolution. Many years later Bush described the process succinctly: 'a psychiatric therapeutic session of many years freed me from the oppression of local rules ...'[10]

A number of unexhibited watercolours of 1947 are more experimental in the description of feelings than are the paintings Bush exhibited at the time. *Tension* (page 195) and *Frightened Boy* (page 194) are two good examples. In them, form is extremely simplified – the figures are like diagrams – and colour is used exclusively for its symbolic, emotional value. Not only does the colour have nothing to do with verisimilitude, but it functions independently of the forms. The sense of strain evident in the drawing of the figure in *Tension*, for instance, is supported by the use of colour, but as a separate element. A red rectangle threatens from one corner, a black laser-like line cuts across the image, a green-turquoise inverted W is superimposed on the torso, descending from the shoulders, the central V cutting deep into the chest. It suggests nothing more than the depiction of 'thought-forms' in early theosophical texts, important images in the genesis of abstract art.

Dr Walters' suggestion to Bush in March 1948 that he turn to 'automatic' painting introduced another historical route to abstraction. It was almost as though the artist were living through a compressed history of the development of abstract painting. He was not alone at the moment in Toronto in pursuing such interests. After a false start in the work of Bertram Brooker twenty years before, abstraction was again in the air. Jock Macdonald (1897-1960), a teacher at OCA recently arrived from Vancouver via Calgary, held an exhibition of his automatic watercolours at Hart House in November 1947. Almost exactly a year later, a large Lawren Harris retrospective exhibition at the Art Gallery of Toronto included eighteen of his big abstract paintings dating back to the mid 30s, which must have given encouragement to those only then in the process of abandoning the national landscape school. For Northrop Frye, reviewing the show in *Canadian Art* magazine, Harris' abstractions were 'a unique and major contribution to Canadian painting.' Describing them, he used words evoking freedom and liberty. 'When we enter the "abstract" room we are conscious first of all of a great release of power. The painter has come home: his forms have been emancipated, and the exuberance of their swirling and plunging lines takes one's breath away.'[11] In the same issue of *Canadian Art*, Andrew Bell, writing of the art scene in Toronto in answer to an earlier article by Robert Ayre that described the artistic vitality of Montreal, warned that: 'Toronto is attentive, as never before, to serious painting. Now, Mr. Ayre, is no time for Montreal to start feeling smug.'[12]

Exactly a year after the Harris retrospective, the Art Gallery of Toronto staged a large exhibition, 'Contemporary Art: Great Britain, United States, France,' which included, among 198 works, radical pieces such as Jackson Pollock's *The Cathedral* and Robert Motherwell's *The Emperor of China*. It sharpened the debate over abstraction, encouraging adherents while hardening the opposition. For a time, the raised voices gave the appearance of confusion. There seemed to be no clear direction. Bell wrote of the Toronto scene again in *Canadian Art* in the fall of 1950, but with an entirely changed tune: 'Painting in Toronto, speaking generally, is still under the thrall of the Group in that it continues to cleave to emphasis on stylized design and heightened colour. There is a lingering underlining, too, of "indigenous Canadian work." '[13] Bell felt that most Toronto painting lacked either a clear purpose or a reasonable universality of appeal. 'David Milne, Paraskeva Clark, Jack Nichols – perhaps the work of these three qualify, but what other?' It would take time.

Although some colleagues condemned Bush's new tendencies, which bothered him, he increasingly took strength from new associations among the abstract camp, the likes of Jock Macdonald and Oscar Cahén (1916-1956), a European-trained designer and painter who moved to Toronto from Montreal about 1946. Bush first visited New York and the Museum of Modern Art in 1950, and that too confirmed him in his new direction. He had returned to exhibiting with the societies following the Gavin Henderson Galleries show, and although he never really questioned the efficacy of this decision, he had to admit that the juries often fostered unpleasant squabbles, and that the actual shows increasingly took on the appearance of two antagonistic forces facing one another across a battlefield.

Bush held another one-man show in February 1952, at the Roberts Art Gallery, then situated on Yonge St. just above Bloor in the location earlier occupied by Gavin Henderson. As before, a small catalogue was published, and again it contained a short statement calculated to give a particular impression of the artist: 'A collection of new paintings by Jack Bush is always a refreshing event. He exhibits infrequently. This is only the second exhibition in some five years in a field of art which is developing as a vital and stimulating force in many other parts of the world. The present collection of twenty-five spirited paintings covers a wide range of subjects, most of which seek to portray a simple truth or emotion, and some of which are pure abstracts, interested in the sheer pleasure of line against line and colour against colour.'

Pearl McCarthy's review appeared the day the show opened. There was a lesson in Bush's new work, she believed: 'In a day when too many people seem to be "going abstract" with the general trend, apparently under the false impression that abstraction is an easy way to reach the public, Mr. Bush paints honestly. He seems to know the simple truth which eludes many, that one must have a rich idea from which to do one's abstracting.'[14] For her, 'the most convincing' of Bush's paintings 'are those which derive from some definite emotion caused by sights observed, or from factual scenes. In the latter category is the brilliantly composed rugby picture called *The Pass*.'

Rose MacDonald of *The Telegram*, who typified Bush as 'always an interesting if sometimes wayward painter,' described the show as 'twenty-five paintings rather closely related in style, and often in mood that enlarges and strengthens the artist's reputation.'[15] There were distinct changes from the exhibition of two-and-a-half years before. 'His colour has clarified, become more brilliant, and in making firmly his own a modified geometrical style, he seems at the same time to have crystallized his thinking in terms of the brush.' Another critic also recognized the marked degree of resolution in the new work, describing it as 'a highly personal integration of mood and form.'[16]

The new work had developed gradually from the old. Paintings in the show like *Release* (first shown in the March 1951 exhibition of the OSA) still displayed dream-like landscapes, similar to the stage-set environments of *House of Doors* or *Exploration* (*Adventure*). The figures had become larger, however, and were more broadly handled, as well as being in themselves planar, generalized forms derived from synthetic cubism. All had been abstracted from still-recognizable objects. His favourite colours continued to predominate, but they were cleaner. Texture was still of great interest to him, but it now related directly to form. Although the mood of the pictures was often sombre, the general impression was one of a freer, more vigorous imagination at work, even though, as Rose Mac-Donald pointed out, the show was admirably coherent. It would not be saying too much to describe the work of the 1952 exhibition as the first in which Bush spoke with a strong, sure, and highly personal voice. He was just about to turn forty-three.

Bush showed only one work in the 1952 OSA exhibition, which opened a week after his Roberts Gallery show closed, a large oil entitled *The Good Samaritan*. It won the J.W.L. Forster Award for best picture. A number of the most recent pictures in the Roberts show, such as *The Old Tree*, were of large figures that filled the whole composition, leaving only a marginal view of a rudimentary landscape behind. *The Good Samaritan* continued in that vein, with the crouched and supine figures almost touching each of the four edges of the picture.

Later that year, in November 1952, Bush again exhibited a single large oil, with the CGP this time. *Summer* was a variation on *The Good Samaritan*, having the same size and showing two large figures, in almost the same positions, which fill the picture. But this time they were a man and woman enjoying a sunny afternoon at the beach. Not only was the subject less emotionally charged, but the forms, though still slightly faceted in deference to cubism, were no longer angular and spiky as in *The Good Samaritan*. His slightly-off-primary colours were unashamedly bright and clear. The up-beat subject (although in an emotional sense it is as neutral as the work of a student's life-class), the substantial forms, and high colouring all reinforce our pleasurable enjoyment of the formal strengths of the larger lines of the composition. This is bold, optimistic work, and it kept Bush among those in Toronto who were in the forefront of experimentation with abstraction.

The abstract painters in the Toronto region had come to realize that the only way to achieve real credibility, even among that small public with a developed interest in art, was to organize apart from the older artists' societies. The first concerted effort in this direction had come in October 1952, when what was billed as the 'Canadian Abstract Exhibition' opened at Adelaide House in Oshawa, where Bush and Winter had exhibited together in 1947. Organized by Oshawa painter Alexandra Luke, it included the work of twenty-six artists from across Canada. Bush showed two of his abstract pictures.

Exactly one year later, in October 1953, he joined with Luke and five other painters from the Toronto area in an even more pointedly 'educational' exhibition entitled 'Abstracts at Home.' The show was the idea of William Ronald, a former student of Jock Macdonald at OCA who worked as a designer at the Robert Simpson Company, and consisted of abstract paintings displayed in modern room settings in the downtown store. There was no specific critical reaction to the exhibition, but the participants had by then become convinced that such non-juried exhibitions, organized by the exhibiting artists themselves, were the best means to establish a viable public forum for experimental art in Toronto. In the following weeks they met on several occasions, and three months later, on 13 February 1954, the first exhibition of Painters Eleven opened at the Roberts Gallery.

Bush had declared fully for the principles of abstract art, and in common with the interests of his like-minded associates in Toronto. By then, in certain of his pictures such as *Holiday* of 1954, he had also cut himself clear of the need to retain in his paintings their apparent pictorial sources. Although the general proportions of *Holiday*, and certainly the strong suggestion of black outlining of its large sweeping forms, relate it directly to *Summer*, and before that *The Good Samaritan*, it none the less must be seen as the basis of even stronger inclinations to the future, to gestural painting of the sort by then firmly established in New York. A closely related painting of the same year Bush named *Stuart Davis*, in homage to a major inspiration for his growing tendency to formal, if not non-objective, abstraction. (There had been two large Davis canvases, *Ursine Park* and *New York Under Gaslight*, in the 1949 exhibition of contemporary international art at the Art Gallery in Toronto.) He had declared then not only for abstraction, but for New York abstraction, and this evident interest would grow to dominate his work for close to a decade. It was a decision that opened fresh new directions in his painting and, what was much more important to a man of forty-three in Toronto in 1954, set exciting new and distant limits to his ambition. Indeed, perhaps for the first time in his painting career, it cleared limits away entirely.

DENNIS REID is curator of Canadian art at the Art Gallery of Ontario, Toronto. He is the author of *A Concise History of Canadian Painting*, and the organizer of the 1972 exhibition *Toronto Painting: 1953-1965*.

NOTES

1 'Reminiscences by Jack Bush,' *Jack Bush: A Retrospective* (Toronto: Art Gallery of Ontario, 1976), unpaged
2 Ibid.
3 *Young Canadian* is in the collection of Hart House, University of Toronto. *Portrait of Professor Felix Walter* is in the collection of the Winnipeg Art Gallery.
4 'Two-Man Exhibit of Painting To Be Seen at Adelaide House,' Oshawa *Daily Times Gazette*, 8 February 1947
5 Lenore Crawford, 'Jack Bush Wins Fame as Artist,' 11 September 1948
6 'Pictures by Jack Bush Typify Deeper Trends,' 15 October 1949
7 'Donges Landscapes at Little Gallery,' 15 October 1949
8 Bush was attracted to a number of these new themes by the work of Ben Shahn (1898-1969). See particularly the American's *The Red Stairway* (1944), *Reconstruction* and *Liberation* (both 1945), for the similar depiction of seemingly innocent, psychologically charged activity within stark, stage-like settings. All three were available to Bush in James Thrall Soby's *Ben Shahn*, published in the Penguin Modern Painters series in 1947.
9 Quoted in Ken Carpenter, 'The Evolution of Jack Bush,' *Journal of Canadian Art History*, IV, 1977/78, 124
10 In *Statements: 18 Canadian Artists* (Regina, Saskatchewan: Norman MacKenzie Art Gallery, 1967), 32
11 'The Pursuit of Form,' *Canadian Art*, VI, 1948, 54-5
12 'Toronto as an Art Centre,' ibid., 75
13 'Yes, Painting might be Better in Toronto,' *Canadian Art*, VIII, 1950, 29
14 'The Lesson from Jack Bush Exhibit,' Toronto *Globe and Mail*, 16 February 1952
15 'At the Galleries,' 23 February 1952
16 'Jack Bush Exhibit,' *Saturday Night*, 29 March 1952

CULMINATION oil on canvas, 1955
36" x 40" (91.4 x 101.6 cm)
Private Collection

FRENCH FACADE oil on canvas, 1957
20" x 27" (50.8 x 68.6 cm)
Jack Bush Heritage Corporation Inc.

CHANSON D'AMOUR oil on canvas, 1958
53" x 89¾" (134.6 x 227.9 cm)
Jack Bush Heritage Corporation Inc.

BREAKTHROUGH oil on canvas, 1958
48" x 72" (121.8 x 183.1 cm)
Robert McLaughlin Gallery, Oshawa, Ontario

24

LET THEM ALL FALL oil on canvas, 1959
69⅜" x 79⅝" (176.2 x 202.3 cm)
Jack Bush Heritage Corporation Inc.

SNOWBALL, PEONY AND IRIS oil on canvas, 1960
60¾" x 85½" (152.5 x 213.5 cm)
Mr and Mrs David Mirvish, Toronto, Ontario

RED, BLUE, GREEN OFF BROWN oil on canvas, 1960
80⅞" x 70" (205.5 x 177.8 cm)
Jack Bush Heritage Corporation Inc.

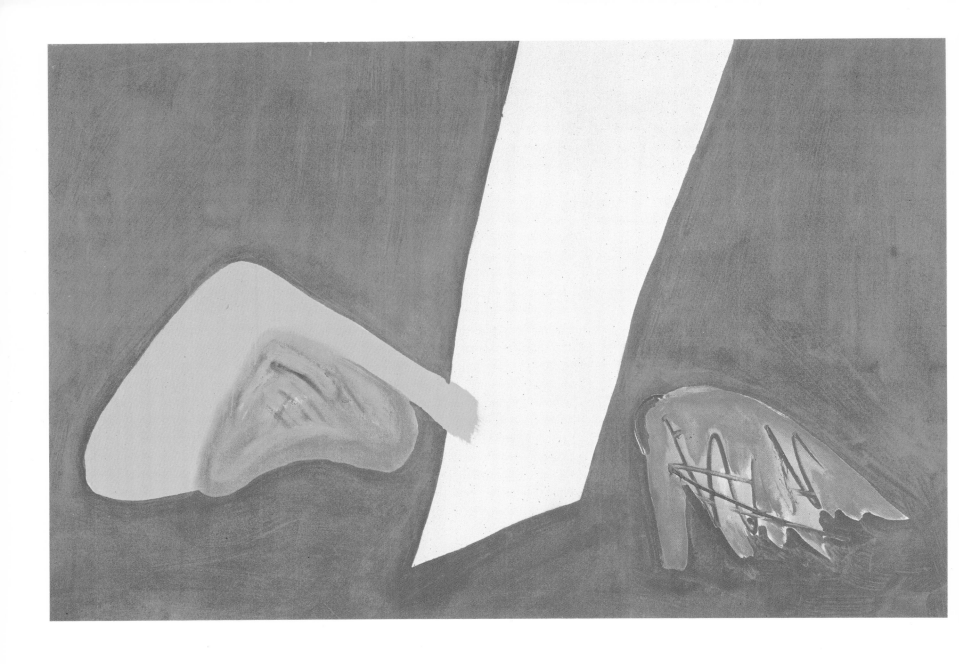

WHITE THRUST Magna on canvas, 1961
37½" x 56½" (95 x 143 cm)
Private Collection

Breakthrough: Jack Bush and Painters Eleven

BARRIE HALE

INCLUDED AMONG THE PAPERS OF JACK BUSH ARE VARIOUS drafts of information forms from the National Gallery of Canada. Taken together, they show Bush in the 1940s and 50s as a member, and often on the executive, of the Canadian Society of Painters in Water Colour, the Ontario Society of Artists, the Royal Canadian Academy, the Canadian Group of Painters, the Art Directors' Club, Painters Eleven, and as the recipient of several medals and awards in both societal and commercial art. It was the record of a typical, albeit successful, artist of his day in Toronto. Abruptly in 1964, however, he resigned from all societies. Painters Eleven, in its short life from 1954 to 1959, had a decided impact on Bush, just as it had marked the beginning of the end of the establishment power embodied in Bush's resumé.

As Harold Town has remarked, Toronto in the early 1950s was the kind of city where people watched the annual Orangemen's Parade without laughing, but it was also, for some, the kind of city Rupert Brooke (one of the few visitors up until then with a kind word for the place) described in his *Letters from America* in 1913: 'It is a healthy, cheerful city (by modern standard); a clean-shaven, pink-faced, respectably-dressed, fairly-energetic, unintellectual, passably social, well-to-do, public-school-and-varsity sort of city.' For a Toronto painter in the 1950s, public school was the Ontario College of Art, with advanced degrees conferred, as it were, by the Ontario Society of Artists. Established in 1872 and exhibiting annually since 1873, the OSA also fostered the creation of the OCA, the founding act (1912) of which stipulated that two members of OSA must sit on the Governing Council of OCA. The OSA, moreover, was not without imperial aspirations; C.M. Manly, president of the society from 1903 to 1905, saw the future in terms of 'the sunrise and full

daylight of a notable Canadian Art which will touch and influence all the land from sea to sea.' Finally, the varsity of Toronto painters since 1933 had been the Canadian Group of Painters, founded that year as a suitable recipient to which the Group of Seven might pass the torch before it was slapped from their hands; but though the CGP had spread its mantle over a remarkable assortment of Canadian painters and painting – Bertram Brooker and Carl Schaefer, Jock Macdonald's 'automatic' work and Lawren Harris's abstracts – by the early 1950s only A.Y. Jackson remained influential. While *Les Automatistes* captured Montreal and Abstract Expressionism took over New York, society art in Toronto was approximately abreast of Manly in 1905.

If it seemed that A.Y. had been around forever, so, too, had the notion of 'the artist as professional man' – illustrator of books and magazines, commercial artist, advertising man, art director – not a tradition so much as a way of life, shared through the generations from Group of Seven to the Canadian Group of Painters to a majority of those artists soon to be Painters Eleven: Bush, Cahén, Hodgson, Mead, Town, Yarwood. There were hotel bars in downtown Toronto where professional artists met to trade news, views, and reviews – kind of clubby, it was. There was also a twenty-year-old bohemia in downtown Toronto, centred on the Gerrard Street 'village,' which by 1930 already had its own little magazines of poetry, art, and opinion.

There were, in short, a number of paths for the young artist to follow in the Toronto of the early 1950s; indeed, if he followed all of them, and many did, life could be quite pleasant. His name and sometimes his photo appeared in the newspapers, with society initials following the name and the photo showing him receiving an award, medal, prize, or plaque – a kind of fame shared almost equally among recipients of OSA awards and Art Directors' medals. In 1954, the year of the first Painters Eleven exhibition

ABOVE Bush in 1949

at the Roberts Gallery, the Sixth Annual Art Directors' Club exhibition featured medal-winning work by Cahén, Town, and also Bush, who was cited for 'finely distinctive, imaginative Christmas design.' There was the friendly life of the artists' bars, Group-of-Sevenish sketching trips in the north during the summer, and life-drawing classes at OCA on winter evenings, where Bush and certain other artists went as if to church. 'Having been born, brought up and taught with a solid academic background,' Bush said in 1975, 'to draw properly – not the way we call drawing today, that's another way of drawing – but to draw the figure in proportion, and to paint landscapes *well*, and to paint portraits *well* – and then to get the urge to experiment with something current, or *challenging*, is a better word ... I run the gamut right clean through ...'

There was a considerable amount of frustration, impatience, and discontent built into the neatly dovetailed collection of fine arts institutions of that time. Of the eventual Painters Eleven,[1] Bush was the only one showing regularly at a private gallery (Roberts, one of only four in the city of any consequence), and he, like everyone else, annually submitted his couple of canvases to the societies in the hope that they would be included in that year's exhibition. The OSA annuals at the Art Gallery of Toronto were *the* events of the season. Though ostensibly democratic, since all comers were invited to submit work, the OSA was an effectively closed society in that work was selected for exhibition by a jury composed of society members. Bush himself achieved juror's status as he made his way along the paths available to Toronto artists and he enjoyed telling an anecdote about his experiences: He, the 'new boy,' and the other jurors were on their way to judge submissions at the Art Gallery in 1944 when Bush spotted a Picasso – his first 'original'; he stopped dead and was gazing at it when one of the older jurors took him gently by the arm and led him away to his duties, murmuring, 'Nothing there for you, Bush.'

It is appropriate to the general ambience of Toronto in the early 1950s that the exhibition of paintings that was to lead immediately to the formation of Painters Eleven took place in the windows of a downtown department store. The exhibit, 'Abstracts at Home,' was organized in October 1953 by William Ronald for Simpson's, where he subsisted as a display artist, and consisted of groupings of modern furniture with abstract paintings discreetly on the walls behind, paintings by Ronald, Cahén, Hodgson, Luke, Mead, Nakamura, and Bush. The seven agreed that they were on to something and at a later meeting at Alexandra Luke's studio, with the addition of Macdonald, Gordon, Town, and Yarwood, Painters Eleven came into

being. Bush arranged for their first exhibition at Roberts, and for the next five years the group showed at private galleries around the province, and, following traditional patterns, around the country as well as on the public museum circuit. By 1959, when they disbanded, the Painters Eleven yeastiness had helped give rise to an entirely different structure of private art galleries in Toronto, galleries interested in showing contemporary work from Toronto and elsewhere. The group had provided an inspirational boost to a new generation of young artists emerging in the late 1950s, as Greg Curnoe, Dennis Burton, and Gordon Rayner have all testified. By the time they were done, Painters Eleven had achieved what they set out to accomplish – first a place in the arena and finally a whole new arena – but some of them were looking far beyond their parochial victories. As Bush wrote to Russell Harper in 1964: '... we were invited to show as guests with the American Abstract Artists in New York, in 1956. This was somehow the first physical contact (which I am now thinking most important) with kindred spirits outside our own parish, or country, for that matter. This sparked the possibility that we lowly Canadians somehow had a real challenge, and a job to do as artists not at all like the local pattern so prevalent for so many years. This in no way made us feel less Canadian. But it was a big job, and lonely, and sure as hell no thanks.'

There are a couple of myths that cling to the art history of Toronto in these years; like all myths they surround enough of the truth to pass for a larger one and they leave out the parts that don't fit. The first borrows a page from the sentimental history of jazz and tells how a handful of Toronto artists brought Abstract Expressionism up the New York Thruway from Manhattan and thereby changed the course of ... The second has to do with Clement Greenberg and how, after wandering the Toronto desert for days and days, he smote Jack Bush on the frontal lobes and thereby released the mainstream of modernism into Canadian waters. Now, as the first myth obscures the free flowering of pronounced individual idiosyncrasy that has been a hallmark of Toronto modernists since the mid 1950s, so the Bush/Greenberg myth serves to shroud most of what makes Bush's work distinctly his own: the conjunction of his quarter century in advertising design, his membership in the Canadian Group of Painters and the various societies of the day, his place in Painters Eleven, and his 'maverick' role, usually understated but always there. 'We paint not intellectually at all,' he said in 1975, 'at least I don't. I paint from my belly, it's instinct, plus a gut feeling. My earlier absorption with figure painting and the Canadian landscape, let us say, seems to persist ... even I'm surprised at some of the things I'm

MUTE BEGINNING oil on canvas, 1958
34" x 40" (86.4 x 101.6 cm)
Private Collection

doing today, you can trace it in works that I did twenty or thirty years ago.'

Clement Greenberg, seven years before his 'Post Painterly Abstraction' exhibition was shown at Toronto's Art Gallery, came to town in 1957, his interest in the painting community here excited by the presence in New York of William Ronald (who that year signed with Kootz Gallery) and by the works of Painters Eleven at the American Abstract Artists' show. He spent most of a day with each of the Eleven who agreed to see him (Town and Yarwood declined the opportunity) and it appears from what four have since reported – artists as distinct from one another as Macdonald, Luke, Mead, and Bush – that he said much the same sort of thing to them that he was saying about, and to, most of the ten thousand New York painters of the day who, as Ronald observed, 'were all doing de Koonings.' More than a decade after this first meeting with Greenberg, Bush would recall: 'I remember well the half day I spent with him. I was proudly showing him all my work, see, which was Abstract Expressionist in influence, and he looked out the window and said, "How old are you, Jack?" And I said, "I'm 48." "So am I," he said, "and you should know better." He said, "Look at what you're doing. You people up here are scaring the hell out of me, you're so good, but what you're doing, Bush, is just takin' all the hot licks from the New York painters, which are so *easy* to do."[2] Greenberg had praise to offer as well, especially for a group of watercolours Bush had done and then set aside. 'They were so simple,' Bush said later, 'that they scared me.' He began to strip his art down to basics, to determine what he, as a painter, was all about: 'You know,' he said, 'from the very beginning my worry had been to try to paint like the boys, to fit in with the crowd, and, fortunately for me, I could never quite do it. Every goddamn time I showed a painting at one of those shows, there it was: not like everybody else's. The difference was *Bush*, and I just couldn't get rid of it … fortunately.'

By the end of Painters Eleven, Jack Bush still had about a decade to go before his perceived image as the postpainterly patriarch of Canadian art truly flowered, but there were already indications of the individual, mature artist he was shortly to become. His long-awaited retrospective (1976-7) did Bush the disservice of implying (by showing none of his pre-1958 work) that maturity was conferred on Bush by Greenberg during his 1957 visit to Toronto, but of course the watercolours were already there for Greenberg to discover and encourage. Similarly, many of the elements that were to give formalist critics of the 1960s and 70s trouble with Bush, the elements that were to distinguish him from other post-painterly artists, had

already appeared in his society landscapes and waterscapes. For one example, the startling, free-floating ovoids and the ambiguous space in which they float above quivering horizontals, seen in the Spasm painting *Onslaught* (1969), are presaged in 1950s watercolours such as *Sailboats – Lake of Bays* (1953): both are characteristic of Bush, but while the content of the later painting was prompted by the onset of the angina pains that were to plague him for the rest of his life, contrary to the watercolour's sensual response to the fuzzy, sweet ambience of a summer's day, the pictorial strategy, the choice of shape, and gesture of the watercolour are clearly those of the hand and mind that radically simplified them in *Onslaught*. Similarly, the expressive, swooping curves that dominate such abstract work as *Bend* (1970, page 139) may be seen in the CGP painting *Engine House*, done nearly thirty years earlier. Pre-and post-Greenberg Bush, so to speak, meet on equal terms in the aptly titled *Breakthrough* (1958, page 24), in which stormy, northwoods clouds are swept aside by sailing bands/stripes/banners of bright primary colours, subtly Bushstroked so that they appear as no one else's primary colours.

Critical response to Bush's work of the late 1950s and

THE FAMILY oil and graphite on canvas, 1959
80⅝" x 70⅛" (204.8 x 178.5 cm)
Jack Bush Heritage Corporation Inc.

early 1960s – in a Toronto in thrall to the extravaganza of Harold Town at home and William Ronald in New York – was lukewarm at best, spiteful at worst. In Toronto in 1957 anyone who believed that Clement Greenberg had anything of value to say was beleaguered; but the maverick streak that had led Bush to embrace the Painters Eleven idea now set him in pursuit of a simpler, clearer way of painting, in spite of what Toronto critics, claques, and comrades had to say about it.

The patriarchal Bush also began to emerge at this time. Gordon Rayner, in the Mnemonica section of his Robert McLaughlin retrospective catalogue (1978), recalled his days as a young apprentice to Bush in his commercial studio: "I'd wander into Jack Bush's office, for example, and he'd be doing Harvey Wood's underwear ads for men

and women, and talk about the importance of drawing as the basis of all art. He experimented with various paints that were coming out at the time ... He'd talk and I'd ask questions. Once, he put down his brush and said to me, "Young Gord, if you are going to be an artist you must think of art all the time, it must be uppermost in your mind, you must rediscover your eyes, even when they are sleeping you must be looking."" Before his death in 1977, Bush would help to make generations of Toronto painters beyond Painters Eleven feel the weight of such words, the profit to be had from his experience.

BARRIE HALE writes frequently about cultural phenomena. In 1972 he wrote the catalogue essay of the exhibition *Toronto Painting 1953-1965* for the National Gallery of Canada.

NOTES

1 In order of birth: Hortense Gordon (1887), Jock Macdonald (1897), Alexandra Luke (1901), Jack Bush (1909), Oscar Cahén (1916), Walter Yarwood (1917), Ray Mead (1921), Tom Hodgson (1924), Harold Town (1924), Kazuo Nakamura (1926), William Ronald (1926).
2 In June 1982 Clement Greenberg read the articles in this book in manuscript. 'Barrie Hale's piece,' he replied, 'has me saying, "You people up here are scaring the hell out of me, you're so good." I've not before had the chance to correct that: Jack was dead before I saw this in print, in the catalogue of his restrospective, and then elsewhere. Jack had, like most people, a poor memory. I said nothing of the sort – anyhow I don't think Jack's memory was altogether responsible;

something got garbled, & Jack let it go. Nor did I see that show in NY of the American Abstract Artists in which Painters Eleven was represented. Nor was my interest in Toronto art "excited" by the New York presence of Ronald, though it was he who got Ptrs 11 to invite me to come to Toronto to look at their work, about which I hadn't the slightest idea beforehand.'
Barrie Hale replies: 'Bill and Helen Ronald remember it differently, however, recalling conversations with Greenberg in Manhattan in which they described the Toronto milieu and the activities of Painters Eleven prior to Greenberg's acceptance of the P 11 invitation. But then, it was nearly thiry years ago, and yes, memories do falter.'

Jack Bush in Retrospect

KENWORTH W. MOFFETT

JACK BUSH'S WORK STARTED TO COME TOGETHER IN 1958. *Mute Beginning* (page 31), seen in the 1980 exhibit 'Jack Bush: Paintings and Drawings 1955-1976' at the Serpentine Gallery in London, is a good example. The picture shows Jack turning to Robert Motherwell and Clyfford Still and away from the 'gesture' painters whom he had followed until this point. Motherwell and Still meant brighter colour and simpler drawing. Right away, Jack's pictures got better. But paintings like *Mute Beginning* are still in a kind of limbo: they aren't quite yet Bush. When I was hanging the show at the Serpentine and it became clear that we didn't have enough space, *Mute Beginning* and the other two earlier works, *Painting with Red* and *Culmination* (page 21), were the first to go. They didn't have nearly the character or quality of Jack's later work.

In 1959 came the first good Thrust pictures. Then Jack made some detours: the Flower paintings and the Cross or Flag paintings. These have more character, but aren't yet very good and it is only by keeping with the Thrust pictures that Jack finally got going. This happened in 1961. His first mature pictures were done in that year and immediately they remind us strongly of Matisse. It is not only their simplified and cursive drawing but also the way Jack used one of Matisse's chief organizational ideas: basing a large picture on a bold figure-ground opposition in which the figure looks 'negative' because it is less painted or is evenly painted. The best examples available to Bush were *The Dance, The Red Studio*, and *The Rose Marble Table* (page 164), all of which hung in the Museum of Modern Art in New York. One of the finest of the Thrust pictures, *Top Spin* (page 165), looks suspiciously like *The Rose Marble Table*.

In many of these Thrust pictures Jack used Magna paint and it seems that he couldn't quite control the colour,

at least in the brighter range. So, for example, *Bonnet* (page 35) becomes harsh and overbearing, and even a very fine picture like *White Thrust* (page 28) is too grating. Somewhat later Bush started toning down and softening the pictures by using thinner colour and earth tones. It is as if he had received a second message from Matisse, this time an even more specific one. The last of these Thrust pictures use Matisse's browns and pinks and washy blues. They are Jack's first real masterworks, pictures such as *Soar, Green on White* (page 43), *Bilateral with Red*, and *Top Spin*.

I like the early Sash picture *Big One* (page 51) and I always thought it unfortunate that there were not a lot more like it. I felt this way about other pictures (and groups of pictures) that Jack did too. It's as if he often didn't have the patience to exploit fully his own best ideas. I relate it to his incredibly fertile imagination on the one hand and to his being a 'late bloomer' on the other. Jack knew he had a lot to say and was appalled that it had taken him so long to get on track: to discover where painting was at and what was really possible. Once he made contact with the best, he became good right away, but by then he was almost fifty and the oldest member of the generation he had come to paint with: Frankenthaler, Dzubas, Noland, and Olitski (Morris Louis died in 1962). Maybe getting such a late start gave Jack his special sense of urgency. Anyway, he could never stay still for long.

The Sash pictures, like the Funnel and Ladder pictures that followed, all recall the paintings of Paul Klee. Some of the best of these pictures, including *Ochre Up, School Tie* (page 75), *Seven Colors* (page 79), *Sea Deep, On Purple* (page 73), *Color Ladder* (page 118), *Tall Green*, and *Tall Spread*, invoke Klee the most. I don't know if Jack was looking at Klee at this point (1963-7), but it doesn't really matter. There is the same delicate wayward drawing, the same thinned down and blinking colour. There is even the

BONNET oil on canvas, 1961
81" x 95¾" (205.7 x 243.2 cm)
Mr and Mrs David Mirvish, Toronto, Ontario

same emphasis given to canvas as texture and painted cloth. If Jack wasn't looking at Klee, he certainly had backed into him. Of course, Jack's scale is commanding while Klee's is almost that of a miniaturist, Jack's colour is far more full bodied, risky, and intense – but their expressive affinity is unmistakable. Nor is it limited to only these particular pictures of Bush. There is a more general similarity of feeling which results in part from the oblique and playful way both painters use motifs drawn from nature to make their abstract – that is, flatly conceived – pictures.

Taken as a whole, the paintings of this second mature period are a wonderful group and enough to establish Bush as a painter of international importance. What can occasionally detract from their quality is Jack's impulse to centre. This happens with a number of his most beautifully painted early Funnels (I'm thinking of pictures like *Orange Centre* (page 55) and *Cerise Band*).

At the end of this period, Jack switched to water-based

IRISH ROCK #1 acrylic on canvas, 4-20 October 1969
91½" x 68" (232.4 x 172.7 cm)
Wellesley College Museum, given in memory of Dorothy Vye Gage, '29, through the New Hampshire Wellesley Club

acrylic, which he used until the end. Acrylics gave him brighter, more evenly painted opaque colour. The general feeling of the Funnels had a lot to do with oil paint: the soft, cloudy, slightly yellow glow and 'worked' look. Now, with acrylics, his colour began to crackle and dance. The format became larger and very geometric. Jack had decided to take on New York. He was going after the big, bright, powerful impact that he admired in the paintings of Kenneth Noland and Frank Stella. But these 'geometric' pictures are not as successful; their often brilliantly devised colour sequences seem trapped in unsympathetic and vise-like designs.

In 1968 Bush got control of the dazzling acrylic colour by using a dominant 'field.' The effect is of a gay little sequence of angles and colours shouldering a big blast of monochrome. The example I know best is *Blue Studio* (page 119), but there are others which are probably just as good, such as *This Time Yellow* (page 116), *Burgundy* (page 121), or *Fringe on Blue Grey*. As a group, they show a power and bold assurance new in Bush's art. From now on he was after the big broad contrasts and a forceful impact.

In the 'calligraphic' pictures of 1969-71, Jack used the field-plus-fringe idea as a ground on which he plastered a big, incredibly powerful calligraphic flourish right in the middle. He was returning to Matisse for the sake of impact. And what impact they have! In *Bend* (page 139), *Zip Red* (page 61), *Red, Blue #3*, and *Irish Rock #1* (page 36) the figures jump right off the ground. In the *Irish Rock* paintings he went back to white, which he hadn't used since the late 50s, and in *Hook* (page 138) and *Sudden* (page 127) he used big areas of unpainted canvas for the first time also since those years. Jack was looking for ways to escalate contrast for the sake of impact. He heightened oppositions of light and dark but also of application. The figure is brushed, the ground rolled on. I remember worrying at the time about the graphic feeling of these pictures and whether they were too poster-like, too forced in their drawing and design (they weren't). Except for *Scoop* (page 124), which is very small, most of them seem slightly faulted and yet so stunningly original and so vibrantly alive that they leave you with your mouth open. They are also much rougher and more differentiated than what Jack did in the 'field'-type pictures.

Clement Greenberg gave Jack two suggestions at about this time which I would like to mention here. Clem had noticed that Jack's pictures often looked better in the studio before they were stretched and framed. He had the idea of leaving some unpainted canvas visible when the pictures were stretched. Jack tried this suggestion and it worked so well that he used it until his death. Right away it became a new variable to play with. Sometimes he would

TEXT CONTINUED ON PAGE 41

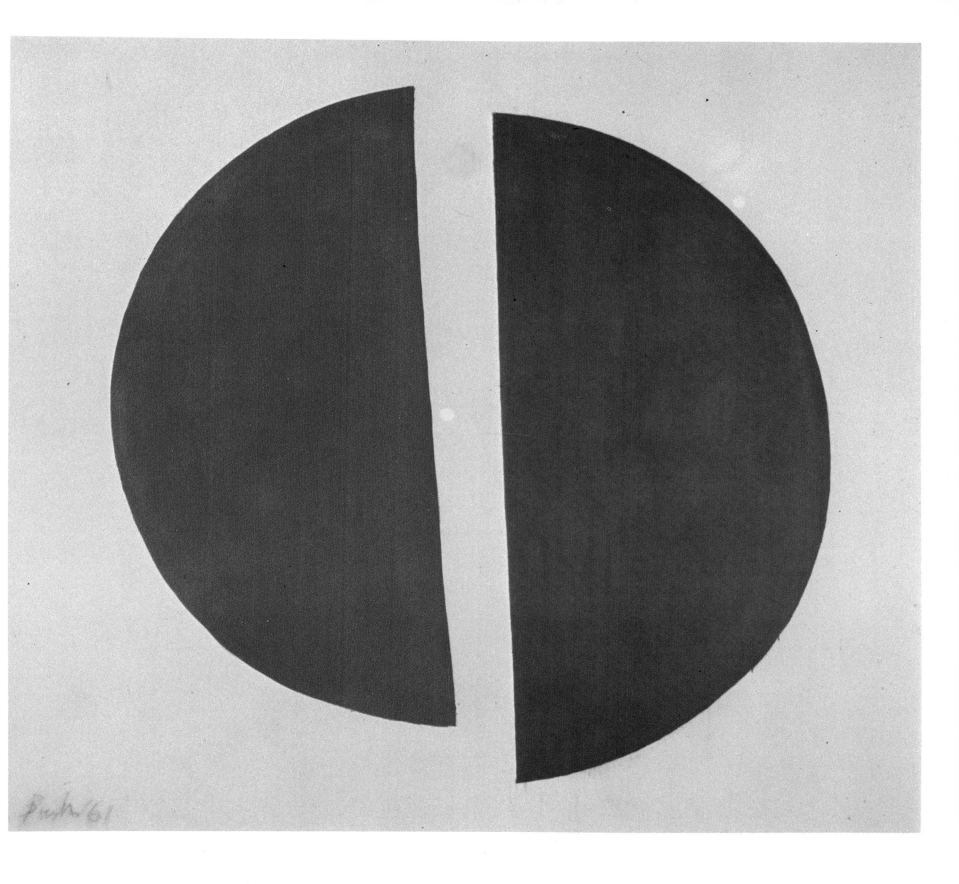

SPLIT CIRCLE #2 oil on canvas, 1961
80⅛" x 88½" (203.5 x 224.8 cm)
Jack Bush Heritage Corporation Inc.

SUMMER TAN oil on canvas, 1961
78¼" x 97⅜" (198 x 247 cm)
Gene and Bettye Burton
Pasadena, California

RED ON PINK Magna on canvas, April 1962
81" x 70¾" (205.7 x 179.7 cm)
Private Collection

ASCENSION #2 Magna on canvas, July 1962
69¾" x 87½" (177.2 x 222.2 cm)
Mr and Mrs David Mirvish, Toronto, Ontario

40

leave a margin, other times none at all. Sometimes he would make the border even and neat, at other times it would be ragged or appear only at one, two, or three sides. Only rarely did he use it to 'package' the picture. Clem's suggestion led Jack to think of his ground as separable from the picture's shape and this in turn led to new compositional and chromatic ideas (see, for example, *Woodwind* (page 191).

Around 1971 Clem made another suggestion. He advised Jack to keep his figure or figures out of the centre and towards the sides. Again, Clem was trying to get Jack's pictures to 'sit' better. Jack experimented with the idea and it worked well (*Two Greens*, page 156, *Yellow Right*, and paintings of the Bar series such as *Snowspread*), but he could never stick to the same layout for very long. Here was his restlessness again. The idea did, however, get Jack to modulate the focus in his pictures and to be more inventive in composition.

For some reason, Jack didn't go directly from the 'calligraphic' pictures of 1969 to the great figure-ground paintings of 1971, but made an odd detour in 1970. These are the so-called Series D pictures (pages 47, 140, 141) which came from some watercolours he did in 1969. Why he painted these pictures is a mystery to me. They seem so obviously a step backward to 1967, a reversion to geometry and to the use of multiple colour areas all of similar size and proportion. They aren't even up to his 'geometric' pictures, and their abrupt appearance in 1970 demonstrates once again Jack's restlessness and eccentricity.

Something that may have affected Jack at this time was the Larry Poons exhibit at the David Mirvish Gallery in early 1972. After that show, Bush started to stress the broad and heavy directional movement of his rollered-on grounds. Mirvish has recounted how affected Jack was by the Poons show and Jack was certainly open to learning from anyone, even from a painter so much younger than himself.

By eliminating the fringe, Jack had given up the last vestiges of an all-over kind of organization and gone straight back to the figure-ground layout of 1961. What he did with it now was very like what Miró did with Matisse: he created a broad, figure-ground relationship of active, weightless, and freely disposed graphic elements on a field. But Miró, not having anything like Matisse's colour, could not exploit this idea the way Bush did.

The late work is a fulfilment and further maturing. During this period, Jack worked along fairly smoothly, much as he had done between 1963 and 1967. His main preoccupation was with contrasting the figure and the ground in colour and density. The colour of the figures is uniformly opaque and often chalky. The grounds are broken, roughly textured, and usually of some subdued, neutral, or earth colour. At first they were rollered on, later they were sponged on. The figures go from the carefully drawn to what look like pastel slashes, swaths, or smudges. It's probably too early to be able to sort out these later pictures completely. An extraordinary group of them was found in Jack's studio after his sudden death in 1977, and Clem baptized them the 'posthumous pictures.' They were not totally new or different from what Jack had done before, but they were especially free and resolved (maybe Jack had received a boost from his retrospective and from being on the wagon). Clem's favourite was *Mood Indigo* (page 189), a picture later considered and refused by New York's Museum of Modern Art (they still don't have one). *Mood Indigo* is an especially refined and haunting example of Jack's last, great group of pictures, the Handkerchiefs. Another wonderful example is *Sharp Flats* (page 99), which is much rougher and more active. The Swords of 1974 are also a remarkable group. Several of the best ones, *Gold Corner* or *Hi Lo* (*Top Bottom*), as well as many of the big, long Bar pictures of 1973-4, seem almost like parodies of Jules Olitski's famous layout. Then there are the 'schooling swaths' with their wonderful soft, dense richness. (I'm not keen, however, on the big overloaded ones like *Concerto for Two Violins*, page 185.) Next to the Handkerchiefs, the Swords, the Bars, and the 'schooling swaths,' the 'sun' pictures that Jack did in 1976 are generally less successful, although there were some good ones, such as *Sundance*. Sometimes Jack's 'imagery' became too specific.

The late Bush paintings that impress me most came in 1973, are high in key, and have a coarse and heavy look. The best of them may be *Totemspread* (page 175), where Jack achieves a dense, rough richness matched only in the most recent work of Poons. Here is a new range of feeling for abstract painting. And there are other startling pictures in this group, such as *On Line, Red Pink Cross* (page 172), or *June Garden* (page 178). The drawing is freer and more spontaneous than anything Jack had done before, and the colour is more saturated, dense, and dominant. Never were his hues hotter, jumpier, more intense and glowing. Why aren't there more pictures like these? The finest of the first group he completed was *Totem with Green* and I remember Clem advising Jack to do more. As usual, Jack did a few and then went on to other things. It is interesting, though, that in what appears to be his last completed painting, *Woodwind* (page 191), Jack returned to the rollered ground and the warm, broad, rough feeling of the Totem pictures.

One way to see Jack's work is as the fulfilment of

promises made by earlier modernist painters. The Thrust pictures and many of the later ones could be said to complete Matisse's notion of the large-scale colour picture. Matisse, after all, didn't succeed very well with his large pictures: most of those best known are more promise than fulfilment: *The Red Studio, The Dance, Music, The Piano Lesson, The Moroccans, Bathers by the River,* the late collages, except for one or two. Jack, in fact, did 'beat' Matisse, at least when it comes to big pictures. Bush's middle period, the Sashes, Funnels, and Ladders, 'fulfils' Klee's delicate art by making it bold and monumental (something Klee himself despaired of ever being able to do). And Bush's late style 'fulfils' Miró's broad, simplified figure-ground painting, fulfils it with colour. Certainly the last Handkerchief pictures can easily be seen as the realization of ideas present in the work of all three European masters.

At the same time, Jack can be said to have added a range of expression to North American abstraction that we find elsewhere only in the work of Gottlieb and the early Olitski. It's the whimsical, playful, bouncy feeling we know from Miró and Klee. Deadpan, cartooney, and 'childlike,' this range of expression insists on the hand-drawn and it gives to the abstract elements an animated life, a personality of their own. Klee talked about 'taking a walk with a line,' Bush about 'Mr Blue' and 'Mr Green.' Bush rarely puts in a colour without giving it its own character, without making it a different shape and size from all the rest, and, as Terry Fenton once pointed out, he rarely repeats a colour within the same picture.

One thing that struck me in the early 60s was that Jack didn't usually leave bare canvas as the other stain painters did. He liked to cover the whole surface and thereby get a more saturated effect. It is this taste for saturation, and what could be called the 'density' of colour, which led Bush to hang on to oil paint longer than the other painters of his generation and which distinguishes him most as a colourist.

Jack's colour is not only saturated and dense; it is also prismatic, bright, and often very hot. It is Fauve-type colour with lots of ringing contrasts, and in this it relates to Noland's colour and to Hans Hofmann's. But Bush has more range as a colourist than Hofmann (but not more than Noland) and more range of handling and drawing than Noland (but not more than Hofmann). Expressively, Bush's art seems closer to Hofmann's. Both created a big, bright, free-swinging chromatic art and both loved to play with all of the elements at once; neither worked in series in any strict or sustained way. Both were late bloomers and their mature art comes as an exalted bursting forth, a joyous celebration.

KENWORTH W. MOFFETT is curator of twentieth-century art at the Museum of Fine Arts, Boston. In 1972 he organized an exhibition of paintings by Jack Bush to inaugurate the Boston Museum's new contemporary art galleries.

GREEN ON WHITE Magna on canvas, 1961
79¾" x 93½" (202.8 x 237.5 cm)
Private Collection

A Dealer's Memoir

DAVID MIRVISH

MY MEMORIES OF JACK BUSH ARE NOT SO MUCH OF ANY one special moment spent together, or of any particular incident, though certainly I have my specific memories. I remember Jack as a friend, supportive and encouraging. Our relationship began shortly after I opened my gallery in October 1963; I was eighteen years old. At that time Bush was a frequent visitor to the Toronto galleries. As a small but lively art community in the early 60s, most of the galleries exhibited European and young Canadian artists, although there was an awareness that something was happening in art in the United States and had been happening since the Second World War. In the fall of 1963 Jerrold Morris Gallery held a comprehensive exhibition of Pop Art, and by March 1965 Toronto had seen the work of Donald Judd at the Isaacs Gallery. As late as 1964, however, no Toronto gallery had committed itself to exhibiting the work of an American abstract artist on a continuing basis.

In the spring of 1964 I held an exhibition called 'XXIX International Artists' at my gallery. Toronto and New York dealers generously lent works by some of the most prominent Canadian, European, and American artists, many of whom had never been shown before in Toronto. Arman, Francis Bacon, César, John Chamberlain, Richard Diebenkorn, Jim Dine, Hans Hofmann, Jasper Johns, Willem de Kooning, Louise Nevelson, Jules Olitski, William Ronald, Michael Snow, Jean Tinguely, Harold Town, and Tom Wesselmann were all part of the exhibition. I wanted also to include Jack Bush, and through the kindness of a Toronto collector I borrowed a 1962 Flag painting, *Paris #2*. For me that show was a very exciting event. During the following two weeks I had the opportunity to see which of the paintings I liked the most. The

show was very well attended and I was exposed to a constant barrage of opinion as to what was best. The Bacon, de Kooning, Nevelson, and the two Hofmanns drew the greatest amount of favourable comment, but to me, the Olitski and the Bush were the biggest surprises. They were not the best-known artists but their work commanded my attention – so much so that my view of what I liked began to change. Although none of the paintings sold, I felt encouraged by the attention the exhibition had received. Jack Bush, Jules Olitski, and Hans Hofmann were the artists whose work I wanted to know better.

That summer I visited the Venice Biennale and was immediately attracted to the work of Noland, Louis, and Stella. In fact, their work filled me with such enthusiasm that I was determined to be their Canadian dealer. Upon returning home I arranged exhibitions for both Kenneth Noland and Frank Stella for 1965, and concluded arrangements for a show of Jules Olitski's work. It had been a wonderful, formative summer. Many of the exhibitions I had planned for fall would be the first one-man shows for these artists in Canada.

I wanted to represent Jack Bush as well, but he was unwilling to commit himself to an exhibition at my gallery in 1965 because at this time he was still working at his advertising job and preparing for major exhibitions in New York and London. He had set himself the task of producing thirty large paintings, which he did on Sundays in a small studio at his home. As an exhibition was not possible, I suggested, and Jack agreed to let me publish, a portfolio of silkscreen prints. We intended to present a synopsis of his work from the three previous years. The success of this project was of real importance to me as I wanted Jack to realize how much I cared about his work. The portfolio, based upon existing gouaches, with an introductory essay by Andrew Hudson, was published in

UP TO acrylic on canvas, August-October 1969
105½" x 65½" (267.9 x 116.4 cm)
Mr and Mrs David Mirvish, Toronto, Ontario

December 1965. In January 1966 Jack Bush joined the David Mirvish Gallery and in November of that year the gallery held its first one-man exhibition of his work.

In the period before he began to show at my gallery we had shown many artists to whom Jack was very sympathetic, people he knew or whose work he knew and admired: Jules Olitski (1964, 65, 66), Helen Frankenthaler (1965, 66), Kenneth Noland (1965), Frank Stella (1965), Milton Avery (1966), and Anthony Caro (1966). It was my intention to provide the work of Jack Bush and all the gallery's artists with a mutually supportive context. I think Jack found this approach attractive and for this reason wanted to be part of my gallery. Public support was still limited, but I had confidence in the artists I had chosen to show. I had already begun to purchase their work.

One of the big advantages of buying the paintings was that if someone came into the gallery and wasn't familiar with an artist's work, I could show him examples covering three or four years. I didn't simply show him this year's batch of paintings and expect him to make a judgment. He could begin to understand that the artist had some reason for painting the way he did, by seeing his evolution and consistency over a period of time. This perspective was a great help in putting Jack's work across and making people see that it wasn't arbitrary.

Exhibitions by Jack Bush were held at the gallery in 1966, 1967, and 1968. They were well received critically by the three local newspapers but it was not until 1968 that more than three or four paintings a year could be sold. This reticence was in marked contrast to the years after 1970 when all the exhibitions were well attended and the paintings were often sold before the openings.

In making his paintings, Jack looked everywhere for stimulation. If he saw a good idea, he would go back to the studio and make it his own. Sometimes the drawing came from art, but it could as easily come from a dress model, marks on a rock, or flowers in his garden. I remember his response to the Frank Stella exhibition held at my gallery in April 1966. These eccentric shaped paintings with large bands were the first in which Stella had used more than one colour since his 'Black' paintings of 1959. Jack made his great 'Criss Cross' and 'Multi-Striped' series (pages 109, 110, 112, 114) following this exhibition. Taking Stella's drawing as a point of departure, Bush rearranged it and then packed more colours into his painting than at any point up to this time in his career.

At my first Anthony Caro exhibition in 1966, Kenneth Noland and Jack Bush helped with the installation. Then everyone present helped to paint and touch-up the pieces. Several years later Bush sent a painting to me at the gallery called *Tony's Horse*. It included all the colours Caro had used on pieces in his exhibition. Jack found successful

paintings in amazing places. Style was just a way of getting elbow-room. Feeling, not style, was Jack's subject matter.

In the mid 1960s ambitious artists had become aware of the importance of seeing what was being painted; they knew that first-rate work was not done in seclusion, that by attending exhibitions they could learn something of what they wanted or did not want to paint. For the thirteen years that I knew Jack Bush, he was always interested in what was on view and made a point of seeing as many exhibitions as possible. He was a sophisticated man in terms of his art, with the ability to pick out the best of what he had seen and utilize it. At the same time, he always retained his own identity. It was his inquisitive nature and strong sense of self that I believe allowed Jack to make the major transitions of being first a Canadian landscape artist, then an abstract artist and member of Painters Eleven, and finally an independent, mature, and truly international artist.

He was able to get a warmth from his paintings in the early 60s, a richness, a sensualness that is different from any other painter's, and in his late paintings of the 70s he was able to create a complexity of colour which sets him apart. He worked with a great range of colours, with light and dark, with complicated grounds and surprising composition in terms of shape, and he made it all like a song. Jack was able to transform colours that by themselves you might not respond to. I would notice it with people coming into the gallery who would say, 'I don't like green pictures,' but the way Bush used a colour, it was no longer a question of a green painting. The viewer thought of it as a whole, the green as simply a part of the painting. Even if it was the dominant part, it suddenly became something very beautiful, not just something green. That was his mastery of colour.

Six years after Jack's death I am as convinced as I was in the mid 60s that Jack is the finest artist Canada has ever produced. In terms of the painters of his own generation, internationally, his paintings today look as fresh as the day he painted them. I look about me now at many of the new painters who interest me and I see Jack very much alive as the inspiration for many young artists in England, Canada, and the United States. What a small audience once saw in his work is now communicating itself to a much wider group of people.

I was Jack Bush's dealer for eleven years. It was during this time that resistance to his work melted. He received the Order of Canada and had a major retrospective at the end of his lifetime. He was the equal of any artist I showed and a man deserving of his international stature.

DAVID MIRVISH was director of the David Mirvish Gallery, Toronto, from 1963 until 1978. He is a major collector of contemporary art.

MAY RED acrylic on canvas, May 1970
68" x 164½" (172.2 x 417.8 cm)
Mr and Mrs David Mirvish, Toronto, Ontario

Jack Bush in the 1970s

CHARLES W. MILLARD

JACK BUSH'S ART BEGAN TO BREAK OPEN IN THE LATE 1950s. Departing from an Abstract Expressionist style that involved broadly brushed, rough-edged forms carried out in modulated, occasionally shaded colours, Bush moved toward a more personal idiom involving flatter, more idiosyncratic colour, and clearly defined, regular, and larger-scaled forms. By the mid 1960s he had arrived at artistic maturity in masterful compositions, completely stamped with his individuality, which were free and open in effect yet totally controlled. These pictures were generally composed of vertical stacks of stripes executed in high-keyed colours such as lime greens, pink-purples, and rich reds and blues. Their colours were thinly applied, often in inflected washes reminiscent of watercolour. At first centred on the canvas and constituting an image clearly distinguishable from the ground on either side, the stacks showed an increasing tendency to shift sideways and attach themselves to the edge of the canvas, leaving a residual ground next to them. This move increased pictorial scale and tightened the surface of the composition.

The extremity of this shifting tendency, and of the bowstring tautness it encouraged, came around 1967 in a series of compositions, generally horizontal in format, in which the grounds were eliminated and several stacks of stripes were tipped at antic angles to one another. The bright, flat colours of the individual stripes, sometimes angled against the stacks they composed, and the irregular relationships of the stacks themselves, made for compositions that were extremely active visually. It is a measure of Bush's mastery that he could juggle the elements of these compositions into expansive and unified entities. The years 1968, 1969, and 1970 were particularly prolific for Bush (his annual output almost doubled), and it was then that he laid the pictorial foundations on which his final

accomplishment was to be built.

During 1968, Bush created several pictures in which solid-coloured grounds reappeared, often occupying half a narrow composition of which the other half was a single row of stripes. The stripes, reduced in number, no longer read as stacks and were seen in partnership with the grounds rather than as superior or subordinate to them. Pictorial equality was maintained by softening the ground colour and intensifying the colours of the stripes, which tended to interact with some liveliness, as well as by adjustments of the relative sizes and shapes involved. Since the stripes were not seen against the larger colour areas in these pictures, 'ground' is an approximate, not to say misleading word for these areas. It does, however, suggest something of their origins and point to something of their future function. Although the grounds were applied flat, occasional accidents of application resulted in inflections amounting almost to mottling, an effect absent from Bush's painting since about 1960, when it had been caused by residues of pigment in his thin paint or unevenness in the canvas surface. In the late 60s it was due to the hazards of applying paint with a roller and was significantly prophetic. *Fringe on Blue Grey* (1968) has such an inflected ground, and exemplifies a new, strongly vertical format in which narrow stripes are arranged as an upright fringe across the bottom of the composition.

After he had restored large single-colour areas in 1968, Bush began to experiment in 1969 with taking the elements of his pictures apart. What had previously been stripes became colour bars, detached from one another and arranged in diagonal juxtapositions across the entire surface of the canvas, as in *Upway* (1970). Bush's increasing interest in forceful shape, suggested in the narrow formats of 1968, now invaded the canvas itself in the form of these bars, which were subtly varied in width and length. Although the bars were wholly contained within the

ABOVE Bush in 1971

TEXT CONTINUED ON PAGE 57

SPAIN #3 Magna on canvas, July 1962
74" x 45" (187.9 x 114.3 cm)
Vincent Melzac Collection, Washington, DC

BILATERAL WITH GREEN oil on canvas, 1963
57½" x 57½" (147.3 x 147.3 cm)
Westburne Collection
Montreal, Quebec

BIG ONE oil on canvas, 1963
106" x 69¾" (269 x 175 cm)
The Canada Council Art Bank/la Banque d'œuvres d'art du Conseil des Arts du Canada
Ottawa, Ontario

TIGHT SASH oil on canvas, July 1963
69½" x 42¾" (176.5 x 108.6 cm)
Jack Bush Heritage Corporation Inc.

52

BLACK VELVET oil on canvas, fall 1963
82" x 60" (203.2 x 152.3 cm)
Art Gallery of Hamilton, gift of Wintario, 1980
Hamilton, Ontario

ORANGE, PINK, GREEN oil on canvas, January 1964
70" x 43" (177.8 x 109.2 cm)
Private Collection

ORANGE CENTRE oil on canvas, summer 1964
81" x 68½" (205.7 x 174 cm)
The Edmonton Art Gallery, purchased with funds donated by the Women's Society and The Winspear Foundation
Edmonton, Alberta

STRIPED COLUMN oil on canvas, summer 1964
88" x 70" (223.5 x 177.8 cm)
Museum of Fine Arts, Boston, anonymous gift, 1973
Boston, Massachusetts

confines of the canvas, something that might otherwise have reduced the scale of the pictures in which they appeared, their extent and their carefully calculated relationships to the formats that held them assured enlargement rather than diminution of pictorial scale. Precisely ruled on their long sides, they were generally left ragged at the ends, introducing a kind of drawing or calligraphy that had not been seen in Bush's work for almost a decade. More freely devised internal shapes appeared at about the same time, first in the form of simple signs derived from road markers, banners, and other pedestrian sources, then as knots, loops, and free forms that Bush invented. These were generally isolated in the upper portions of squared rectangular canvases whose lower extremities were occupied by fringes of vertical stripes, and were often executed in light colours, frequently white, against dark neutral hues, which became grounds in the true sense.

Having allowed the ends of his colour bars and other shapes to go ragged, Bush now began to explore less pristine application of his grounds, following a general trend toward more visible facture in the paintings of the later 1960s and 70s. He discovered that if the thinly rolled paint of the grounds contained a certain amount of unassimilated pigment, the result was a pleasing modulation that produced a yielding, although not atmospheric, foil for the flat shapes on top of them. By 1970 this combination of open ground and carefully described colour areas, which first appeared in 1969, had become prominent in Bush's work, and from 1971 until his last paintings in December 1976 it was his exclusive format.

In the early pictures in which it was used, the juxtaposition of the modulated ground with a fringe of stripes at the bottom threatened to subvert the declarative flatness that Bush consistently sought in his mature work. Even in such a fine picture as *Strawberry* (1970, page 57), the stripes tended to become a foreground fence beyond which the softened ground seemed to want to drop off. Such spatial implications, however, were avoided in *Strawberry* by the assertiveness of the freely drawn 'u' on top of the ground, which pulled the upper part of the composition to the surface of the canvas and held it there in tension with the stripes. Nevertheless, the threat of striped fringes attached to the edges of the canvas acting as *repoussoirs* remained. Moreover, combined with the vertical rolling of the grounds, which became visible when they were no longer uninflected, such fringes introduced a directionality at odds with Bush's basic quest for equilibrium. Running the stripes horizontally and sweeping a governing shape from the top edge of the canvas to the bottom, embracing both ground and stripes, was an unsatisfactory long-term solution, although it might work for individual compositions (*Bend*, 1970, page 139). In the end, the most viable solution was that suggested by the large compositions of detached colour bars – to cut the stripes loose from the edges of the picture and from one another, permitting them to interact as discrete shapes with other forms and allowing the grounds to take over the entire surface behind them.

As the grounds became more unified and their rolled facture increasingly seamless, they placed substantial pressure on the forms on top of them. This pressure was intensified during 1972, when Bush began strengthening his usually neutral (brown or grey) grounds by the addition of larger amounts of unassimilated pigment, usually titanium and umber, which gave the appearance of white and black flecks and splotches. Although they continued to be thinly applied, and what seem to be flecks of white sometimes turn out to be areas of unpainted canvas, these grounds gave an impression of great substance.

Bush then decided to contain the grounds entirely within the confines of the composition, stretching his canvases so as to show the uneven edges of their rolled paint application, a move perhaps suggested by the ragged ends of his stripes and the growing freedom of his calligraphy. The narrow margin that remained was often toned down with either a neutral hue or a lighter version of the ground colour. At one point Bush worked on linen, automatically providing himself with a toned edge. Pulling the grounds away from the edges of the canvas gave them shape and suppressed suggestions of infinite extent. It also made scale easier to manipulate but harder to control, for the ground became yet another defined variable to be juggled with the forms on top of it. Those forms tended to

---

STRAWBERRY acrylic on canvas, March 1970
68" x 91¾" (172.8 x 233.1 cm)
Mr and Mrs Alan Kotliar, Toronto, Ontario

respond to the pressures exerted on them by fleeing to the edges of the canvas, venturing across the centre of a composition only when the verticality of its ground application was countered by one of the sharply horizontal formats that now became as common in Bush's work as vertical formats had been previously (*Island*, 1973, page 169). Until well into 1972 Bush's repertoire of shapes continued to include the bars and rectangles of the liberated stripes, as well as knots, boomerangs, ovoids, and more fanciful configurations executed in the mixed and sprightly hues he favoured. If the shapes were small, weak, or too congruent with the striated ground application, or if their colours were too dull, they were in danger of being swallowed up by the ground, a deficiency that Bush almost always managed to avoid. Similarly, if a ground was separated from the edge of the canvas by too wide a margin, it lost control and the entire composition shrivelled.

In 1973 the coloured shapes began to move back toward the centre of Bush's increasingly square canvases, attaching themselves to one another as if for mutual support. In the Totems of 1973-4, two series of narrow rectangular shapes were criss-crossed at roughly right angles parallel to the sides of the canvas, giving the effect of two intersecting multicoloured bars (*Jay Totem*, 1974, page 177). A straight line defined one side of these bars, while the other was irregularly feathered, modulating it more gently to the ground. A horizontal variation of this generally vertical format involved an imaginary line above and below which were strung colour areas that might have been insufficiently strong as independent units but became assertive in their conjunction (*Blue Tee*, 1973, page 174). One or more ends of the colour sequences in both of these formats were sometimes attached to the edges of the canvas, giving them greater stability and increasing their scale. In a few of the horizontal pictures, a colour bar entering from one edge of the canvas ended in a curving shape (*Dipper*, 1974). Although all these formats continued to be developed by Bush well into 1974, the dipper configuration suggested new possibilities that he decided to explore in depth, first announced in the London series of over a dozen canvases begun in the summer of 1973 (*London #13*, page 173). In them, the scoop of the dipper takes on independent life, becoming the broad arc or lazy 's' that appears in so many late works. As 1974 progressed, Bush's colour areas once again detached themselves from one another.

Bush's mastery is evident in the way in which he played with the interaction between his grounds and the shapes on top of them in these pictures. Varying the amount of unassimilated pigment he rolled on, he allowed his grounds to go matte or out of focus behind higher valued shapes, permitting the grounds to reassert themselves when they spoke alone. If his colour shapes were limited to one area of the canvas, he might alter the value of the ground elsewhere, giving it greater variety where it was otherwise unaccented (*Arabesque*, 1975, page 181). This process was made considerably easier when he began applying his grounds with a sponge, which freely followed the gesture of his hand, rather than with an inflexible roller, which necessitated long, symmetrical strokes. The sponge-applied grounds quickly began to have swirling rhythms that matched the rhythms of the curving colour shapes, at once assimilating those shapes and giving them greater importance by more closely approximating their scale. Without losing their presence or substance, the grounds also became increasingly integrated and yielding. This was accomplished both by reducing or eliminating the amount of unassimilated pigment they contained and by making them even thinner and washier in effect, with the broad linear patterns created by the sponge application less distinct. The resulting harmony gave Bush's painting a subtle unity that characterized it until the end.

Beginning in late 1974, Bush was inspired in his work by music, an interest reflected in the titles of his later pictures. He had always had specific referents for his imagery – the Thrust paintings developing out of flower shapes, the pictures of the early 70s out of road markings – and his musical associations were quite exact. *Chopsticks* (January 1977, page 192), for example, is composed so that the shapes that move from left to right across its surface almost precisely reflect the number and tones of the notes in the opening figure of the piano exercise after which it is named. Always able to abstract and transform his referents into satisfying aesthetic material, Bush's turn toward music in preference to more concrete sources indicated a new degree of integration, embodied pictorially in increasingly complex contrapuntal movement. His development was from lively contrast toward harmony, but with no sacrifice of clarity.

The pictures Bush produced during 1975 and 1976 reach a consistent level of quality matched by few artists in the twentieth century. During those years his colour shapes rapidly developed from feathery arcs toward more clearly identifiable, even hard-edged, rectangles. Sometimes spun out from a circular centre across a square canvas (*Day Spin*, 1976, page 187), or erupted from the bottom of a squarish horizontal (*Spring Sonata*, 1976), they were generally wafted across the surface of the picture in loose and irregular, almost playful, configurations (*Windsong*, 1976). Whether touching or not, attached to the canvas edge or not, they were disposed with a freedom which, while rigorously pictorial, suggests that Bush had risen far above rules and necessities in determining their placement.

Although he never abandoned the high-keyed colour of which he was the master, there is a noticeable darkening in Bush's late pictures. This deepening is less apparent in their grounds, although they too become richer and more moody, than in the shapes on top of them, which are increasingly worked out in muted mustards, rusts, and dark values of the mixed hues he had always preferred. In his larger compositions, Bush often clustered higher tones toward the ends and lower toward the middle, or vice versa, which gave variety to the unity of the last paintings, while continuing to be a danger if pushed too far.

In the fall of 1976, a few months before his death, Bush made sketches for compositions involving circles. The few paintings that were actually finished suggest his awareness of Adolph Gottlieb's accomplishment, especially *Moon Gust* (October 1976), the central circle of which is halated much like the circles in Gottlieb's bursts. Among the sketches that were never executed are some using triangular, semi-circular, and circular forms that would have complicated the relationships among the colour shapes, and between them and the shape of the canvas itself. Another hint of the direction in which Bush might have gone is to be found in *Gay Day* (December 1976), the ground of which is a high-valued, almost yellow hue that occasionally seems to glow. The resulting disembodiment substantially alters the nature and function of the ground, introducing yet another pictorial variable. Both developments would have led to even greater freedom and complexity in Bush's compositions, and to more daring and impressive pictorial accomplishments. It is characteristic of him that he should have pursued such difficult problems with abandon.

Bush was an entirely methodical and non-secretive painter. Each of his compositions was first planned in a tiny pencil sketch filled in with watercolour, felt-tipped pen, or pastel. There were seldom major changes between these sketches and the final work, which Bush was able to transfer without hesitation to the impressive scale he preferred. For his later pictures, the ground was prepared by mixing water, paint, and tension breaker, and rolling it on in parallel bands, alternating down to up and up to down. Shapes would then be drawn in chalk and brushed in with colour, as in the sketches. Although there were occasional alterations in form, colour, cropping, or orientation, they were few, and those who saw Bush work were uniformly astonished at the accuracy of his intuitions and the rate of his success.

Behind the simplicity that radiates from his work and informs his method, however, lies extraordinary knowledge and control. This expertise allowed him to mix unassimilated pigment into his paint and roll it on, confident that it would behave as he wanted it to, going soft where he needed softness and retaining its bite where he needed presence. It also permitted him to pre-plan the mixed and highly personal colours he applied at intervals across surfaces often ten or more feet wide, knowing they would speak to one another and hold their own against a powerful ground. The pictorial premises with which Bush worked remained basically the same for almost the last two decades of his career. His development during that time was not a progress from novelty to novelty, but a steady refinement toward a richer, subtler, and more relaxed and complex art. Using forms that overlap and open out without suggesting depth or infinite atmosphere, and using colours, be they brilliant or muted, that neither advance nor recede but pulsate laterally, Bush created pictures that are unobscure and wholly present, surfaces on which everything is visible. He was an artist whose work is filled with the unexpected, the result of his eagerness to experiment, and one blessed with the extraordinary grace that makes complex and sophisticated solutions seem effortless, almost accidental.

One of the most frequently repeated anecdotes concerning Jack Bush recounts his ambition, encouraged by Kenneth Noland, to rival the quality of Matisse's painting. How far he succeeded in that ambition will only be apparent with the passage of time, but a review of his mature accomplishment suggests that it was a great deal further than even his most fervent admirers have heretofore imagined.

CHARLES W. MILLARD is chief curator of the Hirshhorn Museum and Sculpture Garden, Washington, DC. He writes frequently about nineteenth- and twentieth-century art and is the author of a major study of Degas' sculpture.

The Red Barn: The Search for a Formal Language

DUNCAN MACMILLAN

In the early days you see, the subject was the landscape ... so you can abstract that only to a certain extent and it's still a landscape. Well, what happens when you abstract the *feeling* of the landscape, but the landscape does not appear? Then you are into a music sort of thing, if you follow me, and that's a hard step for the public to take, not have the red look like the side of a barn, but let it be red for its own sake [and] for how it exists in the environment of that canvas.
Bush to Art Cuthbertson, September 1976

Derive happiness from yourself, from a good day's work, from the clearing that it makes in the fog that surrounds us. Think that all those who have succeeded, as they look back on the difficulties of their start in life, exclaim with conviction, 'Those were the good old days!' For most of them success = Prison, and the artist must never be a prisoner. Prisoner? An artist must never be a prisoner of himself, prisoner of style, prisoner of a reputation, prisoner of success, etc. Did not the Goncourt brothers write that Japanese artists of the great period changed their names several times during their lives? This pleases me: they wanted to protect their freedom.
Matisse, *Jazz*

MATISSE WOULD HAVE APPROVED OF BUSH, FOR ON THE road to success and recognition, and approaching middle age, he changed his way of painting and seemed to throw away everything he had gained as he turned from landscape to abstraction. It was not an easy change, nor did it take place overnight. There are diversity and signs of struggle in his painting from the late 40s through the mid 50s and it is clear that although Bush was looking for change in his art, he was not looking simply for a new style. It was rather that he wanted to evolve a new instrument to realize more fully an old objective. When at the end of his life he talked about the red of the side of the barn, he was no longer in any sense a landscape painter, but there was still some kind of expressive equation

ABOVE Bush at the opening of his exhibition at Robert Elkon Gallery, NY, spring 1962

between his painting and the natural world. Expression cannot exist in a vacuum, but must have its origin in some actual feeling or ideal. In Bush's struggles he could only see his way clearly when he was convinced that what he was doing was meaningful as an expression of actual experience. As the sincerity of his struggle is manifest in his early work, so it underlies all of his later painting. The history of its iconography is therefore not a simple catalogue of themes and variations, and goes much deeper than the polite formalities of paint and canvas.

The clarification of Bush's style first began to be apparent in 1955-6, particularly in his small paintings on paper of the latter year. By his own account, Bush found the cost of canvas inhibiting; working on paper freed him from this restraint. The watercolours of 1956 have a new freedom, spontaneity, and assurance, a manifest delight in the sensuous beauty of contrast between light and dark, opacity and transparency, colour and its absence. In November, Bush was also working from the nude in a Toronto art-school studio. He returned to the nude two years later and again produced an important set of nonfigurative works on paper, marked by the same freedom and expressive power as those of 1956. While there is no conceivable link in the imagery of the paintings and the rather prosaic life-drawings, the coincidence of two such different kinds of activity at a crucial creative moment cannot be casual. The pictures themselves are evidence that Bush was already committed to the creation of an autonomous abstract language capable of bridging the gap between perception and feeling. If the nude drawings were the perception, the paintings were the expression of feeling.

For three or four years following 1956 Bush's idiom remained that of Abstract Expressionism, relying on rhythms stressed by the use of black and spontaneity achieved by the image of manifest haste. To capture a sense of excitement, he had constantly to bring the image

ZIP RED acrylic on canvas, February 1971
67½" x 164½" (171.4 x 417.8 cm)
Private Collection

to the edge of disorder. The watercolours of 1958, however, are marked by a new simplicity which is no less immediate in effect. Many years later Bush described his Abstract Expressionist work as chaotic and undisciplined: 'It didn't mean anything! You could just let go! Throw paint on the canvas! Do anything!' Greater painters than he, Cézanne, Rembrandt, and Delacroix, had recognized that expression pursued simply in its own terms is ultimately self-defeating. Unless intensity is harnessed to a formal structure, there is no barrier between coherence and chaos. To realize the ambitions inherent in the 1956 watercolours, Bush had to find a formal language that could recapture coherence back from disorder, without losing intensity of feeling.

Between 1958 and 1960 Bush worked toward this greater formal control in his larger pictures. At times he was successful, as in *Chanson d'Amour* (page 23) or *Mute Beginning* (page 31), both of 1958, but despite their greater simplicity, these pictures were still within an Abstract Expressionist idiom and relied on at least the appearance of spontaneous immediacy. In 1960 he produced pictures in which this quality, though present, was no longer of primary importance. In some pictures he took the idea of spontaneous execution and turned it on its head, using brushwork shapes on so large a scale that they could not possibly have been executed at a single stroke.

Bush established an iconographic pattern that lasted until 1962, and that re-emerged at the end of his life. Its basic elements can be seen most clearly in watercolours like *Four in Summer* (August 1960, page 82). Single movements of the hand provide the formal elements of the image; a rectangle is produced by the downward movement of a broad brush, a circle by rotating it. In large paintings these free-hand elements were scaled up and formalized. Bush had been moving towards this kind of image since 1959 in works such as *Let Them All Fall* (July 1959, page 25). The sparseness of the new paintings was partially anticipated, too, in a series of small pictures of late 1959 and early 1960, in which the ground is divided into four by a freely painted cross. The new large paintings, such as *Three Circles* of 1960, are set apart by their simplicity and confidence. Bush seemed to let shapes and colours find their own expression through balance, relative depth, and transparency. He also began to make much more explicit use of the edge of the canvas. Immediately before he began to think of his paintings in such formal terms, however, he painted a quite different set of pictures with explicit reference to the natural world. These are the Flower pictures, including *Bouquet* and *Snowball, Peony and Iris* (page 26).

These paintings, which were never exhibited in Bush's lifetime, are very beautiful. Colour, and to a considerable extent form, reflect nature directly, in a marvellously fresh evocation of flowers in a garden. For the first time, Bush's paintings show the freedom and transparency of colour that would become the most distinctive feature of his work, and their inspiration is located clearly in nature. Significantly, he achieved this new brilliance by imitating directly the methods of watercolour, when painting in oil on canvas. The luminosity of the paintings depends on the transparency of the paint, the fluidity of the medium, and the dominant white of the ground. They invite comparison with the earlier watercolours, for their particular quality of freedom and convincing delight. The Flower pictures suggest Matisse without resembling him. Matisse once said: 'Most painters require direct contact with objects in order to feel that they exist, and they can only reproduce them under strictly physical conditions. They look for exterior light to illuminate them internally. Whereas the artist or the poet possesses an interior light which transforms objects to make a new world of them.' Bush too sought this balance between reality and expression, though there is no clear evidence of the influence of Matisse on his work at this time. As Bush turned increasingly towards Matisse over the next two years, however, he seems to have recognized this coincidence of motive. Though he put his Flower pictures away, he did not turn his back on them.

June 1960 found Bush at a crossroads. He had just completed a series of seductively beautiful pictures in which he seemed to have realized some of his deepest aims, yet a month later he embarked on the austerely formal series represented by *Three Circles* (22 July). The only overt link between them is in the watercolours of August.

It is suggested that Bush was dissuaded from exhibiting his Flower pictures, that he was pushed away from his own inclinations and persuaded to follow a more strictly formalist path. Something of this kind may have happened, but Bush's own sense of the needs of his painting was sufficiently clear for him to have come to this conclusion on his own. Whereas the pictures of the preceding years had leaned too heavily towards expression, these Flower pictures leaned too far towards perception. The objective was a pictorial language between expression and perception, directly beholden to neither and therefore able to deal equally with both. In the marvellous watercolour *Four in Summer*, he is closer to achieving this balance than he had been in any of his Flower paintings. He had decided correctly that it was only by commanding the purely formal language of painting that he could realize fully the ambitions implicit in his Flower pictures.

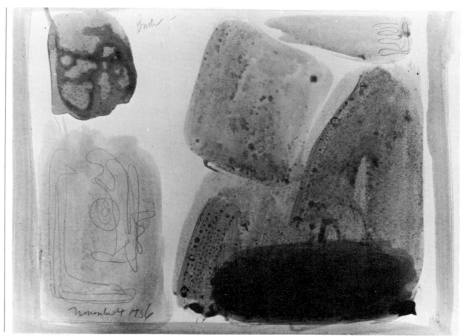

NOVEMBER 27, OSCAR'S DEATH watercolour, 27 November 1956
9¾" x 12⅜" (24.8 x 31.5 cm)
Jack Bush Heritage Corporation Inc.

NOVEMBER NO. 9 watercolour, ink, and graphite, 4 November 1956
14½" x 20" (37.3 x 51.3 cm)
Robert McLaughlin Gallery, Oshawa, Ontario

NOVEMBER NO. 10 watercolour, 4 November 1956
15⅛" x 22¼" (38.5 x 56.5 cm)
Jack Bush Heritage Corporation Inc.

During these years Bush's connections with New York had been growing closer. He visited the city regularly, and, through Clement Greenberg, had met most of the leading figures in the art world. In 1961 he was offered his first one-man show in New York, at the Robert Elkon Gallery the following spring. This was an important event for him and he clearly put a lot of effort into preparation. The pictures that he eventually exhibited were painted between June and December 1961. They all belong to what he called the Thrust series. The dominant motif goes back to *Blue-Green Thrust* of May 1959, but in its fully evolved form it first appeared in a watercolour, *Blue Thrust to Yellow* (page 167), of 1960. In it a long horizontal brush stroke of blue meets a yellow flower-like shape made with a continuous movement of the brush, looping outwards and passing back several times. In the Thrust canvases such as *Top Spin* (page 165), this basic structure is scaled up to give a long shape ending in a flick, or with a series of radiating petal-shaped brush strokes. The shapes used are more explicitly brush strokes, or imitation brush strokes, than they had been in paintings of the previous summer, and because of their obvious basis in movement, there is a tense animation in these paintings. On the whole, the colour is restrained, but subtle variations of warm and cool, flatness and transparency, set up complex vibrations within the shallow picture space.

After the concentrated effort of the Elkon show, Bush needed to pause and take stock. A Canada Council grant allowed him to make his first trip to Europe, in the early summer of 1962. He and his wife, Mabel, travelled to France, Italy, Switzerland, Spain, and England. By Bush's own account, an exhibition of the Matisse paper cut-outs impressed him most. The paintings of the previous years show that Bush had gone to Europe prepared to respond to Matisse above all, and his influence was immediately apparent on Bush's return. Some paintings are straightforward homage, but others show an attempt to grapple with Matisse's complex simplicity. Among the most adventurous are the gouaches painted in the Chelsea Hotel in New York in October 1962 which strongly echo Matisse's *Jazz*. Some are far from successful, but they show Bush struggling to realize the dynamic interaction of simple flat colour that is one of the most obvious features of Matisse's cut-outs.

In New York, Noland and Stella had already gone a long way towards isolating this quality in Matisse's painting, and towards realizing it as a self-sufficient end. It was natural for Bush, who was friendly with Noland, to turn to the work of the younger painters who seemed to be dealing with problems similar to his own. They were exploiting with great success, and considerable public acclaim, ten-

sion between dynamic colour and strict formal control to create pictures that seemed to vibrate with captive energy. Even without the common interest in Matisse, their painting would have been relevant to Bush's own work. Bush allied himself with New York painting and, in doing so, he has been seen as changing his allegiance, as though he cut himself off from his Canadian roots and submerged himself in an alien tradition. No doubt after the difficulties and hostilities that he continued to encounter at home, the excitement of New York painting must have been immensely attractive, but he was very much his own man. The struggles he had with the Canadian public were less significant than the struggles he had within himself. What Bush learned from American abstraction was absorbed into his own art and did not submerge it. This independence can be seen in the emergence of what was to be his best known image, the sash, early in 1963.

The first Sash picture is probably *Tight Sash* (page 52) and seems to date from January 1963. Certainly it represents the resolution of the problems tackled in the Chelsea Hotel gouaches. Its centralized simple structure clearly suggests analogy with Noland's targets, while the diagonal subdivision of the canvas also invites comparison with Stella. It is, however, not a simple variation on a theme set by these two artists. The origin of the sash image is obscure. It appears both as an element in a composition and as a separate image in the Chelsea Hotel gouaches. Bush was deliberately vague about the origin of the image, but the most interesting version is that he was inspired by the sight of a show-window mannequin in a full skirt, tightly belted with a broad sash. This may or may not be apocryphal, but the reference to the figure is consistent with the imagery of the Matisse-inspired Chelsea Hotel gouaches.

In pictures that follow, such as *Orange, Pink, Green* (page 54) and *Black Velvet* (page 53), some kind of figurative inspiration is perfectly possible. The sash figure is the vertical axis, in strong colour, while the rest, being neutral in colour, becomes the ground. About this time, Bush began making small coloured drawings in preparation for his paintings. The sash images amongst them show that although he took great care to wed the image to the ground in the final painting, he conceived the sash structure as a separate image, without any indication of a ground. This method of constructing a composition was very different from that used by the New York painters to whom Bush was otherwise so close. Stella and Noland used formality of structure and execution to stress a painting's radical separation from any contingent reality. Bush, by his deliberate informality and by preserving the distinction of figure and ground, even while uniting them, preserved his allegiance to a quite different set of pictorial values.

Bush's new simplified imagery was the ideal vehicle for his exploration of colour. By the summer of 1964, in paintings such as *Orange Centre* (page 55), the whole picture was animated by the interrelationship of intense and very beautiful colour. Pure colour stained on canvas was a technique that left little room for error. Bush disliked wasting canvas and so it is not surprising that he prepared his compositions carefully, as evidenced by several hundred small drawings in various media found in his studio at his death. They were in no particular order and there was no sign that a conscious effort had been made to preserve them. They were working drawings and Bush treated them as such. The majority of those that survive are from the last two or three years of his life, but a considerable number survive from 1963 on. Some relate to known paintings, and in a few, final compositions are worked out in detail. Bush used to sit and draw in front of the television, and in later life he always took drawing materials on the subway as he travelled to and from the studio. Drawing was therefore a relaxed process and in it his ideas could evolve, freed from the tension and inhibitions that surround the creation of a finished work. As a reflection of his inner life, drawing is the link between painting and music – Bush's favourite relaxation. The drawings perhaps reflect his expressive intentions even more immediately than his finished paintings, and so they can provide vital clues in understanding the logic of his development.

In the middle 60s the drawings confirm vividly his sheer joy in colour. Five or six bars of brilliant colour on a white page are immediate in their impact. They leave no room for abstruse speculation, for they are themselves an absolute. They confirm what the paintings reveal – that the motive force of his work at this time was a love affair with colour and with the possibilities that were opened up to him by a degree of formal control. The extreme discipline of composition based on the tension between colour areas butted together and picture flatness was a source of delight to him. Colour composition in these terms was like the playing of a stringed instrument whose astonishing variety is the product of only four strings under tension, vibrating in a narrow box. Compositionally, his work was less varied at this time than for any other extended period. Between 1963 and 1966 it seemed to follow a steady sequence dependent on the pursuit of the formal possibilities of a given image, the classic form of theme and variations. Bush himself described it this way, and it is easy to see the continuity of idea in the pictures themselves.

Even with this greater formality in the subdivision of

the canvas, Bush kept the figure-ground distinction until 1966, when he began to produce compositions made up simply of vertical stripes. A number of exquisite coloured drawings suggest that the motivation for these stripe compositions was the sheer joy of juxtaposing colour, rather than the influence of contemporary ideas about the nature of abstraction. In March 1966 a picture significantly named *Small Tryout* introduced a new and more rigid structure that suggests he was consciously working towards an all-over articulation. Gradually throughout the year this type of composition became his main preoccupation. Typical pictures of 1967 indicate the influence of Frank Stella, whose work Bush saw at David Mirvish Gallery; *Titan* (*Celebration*) is strongly reminiscent of Stella's output of the previous year, though Bush does not use a shaped canvas. The colours in these pictures are in simple blocks, assembled without the relief of a suggested ground. This is the closest Bush ever came to the hermeticism of contemporary New York painting, but this merely was an episode in his development. Already in early 1968 he was moving back towards a more open type of composition. In pictures such as *Floating Banner* (page 115) he reintroduced a broad ground area, which has a strong spatial feel in contrast to the regular articulation of the colour bars. One painting of this type, *This Time Yellow* (page 116) of July 1968, realized a drawing dated December 1966 and so provides clear evidence of the continuity of his thought.

The very formality of the 1967 pictures is deceptive. They are painted free-hand, consequently the lines are not straight and this implicit instability belies the apparent severity of the image. In the drawings, this underlying tension becomes explicit. Bush used felt-tipped pen, giving each block of colour a strong directional force with the movement of the hand, leaving the ends of the blocks of colour open and feathered, and at times leaving open ground as well. Their dynamic quality is made clear in comparison with works by Morris Louis. When Louis used runs of pure colour starting from a point on the canvas, the result has a beautiful passivity as it is dependent on gravity. Bush preserved urgency by the movement of the hand dominating form and dictating direction. Following the dynamic implications of these images, Bush produced a number of remarkable drawings. In one composition the colour blocks have split apart to create a quite new dynamic image. It appeared as a painting more than two years later, *Spread Out*, the first of the Series D.

Along with seemingly formal paintings, Bush was therefore exploring freer images that reverted to the expressive calligraphic shapes of his earlier career, and at the same time he was also investigating the possibilities of even more organic forms, including the figure. Three drawings dated 18 December 1967 (page 71, top) lead from an unmistakably figurative idea to an abstract composition which emerged two years later as the painting *Up To* (page 45) of August 1969. The diversity of the drawings of these months throws an unexpected light on the paintings and reveals that his search was not just for fresh variations on a theme, but for new expressive possibilities. This search was already leading him in the dramatic new direction that his painting took in 1969-70.

In looking for a way out of the trap of excessive austerity, Bush may have been reminded of his own earlier intentions by the freshness of the paintings of Kate Graham, a close friend and an artist whom he encouraged. Her freely evocative treatment of the natural world was in close sympathy with the expressive side of his own painting that had been kept in check since the Flower paintings of 1960. Moreover, the American pavilion at Expo 67 gave Bush a fresh opportunity to see American painting, and, to judge by some of the drawings, Helen Frankenthaler's free, open pictures very much attracted him.

Against the background of potential change, however, the paintings of 1968 include some of the most serenely beautiful that Bush ever painted. The use of large stained areas suggests the influence of Olitski, but the overall effect of paintings such as *Burgundy* (page 121) is entirely Bush's own. In pictures of this type, the colour bars are parallel to the edge of the canvas, and frequently sit along one edge. This binds their regular complexity into the spatial feel of the broad colour area in a way that suggests the extension of music within a block of time whose mood it colours. Bush frequently spoke of the colour bars as musical, so it seems he was already exploring the analogy of painting and music that emerged strongly at the end of his life. The title of one work in this group, *Blue Studio* (page 119) of October 1968, indicates also that Matisse was still in his thoughts.

While he was working on these calmly beautiful pictures, Bush was looking for a way to open up his work dynamically. The solution appeared in a group of drawings dated 19 March 1968. Two of these compositions he painted exactly a year later. Most of the eleven drawings on the sheet are straightforward colour-bar pictures of the type he had worked on throughout 1968, but two are different: in them he introduced a free calligraphic shape into the open area and the colour bars, while they are freely and openly related to each other, are no longer controlled by the rectilinear structure of the canvas edges. This idea first appeared on canvas in February 1969 in paintings such as *Scoop* (page 124). In this series, loops and curves are scaled up in a way that recalls his practice of nine years

earlier, with the difference that he is now endeavouring to preserve the dynamic quality of drawing in the finished painting.

It is a common mistake of art biographies to read the artist's personal life into his paintings, to say that in such and such a year he went bankrupt, was crossed in love, or lost his mother-in-law, and then to look for the impact of this event in his art. With Bush, however, there is one point where his imagery reflects directly a painful personal experience. In early April 1969 he suffered an attack of angina and, in a dramatic development of the new forms of the previous months, he immediately translated the experience into paint. A drawing dated 7 April and titled *Unexpected Attack* was followed three days later by the beginning of a series of paintings that have titles like *Onslaught, Here it Comes, Tight Band*, and *Spasm #1* (page 126). In all of these pictures, in place of the relaxed curve of the single motif of *Scoop*, he has put a multiplicity of 'blips.' They are arranged all running the same way, either into the painting's colour bars or parallel to them. The result is not only dynamic; it is a tense evocation of an attack on life's most basic and necessary rhythm, all the more telling for its graphic simplicity and lack of melodrama. Such pictures are a stark reminder that Bush's painting was an expressive instrument dependent on experience to give it purpose. It would, however, be a mistake to look more deeply for the effect of this crisis on Bush's art than is immediately apparent in these paintings. The changes that took place around this time were already under way when the crisis hit him, so it cannot be said to be their cause. Nevertheless, such a painful reminder of mortality is not something that a man of Bush's sensitivity would ignore. It would have been surprising if it had not inspired him with a sense of urgency and there is no doubt that the pace of change in his work speeded up at this point.

In September, after his illness, Jack and Mabel Bush took a holiday in Ireland. Although it was only a short break, it seems to have given him the opportunity that he needed to take stock of his painting. The handful of drawings done in Ireland or on his return show that he looked for new possibilities in old ideas, in landscape, the figure, and even the flag motif on the tail of an aircraft. A number of these compositions appeared later as paintings, such as *From England*. The most enduring inspiration is represented by a small drawing dated 4 October, done immediately on his return. It is inscribed twice, with 'On limestone rock – Killarney' crossed out, then *Irish Rock #2* (page 151). Both the painting of this title and *Irish Rock #1* (page 36) were begun this same day. The motif is a roughly drawn white cross. It is taken from painted

ENGLISH VISIT acrylic on canvas, July 1967
82" x 111" (208.3 x 281.9 cm)
Anne Mirvish
Toronto, Ontario

marks indicating grazing boundaries that Bush had seen in Ireland, crude slashes of white paint on grey rocks, elementary even as graffiti but dignified by function. The format of these pictures is the same that he had used intermittently since the beginning of the year. Loosely arranged colour bars at one edge of the picture and a calligraphic image on the picture field remain, but instead of the suavity of the loops and curves of the earlier pictures, the execution of the cross motif imitates the roughness of the original marking on rock while the ground imitates the rock itself. Instead of an unmodulated colour field, the ground is a heavy mottled grey, made by laying on thick, partially mixed paint with a roller.

Though their formal structure appears little different from that of the paintings of six months earlier, the two *Irish Rock* pictures represent a new departure in Bush's work. The handling and colour in the motif and colour bars are quite distinct from that in the ground, so that the whole balance of the picture now depends on unstable rather than stable tension. A margin of bare canvas at the edge allows the ground to keep both its material presence and a spatial feeling, and so compounds this dynamic instability. A superb example of this kind of painting is *Two Roadmarks* of 1970. It is one of a series in which Bush followed the idea of the *Irish Rock* pictures by using Toronto Public Works' street marks. Every element in this painting has an irregular, wanton life of its own, creating a complex and vivid set of contrasts among the image, the ground, and the now tensely present edges of the canvas.

At the same time, Bush began what he called the Series D paintings. The conception of the first of them goes back to 1967 with the drawing for *Spread Out*, and this picture, together with *Walkway*, was begun in September 1969. The series was completed the following year. Like the 1967 paintings, the Series D pictures are composed of simple blocks of colour and are mostly very large, although the colour blocks are set against a ground of bare canvas in an open arrangement. Superficially, they are quite different from the *Irish Rock* and Roadmark pictures, but they share with them an interest in intensely dramatic expression. The colour bars are usually open ended. Their feathered ends, derived directly from the movements of drawing, give a strong directional thrust, reinforced at times by the introduction of secondary elements. Frequently, the colour bars are tapered in a 'perspective' effect and then the composition is made up of groups of bars arranged in opposing perspectives. The result is to suggest the mingling of forces in an orchestral chord, a single unit of sound made by the dynamic concatenation of diverse and individual parts.

The word 'classical' is much and easily abused. It may,

however, be used with some meaning to draw a contrast between Bush's work of the early 60s and the new direction he took at the end of that decade. Between 1963 and 1969 he sought expression in his finished paintings in the refinement of limited means and the exercise of strict formal control, so that richness and variety are achieved within an overall sense of balance in a truly classical manner. The delight that Bush both found, and can give, in his exploration of colour harmony as an active force within an ideal abstract order suggests Mozart. In the paintings that Bush began in September and October 1969, he neither abandoned that discipline, nor lost faith in formal control, but he began deliberately to put them under stress. Balance was now to be achieved by the opposition and matching of increasingly powerful forces, rather than by the harmonious assemblage of parts. This can no longer be called classical. With the new materiality and expressive force that entered his painting, he seemed to be turning his formal language back to expression of explicit feeling.

The interaction of different movements within the picture plane characterize the new freedom in the work that developed from 1969 into 1970. Colour is used to enhance this contrast of movements and evolves a dynamic dimension of its own. This meant a change in the way Bush used colour, and as a consequence the regular colour bars that had been a consistent feature of his work for so long virtually disappeared. They had served as a kind of musical obbligato and this function was now taken over by the dynamic rhythms of the rollered ground. These grounds, however, are made of broken, often intermediate colour: greys and greens are common, for example. The variety of colour that had been the property of the colour bars is now distributed against this surface in much more freely associated shapes, whose high colour key and light texture both increase their animation against the deeper toned ground and accentuate contrasting movements. A vivid example is the horizontal *Zip Red* (page 61) of February 1971. The ground runs vertically and, out of a group of loosely assembled colour bars, a long red streak cuts across the ground towards a yellow flourish on the left that seems to be a projection of all the activity on the right-hand side of the canvas. Drawings for this composition show that the image was conceived in terms of the hand's movement. There is no indication of the ground. This was prepared separately and at a later stage. There was, therefore, an inherent contrast between image and ground, a contrast that Bush clearly appreciated and enjoyed exploiting.

Zip Red brings together elements of both new types of composition, the Series D and the rollered-ground pic-

DOUBLE ROADMARK acrylic on canvas, February 1970
84¾" x 68½" (215.5 x 174 cm)
Lewis Cabot
Boston, Massachusetts

tures. It also suggests a real link back to the paintings of the Thrust series of 1961-2, and from this time forward the use of imagery based on the scaled-up brush stroke once again becomes an increasingly common feature of Bush's painting. In a series begun late in 1971 he put together one, two, or three large shapes that are clearly based on the hand's movement, but rendered on such a scale that no imaginable brush could execute them. Elsewhere, as in *Zip Red* or *Right to Left* (page 154), elements are presented as single brush marks, even though they are scaled up beyond the possibilities of a single movement of the human arm. Bush was not trying to create an illusion of spontaneity in these pictures. What matters is animation and the image of movement – movement of much more explicit kind than anything he had used since the Abstract Expressionist pictures of the late 50s. It depends on the rhythmic properties inherent in the processes of drawing and painting, but unlike the earlier paintings, it is definite, not indefinite. Bush could not conceivably have thought in such a programmatic way, but it is almost as though in his search for an autonomous formal language, having mastered colour, he had moved on to dynamic structure.

An important stage in this development is represented by a group of gouaches painted in the autumn of 1970 and the spring of the following year. These all have the heavy grounds of the larger paintings, but the smaller scale seems to have allowed greater freedom, so that the imagery is varied and inventive, breaking away from the simple brush-stroke shapes of the larger works. In some, Bush had used a cork or potato as well as the brush to give a staccato dotted rhythm. Especially in the group of May and June 1971 the colour is very beautiful and titles indicate that once again the garden is the inspiration. The sequence begins with *Spring Blossoms* (page 196), and proceeds with such titles as *Drifting Blossoms* and *Forsythia*. One of the loveliest of these is *Apple Blossom Burst* (page 197) of May. A complex white shape made with a loaded brush hangs against a cool grey ground in a way that is in no sense descriptive, but which is deeply evocative of the shapes and colours of spring. The success of these small paintings is a measure of the extent to which he has freed himself from the burdens of description and overt expressiveness. The animation of brush stroke and ground and the poetic interaction of colour are an autonomous equivalent to the perceived world. He is approaching the problem of the red barn.

The inspiration of his garden, expressed in irregular shapes and the opposition of short broken rhythms keyed by colour, appeared in larger paintings in June 1971 with pictures such as *Spring Breeze* (page 147). In the early summer of 1972 this direct inspiration of flowers and garden found expression in similar forms, as in *Soft June* (page 83) and *June Bud* (page 108). It is as though these garden paintings were a necessary response to the natural world which overtook him in May and June. The following summer these forms reappeared once more and this freer vocabulary became the main preoccupation of his work.

At the same time, a more formal imagery continued to evolve. During 1971-2 he worked through a series of loop, bar, and hook paintings. Then late in 1972 he began a series whose imagery was even more severely simplified and calmer in effect. Two or three rectangular bars float against the rollered ground. Sometimes they form a loosely constructed configuration; at other times, the basic elements are joined by a group of subsidiary shapes which work like the grace notes or decoration in a musical figure. The apparent simplicity of this kind of structure is the framework for a marvellous subtlety of colour. Frequently the character of the image colour is close to that of the ground, giving maximum value to the other distinctive qualities of figure and ground, their direction and difference of texture, and so giving quiet sensual life to the painting. Subtlety and simplicity allow this intensity to take us by surprise.

The spring and summer of 1973 was a period of considerable diversity in Bush's work. The Bar series that had run through the autumn and winter ended abruptly. In the large painting *Island* (page 169) of February, the dominant green shape that runs right across the canvas has an open edge that gives it a different and more informal character than the simple bar. This informality becomes radical in paintings like *Criss Cross* (page 171). Throughout the summer he experimented with a variety of informal motifs, picking up on images like those in *June Bud* of 1972 that in turn looked back to the gouaches of the previous year. As in these earlier pictures, he seemed to be interested in exploring the interaction of smaller, more complex rhythms of movement, shape, and colour, and from this emerged the first of the Totem series.

From 1971 to 1973 there was a hiatus in the sequence of drawings. This may be an accident of survival, for it seems Bush was making only rough notes with pen or pencil to guide him and then throwing them away. The imagery in the London series of the spring and summer of 1973 (*London #13*, page 173), however, appears to be based on magnified drawing marks, rather like the works of 1975-6. Certainly, by the end of 1973, drawing had re-entered his creative process, for the sequence of drawings he began then runs through without a break to the end of his life. In April he had produced the first of what was to become the Totem series, using shapes apparently

TOP Three Sketches, 18 December 1967
Jack Bush Heritage Corporation Inc.

BOTTOM Two Notes, recto and verso, for unpainted pictures,
June 1976 Jack Bush Heritage Corporation Inc.

made by the relaxed movement of the hand with a pen, but it has a positive structure that relates it back to *Island*. Its central axis and vertical configuration suggest the figure as well as the totem title, and may recall an abstracted figure drawing of 1970. The image in these paintings is built up basically of rectangular elements, in which the fourth side of the rectangle is left open and feathered. This composition relates to the open, loosely structured shapes of earlier paintings, but each element is given more definite rhythmic character. From drawings, it is clear that this rhythm is that of the hand: each element is a small block of coloured hatching. Bush used a felt-tipped pen and the feathering is the result of the natural lack of uniformity at the end of the hand's movement. *Jay Totem* (page 177) offers a good example of how these pictures work. It is built up of a rich set of dynamic relationships whose energy is held within the picture plane but is not neutralized by it. There is a subtle interaction of colour and texture between image and ground, made more subtle by shared colour accents; there is the interaction between the directional thrusts of the image and those of its constituent parts, and there is the interaction between this complex of movements and the quite different quality of movement in the ground.

It only requires the substitution of the dimension of time for that of space to see a vivid and precise analogy between this kind of painting and music – especially jazz – in the way that the rhythms, colours, and subdivisions of the figure relate to the underlying tone and beat provided by the ground. As a jazz musician, Bush would have recognized this analogy, but whether he sought it, or simply found it, in October 1974 it became an explicit objective in his painting. In that month his imagery changed as he began a sequence of paintings with musical titles that continued to the end of his life. It includes almost all the pictures he painted from then until his death. There is plenty of evidence in the paintings themselves that this was more than a titling fad. *Duet* (March 1975), for example, consists of two distinct groups of elements, *Trio* (May 1976) of three. *Bridge Passage* (January 1975) is made up of two groups of elements linked by an arching line, and in case there should be any mistake, the drawing for the painting is inscribed, 'Bridge Passage – between first and second themes'. There are a number of notes of this kind, either on drawings or just fragmentary jottings on scraps of paper: 'consonant chord, combination of tones … in a state of repose – Dissonant chord, harsh, state of unrest'; 'Swing Rubato (freedom of tempo – plus and minus deviations compensate for each other … both melody and accompaniment coincide again'; or 'Keyboard, whole set of keys'. He painted *Swing Rubato* in June 1975 and *Keyboard* in November of the same year.

One of Bush's sons gave him a musical dictionary about this time and these musical definitions show that he studied it carefully, but together with this interest in the forms of music he was also looking for equivalents to the mood structure of particular pieces of music. Titles from jazz, folk-song, and classical music appear frequently in his work throughout the last two years of his life. In an interview he described how he sought equivalence in a very particular way and among his notes are jottings that reveal him reflecting on pieces of music in the search for this kind of equivalent. One note reads: 'Middle to deep held single piano note, slow held temp, velvet fiddle background'. Elsewhere he wrote, 'Kiss me Kate, So in Love – deep piano single notes – High piccolo'. In both, the language he uses to describe music could equally apply to qualities in painting and so seems to relate to a process of translation.

Without even looking at the paintings, therefore, there is evidence that he was deeply interested in the age-old problem of synaesthesia – the analogy of music and painting. It is an idea that has frequently inspired painters and musicians. Matisse constantly used musical comparisons to illuminate the purpose of his paintings, and explicitly in the title *Jazz*. Music combines a purely abstract language with the miraculous capacity to describe feelings based in the real world and capable of association with it, and so clearly matches Bush's own intentions in trying to create an abstract language of painting. With the 'musical' pictures, if they may be so called, what he was doing related directly to the central preoccupation of all his painting.

The moment of this new departure can be identified precisely from the drawings as October 1974. The common characteristic of the 'musical' pictures is that they consist of a sequence of coloured marks grouped against the ground in a single rhythmic pattern. This pattern is divided up at times into rhythmic sets, as in *Concerto for Two Violins* (page 185), for example, where there are six, but at no time do these sets form a block of colour opposed to the ground as they had done in the Totem pictures. Instead, their structure is open and they stand much in contrast to the ground. The character of the ground itself changes too. In place of the roller loaded with heavy paint which gave a solid expanse, articulated by mechanical movement in long linear or rectangular rhythms, Bush used a sponge. The paint is lighter and the movements in the ground follow the natural circular movements of the arm. This gives a softer, more erratic rhythm, and a turbulent transparency to the surface. The effect establishes a new, closer sympathy between figure and ground. In some paintings the flow of the image, though quite

TEXT CONTINUED ON PAGE 81

ON PURPLE oil on canvas, summer 1964
88" x 68¼" (223.5 x 173.5 cm)
Nahum Gelber, QC
Montreal, Quebec

COLOUR COLUMN ON SUÈDE oil on canvas, April-Summer 1965
90" x 57" (228.6 x 144.8 cm)
Tate Gallery, London, England

74

SCHOOL TIE oil on canvas, summer 1965
88½" x 66" (224.8 x 175.3 cm)
The Edmonton Art Gallery, with funds from Westburne
International Industries, Edmonton, Alberta

PINK TOP oil on canvas, summer 1965
33" x 26" (83.8 x 66.0 cm)
Gary Milrad, Toronto, Ontario

COLOUR PILLAR oil on canvas, 1965
80" x 36" (203.2 x 91.4 cm)
Debut Realty Ltd, Kitchener, Ontario

DAZZLE RED oil on canvas, fall 1965
81" x 104" (205.7 x 264.2 cm)
Art Gallery of Ontario, purchase, Corporations' Subscription Endowment, 1966
Toronto, Ontario

SEVEN COLOURS oil on canvas, fall 1965
92" x 43½" (233.7 x 110.5 cm)
Private Collection

ROSE RED AND RED oil on canvas, January 1966
90" x 70" (228.6 x 117.8 cm)
Private Collection

distinct from the ground, echoes and makes distinct its rhythms.

This kind of unity was an objective of the new paintings from the start. Since he had shifted from overall compositions in 1969, Bush had only indicated the figure in his compositional drawings, not the ground. No matter how fully worked out they were, though he occasionally indicated the ground with a written note, he seems never to have needed to see it with the figure before he started painting. From the first musical compositions, however, he included the ground in the working drawing. He used chalk, a medium he had not used before in this context, but which has obvious sympathy with the effect of his new sponged grounds. At first he only filled in one corner of the composition, but latterly, even though the drawings remained very small, he filled in the whole ground colour, so he had the complete composition before him when he started to paint. Initially, he used chalk for the ground, but retained felt-tip for the figure. Very quickly, however, he adopted chalk for the whole drawing. Chalk gives softer, less positive shapes to the individual elements and also gives the colour its distinct earthy quality.

Drawing played an even more important part in this new iconography of the 70s than it had done before. Its whole basis was the movement of the hand in the act of drawing. Its starting point can be seen in a number of pencil drawings, which consist of small single marks of the pencil disposed in rhythmic groups. One sheet includes four drawings that can be related to specific pictures, one of which, *Pianissimo*, was amongst the earliest of the musical pictures. This small drawing was followed by another in chalk, with the pattern laid out first in pencil. Starting from the basic rhythmic idea of the pencil drawing, he has elaborated it in colour, keeping close to the character of his 'subject' by using soft intermediate colours both in the figure and the ground. In contrast, another drawing uses heavy, regular pencil strokes parallel to each other along the bottom of the composition. In all these compositions, the basic rhythm is established in the same way, even if there is not a pencil drawing detailing it. Each element in the figure is a separate stroke.

The translation of these movements into colour is enormously important. Colour interval, the natural sense of separateness between two colours, was something that Bush understood better than anyone, and had always been central to his art. He began to use it in a new way. In the sequence of colours as they proceed across the canvas, we perceive the actual spatial interval and also the colour interval, which relates to physical distance but is not dependent upon it, as it is the product of colour character and intensity. The effect is analogous to that of music,

where interval has the same two characters and so provides the separation necessary to perceive variety and the basic structure through expectation. Set against the broader rhythms and the unified colour of the ground, these complex and very animated figures opened up enormous new possibilities for Bush, as the volume and variety of work that he produced within this formula clearly show.

Bush's interest in the formal language of music would have had little point if it had not been directed towards exploring new expressive possibilities in his painting. The way his thoughts were leading is apparent in a great painting like *Salmon Concerto* (page 184) of August 1975. Salmon is the colour key. The painting is an autonomous pictorial statement which is indebted to music only by association with its purposes. Music is a formal language in which forms and expression are indivisible. It was this indivisibility and consequent expression that Bush was seeking in his own work. To this end, he seems to have tried to find equivalents for the mood and feeling of particular pieces of music in his paintings. This search gave rise to several brilliant paintings, for example *Basin Street Blues* (summer 1975, page 183) and the miraculous late painting *Mood Indigo* (November 1976, page 189), but the necessary point of departure here and elsewhere was dynamic unity. This unity was essential in order to establish the basic analogy between the flow of music in time and the flow of painting in space. The new features of his practice from October 1974 were all directed to this end. As he achieved unity with increasing confidence, the sympathy between figure and ground began to generate a new kind of energy. It is as though the narrow space of the picture plane was like a sluice to a standing pool. Only through the confinement and direction of its narrow walls can the latent energy of the pool be realized. Like Brückner or Mahler, Bush seemed to harness an elemental energy which, though it may be all about us, can only be perceived as he captured and controlled it in his painting.

His own perception of the scale of what he now had in his grasp seemed to come first in the two paintings *Day Spin* (page 187) and *Night Spin* of May 1976. The circular shapes that suggest the sun and moon are a natural product of the flow of drawing, as a beautiful pencil drawing makes clear. In the paintings they seem like eddies in the picture's field of force. It is almost as though what was happening in the composition was so elemental it was creating its own astral bodies. His titling suggests Bush saw it this way. In *Moongust*, *Windsong*, and *Woodwind* (page 191) he identified this force as the wind, and like the wind it picks up and blows the shapes through the picture's space. In this last picture he returned quite unexpectedly to the use of the roller. He laid a ground at an angle to the edges of the canvas, exploiting its strong directional sense to suggest the extension of the force running far beyond the picture's edge, and carrying the elements of the composition with it.

It might seem with these late pictures that Bush returned to landscape. Though there are echoes of early landscapes, these pictures are pure painting. They are testimony to the unity of the expressive drive that brought him at last to the fulfilment of ambitions that more than twenty years before he had realized were beyond the reach of conventional painting.

A measure of the success of his determined search for autonomous expressive language is given by *Mood Indigo*. It was painted the month after he had made his remark to Art Cuthbertson about separating the red of a barn from the structures of landscape in order to allow it to speak with its own emotive force. The red barn door, if it existed, had the same status in a painting as did the music in *Mood Indigo*. Its emotive force could only be captured in painting by forms of coherence peculiar to painting alone.

Bush's insistence on the autonomy of a painting as the basis of its expressive power is reminiscent of Matisse, whose influence was still important to Bush, as is apparent from the fluttering paper shapes of some of these late works. Bush, however, had begun as a follower of the Group of Seven. Through them he had inherited the ambitions of North American late romantic landscape painting. Jackson Pollock, who was his close contemporary, inherited similar ideas from a different source. Very differently from Matisse and the French tradition, these two artists called for a passionate identification with the natural world, for actual union with nature in feeling. Bush, like Pollock, began from radical dissatisfaction with the means available for achieving this consummation, but he did not in the end question it as the ultimate end of painting.

DUNCAN MACMILLAN teaches art history at the University of Edinburgh and is curator of the Talbot Rice Art Centre. He organized the exhibition *Jack Bush: Paintings and Drawings 1955-76* for the Edinburgh Festival, 1980.

FOUR IN SUMMER watercolour, 1960
20½" x 26" (52 x 66.3 cm)
Art Gallery of Ontario, Toronto, Ontario

STUDY watercolour, May 1958
17" x 22" (43.2 x 55.9 cm)
Jack Bush Heritage Corporation Inc.

SOFT JUNE acrylic on canvas, June 1972
65" x 102" (165.1 x 259.1 cm)
Debut Realty Ltd, Kitchener, Ontario

Triumph over Adversity

KEN CARPENTER

All great works of art are trophies of
victorious struggle. JULIUS MEIER-GRAEFE

THE DEVELOPMENT OF JACK BUSH AS AN ARTIST IS something of a model for the history of Canadian art as a whole. He began in the 1930s with an affinity for the Group of Seven, rightly taking them as among the best and least pretentious artists of the day. Often he would work as they did, painting landscapes outdoors on small wooden panels and building up to larger pictures in the studio. During this decade we can see a particular admiration for Lawren Harris and A.Y. Jackson, and we know that at one time Bush attempted to meet Jackson, although without success. It was only later that he would find the Group of Seven too limited.

From about 1947 to 1951 Bush produced a more private and troubled art aligned with expressionism, which will prove central to this essay. Near the end of that period, we find him taking part in the move by advanced artists in Canada towards abstraction. In the 1950s, as a member of Painters Eleven, Bush emerged as one of the few heroes of Canadian culture – strong and courageous enough to move beyond the parochialism of purely Canadian concerns and ambitions to the international arena, whatever the opposition from the Canadian art establishment. When after 1957 he increasingly opted for the thinner paint surfaces and more open layouts typical of Post-painterly Abstraction, Bush was able to make a very personal and richly varied contribution to what in retrospect seems the best art done anywhere since the mid 1950s. It was one of the few times in the history of Canadian art that a Canadian artist took part, almost from its inception, in a major movement of world art.

ABOVE Bush in his Wolsley Street studio, 1975

But while Bush's development encompasses an extraordinary range of quite different periods, even within single phases there is a complexity, a seeming inconsistency, that has often puzzled his audience. In the early 1950s Bush seemed to be going in a half dozen different stylistic directions at once, and Kenworth Moffett has observed of Bush's more mature work of the 1960s and 1970s, 'It is almost as if Bush begins all over again with each canvas.'

The apparently disconnected quality of Bush's *œuvre* suggests a very open attitude to artistic exploration and also a refusal to repeat himself, such as Michael Fried so properly credits to Jackson Pollock. But more is involved than this. Like that other great and versatile colourist, Hans Hofmann, Bush could say, 'I do not have many styles – I have many moods.'[1] I would argue that Bush's art has all the contradictions of a complex personality and all the ferment of a richly lived life. It is for this reason that *The New York Times* could observe, 'He has taken a style that was often in danger of degenerating into an impersonal exercise and realigned it with the specifications of experience.'[2]

The danger for art of falling into sterile exercise is one of the constants of art history, and so is the struggle by artists to escape it. Particularly helpful antidotes to exhausted convention can be found in 'nature' and in the artist's personality. As Cézanne once observed in a letter complaining about the dullness of exhibitions by the *Académie des Beaux Arts* in the so-called Salon, 'It'd be better to introduce more personal emotion, more observation and more character.' Then he went on, 'The Louvre is the book in which we learn to read. But … let us go out and study beautiful nature … let us express ourselves according to our temperaments.'

But creative expression cannot simply be willed. It requires, as Kandinsky so well put it, 'pure inner necessity.'

TEETER acrylic on canvas, November 1976
78¼" x 77¼" (198.8 x 196.2 cm)
A.J. Pyrch
Victoria, British Columbia

Such necessity has for centuries been connected with some vague dissatisfaction or irritation felt by the artist, a 'divine itch' that both drives him on and supplies invention seemingly beyond his powers; in earlier times it was often called his muse. Philosophers have commented on the artist's uneasy disposition at least since the time of Aristotle, who observed that genius is allied to melancholy. Hence Picasso's statement about Cézanne, 'Ce qui nous intéresse, c'est l'inquiétude de Cézanne.' ['What interests us is Cézanne's anxiety.']

Such anxiety stems from the artist's distinctive ability to face reality unblinkingly, even in its ugliest and most disturbing aspects. We can think of 'the ugly' as Ella Sharpe does: that which 'is destroyed, arhythmic, connected with painful tension.' To Rodin the ugly was 'that which is formless, unhealthy, which suggests illness, suffering, destruction, which is contrary to regularity – the sign of health.' In successful art, various ugly qualities are present, but they yield to 'the beautiful': that which is whole, complete, and rhythmical. Thus to Hanna Segal, both the ugly and the beautiful are necessary aspects of aesthetic experience, but by a process of 'reparation' the ugly is made beautiful. This transformation is, she feels, at the heart of art *as art*.

Segal's analysis, which I will not attempt to spell out in detail here, can help explain why new art so often looks ugly at first and also why artistic creation is so often connected by theorists like Sharpe with 'a nullification of anxiety' – why Matisse and so many other artists identify artistic creation with 'getting free' of tension,[3] even though they can by no means always specify what those tensions are. Perhaps the great critics have intuited something similar as well, for Julius Meier-Graefe has emphasized the 'obstacles we must feel to appreciate the gift' of coherence in the work of art, and Clement Greenberg reserves his highest praise for a 'hard-won' unity.

In our day, to specify these cathartic processes as the essence of art invites a further elaboration of them such as could only be drawn from psychoanalytic theories of art and creativity like Segal's. However, this is not the place for such a demanding enterprise, and in any case, traditional aesthetic theory was able to specify some of the vital aspects long before the neo-Freudians worked out a more comprehensive theory of art. I would prefer here to appeal to that seminal concept, 'aesthetic distance,' which for many aestheticians and critics is the essence of art.

The act of distancing was first described by Edward Bullough. He argues that 'in instants of direst extremity ... our practical interest snaps like a wire from sheer overextension.' Our perceptions are put 'out of gear with our practical, actual self ... outside the context of our personal needs and ends.' Accordingly, aesthetic distance entails a certain kind of objectivity. It is because of such objectivity that the artist is free to elaborate his experience in a new, creative way.

The distancing activity is not, then, an impersonal or intellectual one. Rather, it is necessarily an affective response, often highly emotionally coloured, but of a peculiar filtered quality. To Bullough, 'the artist ... will prove artistically most effective in the formulation of an intensely personal experience, but he can formulate it artistically only on condition of a detachment from the experience *qua personal*.'

The artist's detachment should not, however, suggest that successful art is not deeply felt. Even critics like Clement Greenberg who emphasize 'form' or syntax above all other analytical concerns frequently argue that 'feeling is all.' They take it for granted that the artist 'always has to work from his life.'[4] The Italian philosopher, Benedetto Croce, put it very well: 'Those artists who embrace the creed of pure art or art for art's sake, and close their hearts to the troubles of life and the cares of thought, are found to be wholly unproductive, or at most rise to the imitation of others or to an impression devoid of concentration ... The artist ... must have a share in the world of thought and action which will enable him, either in his own person or by sympathy with others, to live the whole drama of human life.'

Croce seems to have reached this conclusion by an elaboration on the concept of distance. He implies that we care about successful art because the artist has experienced feelings in his own life that *need* to be 'resolved' or 'distanced,' and we can sense that his effort to do so has been successful: ' ... in effect, the feeling is altogether converted into images, into this complex of images, and is thus a feeling that is ... resolved and transcended.'

While Bullough, Croce, and the rest can be frustratingly imprecise about the source and exact nature of the feelings the artist distances, and while they scarcely consider whether there are unaesthetic kinds of distancing, they do agree that art is, in effect, a way of overcoming. Croce calls it liberating. It is on this basis that I am prepared to argue that Jack Bush, and perhaps all great artists, have not only painted from their feelings, but have also painted their feelings out. Hence we might have grounds for distinguishing between an empty formalism on the one hand, and the deeply felt, inspired modernism of a Jack Bush on the other.

The place of feeling in Bush's art might become clearer if we look briefly at some other artists who could be said to have painted their feelings out. History is full of documented examples, not all of them entirely successful. Vincent van Gogh found art to be a 'lightning rod' for his illness, but for a relatively brief time. Edvard Munch was an important artist when he dealt with themes of jealousy and despair, but his art declined drastically in quality after his mental collapse in 1908 and subsequent therapy. He then withdrew from his former, emotionally charged subjects and turned to the dullest of cows and other drably bucolic things. Munch would seem to have lost the ability to confront and transcend the cares of life in his art, and in the end could only deny them. Paul Cézanne and José Clemente Orozco offer healthier examples, and they were more successful in sustaining their creativity over a long period. I will therefore compare their creative processes with those of Bush.

Of the two, the Mexican muralist offers the more straightforward example. Orozco had an unfortunate accident in his youth while studying at an agricultural college between 1897 and 1900. As his biographer, MacKinley Helm, observes: 'In a playful experiment involving gunpowder, three fingers of his left hand were blown off and his eyes were damaged. Infection and subsequent surgery left him for life with a fingerless stump. But Orozco not only stood up to the damage. He used it. Many iconographical elements in his subsequent work may be traced to the accident. One observes, for example, his preoccupation with ideal, Herculean hands ... expressive ... strong ... and whole.'[5] Orozco, then, was not only an artist with great courage in the face of misfortune, but also one who – like Bush – knew the uses of adversity.

Paul Cézanne's creative processes and development are even more akin to those of Bush. Cézanne, like Bush, dealt for a while with highly dramatic subjects before achieving a calmer, more mature mode. As Theodore Reff has observed, Cézanne's 'early works ... portray with an outspoken, often crude realism the artist's own obsessing fantasies or fears. Primarily about women, they project conflicting attitudes.' Reff identifies three main types: overt sexual desire, a violent aggressiveness, and an ironic adoration. Among Cézanne's early subjects were *The Orgy* (circa 1864-68), *The Murder*, and *The Rape*. Lying behind all this is a fear of the fatally attractive woman, who – Cézanne felt – 'wanted to get her hooks into him,' and also considerable sexual guilt. Clearly Reff is correct to observe that 'the erotic and the painful are not easily distinguished in Cézanne's imagery.'

The most important of Cézanne's early subjects was *The Temptation of St. Anthony*, of which there are three paintings and at least four drawings between 1869 and 1875. The first of these paintings (page 96) shows the tempted saint drawn off to one side and recoiling in horror.

In the centre, three women unrelated to the traditional theme dominate the composition. The two on the right are clearly androgynous, and that on the extreme right is identified by Reff as Cézanne himself in a remorseful pose. Reff sees in this figure 'a sudden shift from the third to the first person.' Together with 'the eccentric design and macabre mood,' that shift reveals to him an intensely personal content and a deep involvement with the theme.

Perhaps an equally important subject for Cézanne at this time was his bathers, which he also treated in a very personal way. While a painting of bathers by Renoir, for instance, is a scene of relaxation and pleasure in contact with nature, Cézanne's early bathers have an air of tension. The figures are isolated from one another, and they, too, can be ambiguous in gender. Among the paintings and drawings of bathers, there is one recurrent image of particular importance – that of a solitary standing male figure. On a number of occasions Cézanne depicted him, with one arm raised high and the other stretched down on a level with the genitals. As the artist's biographer, Jack Lindsay, sees it, 'the line of the two arms is one of tension, creating an intense conflict in the figure.' In this and related works, 'the tension is centred in the neck, as if the head is trying to tear itself away and disown the rebellious energies of the body; the image expresses an extreme dislocation of impulses, especially a dislocation of cerebral and sexual elements.'

It seems to have taken him almost a decade, but Cézanne resolved the tensions we have noted in his treatment of these two subjects. Meyer Schapiro believes he did so by the 'repression of a part of himself which breaks through from time to time.' There are numerous clear examples. In *The Black Clock* (circa 1870) the temptress is no longer present, and the menace of her sex has been displaced to the red mouth of the shell in the foreground. If there is anything out of control now, it is the various objects in the still life, which threaten to topple off the table. In the *Bathers at Rest* of 1875-76, the figure of St Anthony has evolved into that of a tree, although its gesticulating branches still convey something of the saint's anguish.

The increasing aesthetic distance and refinement in Cézanne's work at this time may owe something to his meeting Hortense Fiquet, his future wife, in 1869, although the frequent separations of their troubled relationship could suggest otherwise. Cézanne's ability to resolve the tensions in his art was more certainly enhanced by his meeting the Impressionist, Camille Pissarro, with whom he experienced his only apprenticeship (1873-74). Lindsay tells us that in giving Cézanne the technical possibility of mastering his medium, Impressionism also gave him the power of resolving his deepest conflicts. Cézanne was soothed by its essentially harmonius or idyllic world.

The result of this process has been well described in Lindsay's biography of the great master, where he emphasizes Cézanne's changing treatment of the standing male bather:

About 1878 he seems to gain a certain self-control. The helpless surrender to dislocation and disharmony gives way to something like a successful containment of energy in a less distorted body; the conflict is still there, but no longer in such a destructive form. At the same time ... he feels linked afresh with the world of nature. The tensions ... flow out and affect the landscape ... and this ... eases the tautness of his pain ...

Thus, as his art matures, he transfers to nature the tensions and resolutions which he feels in his own body ... What he does is in no sense a mere imposition of an abstracted pattern.

Over the years this process continued. Cézanne's early, Romantic mode of untempered self-expression was slowly converted into a mature classicism, and the passionate content submitted to an ideal of order and proportion without being sacrificed. The culmination is those late Apollonian masterpieces, *The Great Bathers*, of which there are several versions (page 95). His triumph, like that of Bush, is all the more moving for being so hard-won.

Upon first examination, Bush's work of the 1930s and 1940s seems fairly typical of that motley collection of heirs to the Group of Seven, the Canadian Group of Painters, but it was not truly in keeping with their more conservative spirit. Bush already had an urge to declare the surface of the painting rather than spell out the subject. Like Cézanne, Bush had a preference for subjects just a little out of control – in his case, leaning farmhouses, sagging barns, and the like. Accordingly, the surface of his paintings has a tendency to pulsate and warp in a way not typical of the Group, and there can be a considerable freedom to the elements, which tend to separate from their surroundings and to float. In some cases he also allowed the colours to mix on the surface, as he later did so successfully in his paintings with rollered fields.

On occasion there are even more striking indications of his mature work, but only in a fragment of the painting: in a corner or within a portion of some object we see a few free lozenges of colour divorced from representation, and we know, in hindsight, that Bush was nearly ready for abstraction without really knowing what it was. He seems, then, to be developing an interest in pure form, and there is little pressure from his personal life on his art. However, in one instance we can see a clear suggestion of phalluses in what are ostensibly farm implements (*Farmyard*, 1933), and there is also a certain penchant for the cover of

darkness and brooding, ominous clouds, especially around 1946.

This more personal and rather melancholy aspect of Bush's art came to a height in 1947, the year he consulted Dr Allan Walters for help with a number of medical problems that could not be diagnosed physically. That September, Walters encouraged Bush to paint directly from his feelings. The occasion is recorded by the artist in the first of three notebooks in which he kept a running inventory of all his art after 1930:. 'Experimental work suggested by Dr. J. Allan Walters, and commenced in Sept. 1947. The idea being to paint freely the inner feelings and moods. Around March 1948 he further suggested starting from scratch on a blank canvas with no preconceived idea, and just let the thing develop in colour, form, and content.' There is a certain irony that a medical doctor, albeit a well-informed lover of art, should have been the one to suggest so major a change in creative procedure. For Bush it was of such significance that he began a new set of entries in his record book immediately after the above reminder. He was on a course that would stamp the next three years or so as an important and singular phase in his art, however brief it may have been.

Dr. Walters' suggestion was not only to paint 'automatically,' but also to work without consideration for what should and should not be shown. Bush was therefore freed from any fear of doing bad, unshowable work and was able to paint without any shyness or self-consciousness about revealing himself. (From that time on, one of his greatest strengths as an artist was his honesty, his lack of any

TEXT CONTINUED ON PAGE 93

HOUSE OF DOORS gouache, 1947
17⅜" x 23¾" (44.2 x 60.3 cm)
Jack Bush Heritage Corporation Inc.

MABEL'S RELEASE #6 acrylic on canvas, March 1966
45" x 70" (114.3 x 177.8 cm)
Edwin L. Stringer, QC
Toronto, Ontario

LILAC acrylic on canvas, May 1966
81" x 87" (205.7 x 221.6 cm)
Mr and Mrs David Mirvish, Toronto, Ontario

AWNING acrylic on canvas, June 1966
90" x 67" (228.6 x 170.2 cm)
Department of External Affairs, Canada

ROSE acrylic on canvas, July 1966
89" x 57" (226.1 x 144.8 cm)
The Toronto Dominion Bank Contemporary Art Collection

pretence or self-deception.)

Bush's procedure was to work primarily on paper, especially paper of low quality such as newsprint. His friend and colleague on the executive of the Ontario Society of Artists, R. York Wilson, saw many of these paintings. As Wilson remembers it, Bush might do twenty or thirty of them in an evening, and 'they started off in the most morbid colours.' A number of pictures from these years survive, for example *House of Doors* (page 88), a watercolour done perhaps as early as a month after Bush's first conversation with Dr Walters. It is a surprisingly careful rendering, not at all consistent with automatism, and has a relatively calm if *triste* tone. While Bush recorded beneath its title, 'Experimental expression as suggested by Dr Walters,' it clearly precedes the automatist exercises recalled by Wilson.

None the less, Bush seems to have transcribed his feelings rather directly even into the more finished works that do survive. The titles themselves are indicative: in September 1947 there are *Tired, Weary, Whither,* and *Stomach Pain*; and in October we find *Indecision, Panic, Tension* (page 195), and *Afraid.* Wilson remembers Bush at the time as 'searching for a door, a way out,' and in some of the paintings all the doors are frustratingly closed. In later works from this phase of his art, Bush frequently depicted figures under constraint – buried, muffled, and the like.

At other times, we see less of Bush's suffering and more of his response to it, for Bush appears, quite unconsciously, to have protected himself from his discomfort. Even in *House of Doors* a few of the doors are open in a kind of wish fulfilment. In *Exploration (Adventure)* (February 1948), the protagonists have evolved through a kind of displacement, reminiscent of Cézanne in the early 1870s, into playing children, and they have climbed various ladders to surmount walls and other barriers, although there seems as yet no exit for them.

Occasionally Bush responded to his situation with considerable aggression. Alex Cameron, who worked for some years as Bush's studio assistant, recalls that in one painting Bush depicted a colleague, with whom he was angry at the time, eating out of a trash can. In *Struggle* (May 1948), two figures of anonymous, incomplete visage hold each other's throats in a deathly grip. *Struggle* might not be major art by a mature artist, but it is a deeply felt work that emerges directly and honestly from a major artist's life.

Sometimes, however, Bush was less successful in resolving tension in his art. In *Release* (1950), for instance, the artist's own feelings are both reversed and denied by the leaping, almost triumphant central figure, but the result appears more wilful than convincing. The artist has achieved a certain amount of distance, but it is not an artistically meaningful distance.

Perhaps the major painting of this phase of Bush's art is *The Long Night* (1948). It is a dark, allegorical work, probably a biblical subject such as Christ in the Garden of Gethsemane. In it, various figures sink in despair or rise in murderous gesture. The moon appears as a disembodied eye in a swath of colour running across the sky. This troubled, extravagant work, so evocative of guilt and remorse, is also replete with shapes typical of Bush's mature vocabulary: the colour swath is an ancestor of those in Bush's Thrusts; under the arm of the deadly figure third from the left we see Bush's omnipresent crescent shape. Clearly Bush is shifting his attention away from his personal difficulties to a concern with his formal vocabulary and, however troubled he may have been at the time, he has portrayed a general situation rather than his particular one. None the less, like Cézanne's *Temptation of St. Anthony, The Long Night* is too close to 'the troubles of life and the cares of thought' to be truly successful. We are struck by it, but it does not move us deeply.

Later in Bush's career there are a number of other examples of work that clearly derive from his feelings, but with increased maturity he more often transcended his feelings, and the pictures are more successful as art. For instance, when Oscar Cahén, Bush's colleague in Painters Eleven, died in November 1956, Bush was driven to paint all day, starting with colours of mourning, such as deep purple. When he continued the next day, the colours had become lighter – without the artist's willing it. Bush later observed, 'it was like a spirit moving up.'

Perhaps the best known example is Bush's artistic transformation of his angina pains. When he first began to suffer from angina in the late 1960s, his doctor called for an electrocardiogram. Both his physical discomfort and the image on the electrocardiogram were frightening to Bush, and in order to come to terms with the experience, he decided, in effect, to paint it. The result was a number of works containing an elliptical shape that was for Bush the way he visualized the pains he was experiencing. (We have seen something like this shape before in *The Long Night*.) There are both works on paper (the Spasms) and such canvases as *Sudden* (page 127), *Onslaught,* and *Flutter* (all 1969). In one instance, *Test* (1969, page 128), the image is reminiscent of the electrocardiogram printout itself.

Like the evolution of Cézanne's bathers, Bush's development of his 'angina' imagery is highly revealing. At first the motif is occasionally too forceful in its suggestion of driving motion. The best canvases of 1969 seem more removed from Bush's original experience with his doctor, and their artistic quality is considerable, but, good as they are, I doubt they show him at the height of his artistic powers. I would argue that Bush is still not distanced enough from his pain, and it is scarcely surprising that at least one careless reviewer has interpreted the crescent shape as a bomb. However, there is little disagreement that the emotional tone of the work is primarily joyous, not fully in keeping with the idea of an attack.

By 1971, in such splendid paintings as *Falling Blossoms* (page 198) and *Spring Breeze* (page 147), Bush has transformed his initial experience into the stuff of great art. The pink and white ovoids at the top of the latter picture read now as theme and variation, and the motif, increasingly broken and incomplete, is no longer fully identifiable. In places the floating ovoids evoke flowers – tulips, perhaps. Elsewhere they appear almost heart-like. A few of them suggest raindrops, or even teardrops. Bush still acknowledges his suffering, then, but what was irregular and distressing in his heart has been made over into something free and pleasurable in the work, commingled with the pleasures of nature. It would seem that, for Bush, art was a way of overcoming, and triumph over adversity was inseparable from his genius.

The greatness of paintings like *Spring Breeze* is underlined by comparison with works in which the artist was insufficiently distanced from the tension underlying the creative process. One example is *Cirr* (1974, page 94). Bush himself observed that the image was suggested to him by a doctor's diagram of normal cells interspersed with dying cells in a diseased liver, and in fact the title is an abbreviation for cirrhosis of the liver. The diagram was intended as a warning to Bush to reduce his drinking, which was a problem for him at various points in his life. Like his electrocardiogram, this image was disturbing to Bush, and his way of surmounting his fear was again to render the image into art. In the case of *Cirr*, however, the artist remains too close to the schematic indication of rupture and destruction. The forceful lines breaking up the occasional 'cell' have a sharpness too suggestive of pain, and the work implies a momentary lapse, a helpless surrender to Bush's troubles with alcohol and with his health. Perhaps it is significant that *Cirr* was done just after Bush had been released from a clinic to which he had gone for help with these problems.

On one other occasion Bush himself may have felt the work was lacking in aesthetic distance. I am thinking of a Sash painting called *Double Martini* (1964). Like so much of his art, Bush's Sashes are fully abstract works that none the less gained their inspiration from what he called 'possibilities' found in his visual experience of the world around him. For the Sashes the stimuli were manifold:

Bush himself suggested a dress on a mannequin, a necktie, the view looking out from a tent, part of an old Chevrolet, and so on. He could find his preferred vocabulary anywhere. In *Double Martini* he seems to have found his motif in a drinking glass. Some time after exhibiting this painting in Montreal at the Galerie du Siècle late in 1964, the artist destroyed it and recorded the fact in his notebook. We can take this editing decision as simply Bush's detached quality judgment on the work. However, the image as Bush recorded it seems much closer to its source than other Sashes, and I would argue that in destroying *Double Martini* Bush was not only responding to an intuitively sensed lack of distance in the work but also asserting his determination to rise above his problem.

If for Bush art was a way of overcoming, that is not to say that Bush or any other artist was necessarily more troubled than your Everyman. The trials of a normal human life

CIRR acrylic on canvas, May 1974
66½" x 45¼" (168.9 x 114.9 cm)
Jack Bush Heritage Corporation Inc.

offer more than enough dissatisfaction and disappointment to feed any artist's creativity.

But even when the artist is emotionally scarred, his problem is transcended in making good art. For instance, Cézanne had a phobia of being touched. As Lindsay tells us, 'For his later life this fear is well documented, but it was known earlier to the Pissarro children, who were warned against touching him,' and Cézanne even required his housekeeper to take special care when serving meals not to brush against him with her clothing. This touch phobia can be traced back to particular incidents in the life of Cézanne: being kicked from behind by a boy at school and almost falling down the stairs; dreams of 'ravishing beings with angelic voices,' of whom Cézanne wrote, 'It's all in vain, my hope of touching them'; and brushing against the dress of a young woman, whose affections he longed for but failed to gain. Cézanne's triumph was the strength he made of this weakness. As his work grew in maturity, his touch became more inventive and increasingly served to establish the planes so essential to the structure of his art. Ultimately, in the 1890s, what and where he did *not* touch took on its own importance as well and led to one of his greatest formal innovations: the breakdown and even the reversal of traditional figure-ground distinctions.

In bringing deeply personal concerns, such as a fear of touch, into his work, the artist often establishes a very personal relationship with his formal vocabulary and may give it a variety of human attributes. In Cézanne's letters we see him responding to planes much as he would to a person, and he is even reported to have talked of 'the souls of the planes.' Similarly, Bush has often been cited for his

Paul Cézanne **THE BATHERS** oil on canvas, 1900-6
51¼" x 76¾" (130 x 195 cm)
National Gallery, London, England

highly intuitive and personal way of disposing colour in his work. He once observed, 'I find myself saying crazy things like, "OK Mr Yellow, what do you want beside you over there?" I try a colour. If it's wrong, it will scream back at you. The painting ... lets you know when what you've done is right or wrong. And you have to listen. To pay attention.' The Canadian painter, Ann Clarke, once asked Bush whether he would still make art if he were isolated on a desert island. He replied, 'Well, of course! I expect I'd find some pebbles and then ask, "Now Mr Green Rock, what would you like to be near?" [and then go on from there].'

This anthropomorphizing of form is no mere eccentricity, although it can seem so; in fact, it leads to the most moving results. The elusive quality of Cézanne's 'lost-and-found' drawing, with all its shifting and uncertain contours, is not just a category of formal analysis but also an unavoidable aspect of human experience. This was especially the case for Cézanne, whose family life was often disrupted and unstable. Meyer Schapiro has gone so far as to wonder if in Cézanne's 'lifelong preoccupation with still life there is not an unconscious impulse to restore harmony to the family table, the scene and symbol of Cézanne's conflict with his father.'

Among Bush's most abstract, most moving, and perhaps even most personal works are his 'musical' paintings. My own experience with them has been both unexpected and touching. In 1976 I drove with my wife from Toronto to Montreal for Bush's one-man exhibition at the Waddington Galleries. The show was a highly successful one in terms of both sales and artistic quality, yet as I spent more time with it, I found myself increasingly uneasy as I contemplated the work. It was only after my wife questioned my reaction that I understood it. Somehow the work was telling me that Bush had but a short while to live. Just a few months later he was indeed gone.

What was I responding to? Perhaps the answer lies in Wilhelm Dilthey's concept of *Nach-Erleben*. His idea is that we can intuitively reconstruct the emotional state of other people from their behaviour and expression. We relive their mental and emotional state by a process of unconscious identification.

But what specifically in the 'musical' paintings might indicate that they are among the artist's last works? One indication is the repose, and also an elegiac quality, that had not been present in Bush before. In the 'musical' paintings the elements have an intensified freedom and float, like something drifting away. In a few of them, such as *Basie Blues* (1975, page 97), the colour strokes seem to have come gently to rest at the bottom of the canvas, and this brings to mind certain later Courbets in which boats have settled on the shore after a storm, such as *The Wave* (1870, Louvre version, page 96). In all of them there is a kind of gentle dissolution, a suffusion of the basic forms by the rhythms of the whole, that is reminiscent of Titian at the end – and the height – of his career.

I later discovered that in his last year Bush was also reviewing various aspects of his earlier life and work. Occasionally he recapitulated an earlier theme, for instance Christmas cards, which had interested him in the 1950s. In *Bull Fiddle* (1976, page 135) one can see an abstract rendition of the earlier funeral scene, *Village Procession* (1946, page 10), with even the picket fence of the latter returning in the configuration of the main elements floating on the colour field.

On first reading, one might think that I am advocating a new kind of representation theory, such as some have attributed to Meier-Graefe. Certainly Bush's work is tied with remarkable clarity to the stresses, and the pleasures, of his existence. But such a correspondence is scarcely the point. Any number of artists have done work bound as closely as one could wish to their daily life, but no degree of congruence between the personality expressed in the art and the personality of the artist himself in his day-to-day existence can guarantee artistic greatness. Jack Bush's painting may emerge directly from a richly human life, but unlike the work of so many currently fashionable artists – Joseph Beuys, Lucas Samaras, Vito Acconci, and the like – it stands first and foremost as art.

Its greatness lies in part in the remarkable acceptance

of reality that, ever since his conversations with Dr Walters, marked Bush's career. In the technical terms of Bullough, Bush's 'distance limit' was great: it encompassed a range of feelings and circumstances that most of us could never tolerate, would never wish to face. This courage showed in Bush's extraordinary candour – in the way he so openly talked of his problem with alcohol and so unselfpityingly remarked on problems with his health. In one instance, he spoke to students at York University in Toronto of his pride in his struggle, by then successful, with alcoholism. He wanted them to know of it and the central role of such struggle with adversity in his life as an artist.

Whatever the personal difficulties he may occasionally have experienced, Bush's art consistently rose above them. We can say of it, as Walter Pater did of Michelangelo's poetry, 'The cry of distress is indeed there, but as a mere residue, a trace of bracing chalybeate salt, just discernible in the song, which rises as a clear, sweet spring from a charmed space in his life.' Never one who 'willfully lived in sadness,'[6] Bush created an art with an unabashed relish for the fulness of colour and all its range. It sings with a glorious, almost exalted sense of freedom in its floating colour shapes and unexpected leaps of colour interval, and yet everything remains consistent with a context of harmony. While the elements in his greatest paintings can have a suggestion of incompleteness that approaches fragility, his colour and his touch provide the work as a whole with an assertiveness and a vitality that are all the more moving for the limitations of the parts.

Paul Cézanne **THE TEMPTATION OF ST ANTHONY** oil on canvas, 1867-70
21" x 28½" (54 x 73 cm)
Foundation E.G. Bührle, Zurich, Switzerland

Gustave Courbet **STORMY SEA** (called The Wave)
oil on canvas, 1869
45½" x 62½" (117 x 160 cm)
Musée du Louvre, Paris, France

Like all great art then, his work is, as Segal says, 'an unconscious demonstration … that order can emerge out of chaos,' that there can be triumph over adversity. Jack Bush persuades me that Meier-Graefe may well have been right when he said, 'The great artist is the great man.'

KEN CARPENTER teaches a course in art criticism at York University, in Toronto, and writes about contemporary art. In 1981 he organized the exhibition *The Heritage of Jack Bush*.

BASIE BLUES acrylic on canvas, August 1975
48½" x 69" (123.2 x 175.3 cm)
Marvin Rosenheck, Montreal, Quebec

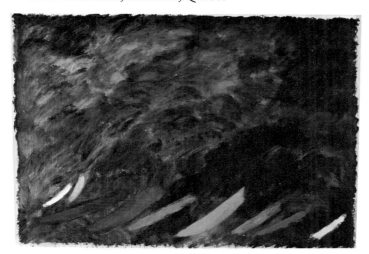

NOTES
1 Paraphrased from quotations in the catalogue for Hofmann's retrospective at the Stedelijk Museum, Amsterdam, 1965.
2 Hilton Kramer, 'Art Opener in Boston: Jack Bush,' 19 February 1972.
3 For some very lucid commentary by Matisse, see Jack Flam, ed., *Matisse on Art* (London: Phaidon Press, 1973), 61-3, 74, and 94.
4 David Smith as interviewed by David Sylvester, 16 June 1961; in Garnett McCoy ed., *David Smith* (New York and Washington: Praeger Publishers, 1973), 171. Smith was justifying his comment, 'There is no such thing as *truly* abstract.'
5 *Man of Fire, J.C. Orozco* (Boston: Institute of Contemporary Art; New York: Harcourt, Brace and Company, 1953), 10.
6 Walter Pater, *The Renaissance: Studies in Art and Poetry* (London: Macmillan, 1873; reprinted New York: Mentor, 1959), 66, 67.

In this essay I have made extensive use of the following sources: Edward Bullough, '"Psychical Distance" as a Factor in Art and an Aesthetic Principle,' *British Journal of Psychology*, V:2, 1912, reprinted in W.E. Kennick, ed., *Art and Philosophy* (New York: St Martin's Press, 1964); Benedetto Croce, *Aesthetic* (London: Macmillan, 1909), and 'Aesthetics,' *Encyclopaedia Britannica*, 14th edition, 1929; Clement Greenberg, 'Feeling Is All,' *Partisan Review*, XIX:1, January – February 1952; Jack Lindsay, *Cézanne – His Life and Art* (London: Evelyn, Adams and Mackay, 1969); Julius Meier-Graefe, *Modern Art* (London: W. Heinemann; New York: G.P. Putnam's Sons, 1908); Theodore Reff, 'Cézanne: the enigma of the nude,' *ARTnews*, 58:7, November 1959, and 'Cézanne, Flaubert, St. Anthony and the Queen of Sheba,' *Art Bulletin*, XLIV:2, June 1962; Meyer Schapiro, *Paul Cézanne* (New York: H.N. Abrams, 1962); Hanna Segal, 'A Psychoanalytical Approach to Aesthetics,' *International Journal of Psychoanalysis*, XXXIII: 2, 1952, reprinted in Melanie Klein et al., eds., *New Directions in Psycho-analysis: The significance of infant conflict in the pattern of adult behaviour* (London: H. Karnac, 1977); and Ella Sharpe, 'Certain Aspects of Sublimation and Delusion,' *International Journal of Psycho-analysis*, XI:3, July 1930.

I have also benefited from extensive conversations with Jack Bush, Alex Cameron, Ann Clarke, Joseph Drapell, Kate Graham, and R. York Wilson.

Where did the time go?

INTERVIEWS WITH FRIENDS AND COLLEAGUES
BY PHYLLIS TUCHMAN

William Winter (b 1909), painter; former partner, Wookey, Bush and Winter

JACK WAS PROBABLY THE BEST COMMERCIAL ARTIST I'VE ever seen. If a woman was holding a tea cup, she was bloody well holding the tea cup. This sounds very simple, but you'd be surprised how many talented people miss that completely. Even in his abstractions, he was objective in that sense. He made strong statements. Jack had a dynamic nature.

I first met him when I was about twenty-one. I worked in Toronto one summer during the Depression. Then, I went back west. After I was married, I came back and got a job the first day in the same place. Later on, Jack and I went out with another lad, a very good layout artist, and we had a company together for about twelve years. We made a happy dollar, and had lots of fun.

We belonged to art societies, of course. They were terribly important in Canada, partly because we have a very big country with a limited number of artists. Belonging to an art society – the Water Colour Society, the Ontario Society of Artists, the Royal Canadian Academy, and the Canadian Group of Painters – was your only chance of showing because there were one or two snobby dealers in town here and they didn't show us. They showed English painting. So, belonging to a society, you had the chance to show and to meet other artists and kick things around.

Jack and I both painted. We would go out on our holidays, on weekends, whenever, to paint. We did all kinds of things. There are places close enough to town like the Caledon Hills where we would go. Jack and I belonged

to what was known as the 'Cold Buns School' – we sat on stony hillsides. The autumn was always a very big thing, and the painting we did was exhilarating. How good it was, I don't know. But this has been a tradition in this country – to sit on stony hillsides and paint whatever you see. Sometimes, the better ones, you would paint them up in big size when you got home. Three or four of us would stay with a widow who had a house and good meals, and we would come in there after a good day's painting. You'd come in from a day like that, and you'd all sit around and have a drink and a lot of ha-ha, and then a good dinner, and it was really rather attractive.

Bush and I both had an exhibition when we were thirty-three. It was a 'retrospective' at Hart House at the university. We both showed about sixty paintings, big and small, which was a damned thing. We were chiefly delighted because two were stolen by a student just before Christmas. We were paid insurance. Well, no one ever sold a painting, and we were paid a big sum: $75.00 each! The people from the university told us with such long faces that this thing had happened. We were so pleased because we never sold anything. No one ever did.

We painted the same kind of thing: a lot of landscapes and things around the town – cafés, bars, whatever came up. The Group of Seven were our predecessors. They were older men, and we were a little put off because it looked as if to be a good painter, you had to handle a canoe. They were all men of the North who would go out and paint our northern country. Alex Jackson would appear anywhere with a bedroll and a set-up, that sort of thing. These men were very good to us; but, of course, Jack and I were city lads. We liked the city, and we had small children and couldn't get away. So, we painted in the streets of the city. We managed very well. We were possibly the best of the lot at that time.

Jack liked the company of other people. He certainly

ABOVE The second anniversary party of Wookey, Bush and Winter, Toronto 1943: (from the left) Les Wookey, Gladys Wookey, Mabel Bush, Jack Bush

SHARP FLATS acrylic on canvas, December 1976
65½" x 80¼" (166.5 x 203.8 cm)
The Edmonton Art Gallery
Edmonton, Alberta

read books, but he was not an intellectual. Jack had this curious objectivity which gave him considerable power. I mean, if the man was drinking out of a tin mug, he was drinking out of a tin mug.

He was a good-looking man, and he dressed well. He was a Montreal man and Montreal men have flair and style. Montreal men have it all over Toronto men, as far as that goes. They have a cosmopolitan feeling about their clothes, about the way that they behave.

He was quite a religious man. He had a whopping big funeral at St Thomas' Church, which is High Anglican. He had very strong feelings. He had a great regard for the opinion of authority. He really did believe that there was a kind of hierarchy and in some ways, he was quite right.

He was extremely interested, all of us were, in what was contemporary. Twenty-five years ago jazz became a very big thing in Toronto; that is, New Orleans jazz and jazz concepts. He was part of his time. We all are. We grow up with our time.

Remember, I came down from the West where I had no support, and I found Jack and other young men who were so warm and friendly. Our experience in commercial art was both good and bad. Good in the sense that it gives you a work habit. You don't sit around waiting for inspiration. On the other hand, there are commercial attitudes which are very wrong, about pretty young house-wives opening their filled refrigerators, which just aren't true. After a while, in commercial work, if you're not very careful, you get to believe in this world. It's a phony world. When we were young men, we would fight to do the ads which would show an arthritic victim whose troubles would be cured by this wonderful ointment. We would be delighted drawing crippled creatures. It was wonderful after months of exposure to the phony world of good-looking people.

Jack was a terribly efficient commercial artist. New York is a different thing – people have been able to specialize for a very long time. It was not quite that way here. We had to do whatever came to town. We got a certain reputation and good prices. Jack had the International Nickel account, which was a good one. It's hard to explain to someone who hasn't been in the business; but when Jack painted an underground miner working at a rock face, he was bloody well working that rock face. There wasn't a dainty bit about it. Jack was always full of talent, dynamic, and atavistic. How can I explain it? Jack was naïve in some ways. For instance, there are many more sophisticated painters than Jack; but Jack had this gutsy feeling towards form and colour that was really quite naïve. Clement Greenberg just adored Jack because Jack had this atavistic kind of freshness towards his paintings.

There are all sorts of competent people who paint very well indeed; but Jack would really get down to basics.

J. Allan Walters, MD (b 1906)

Jack had a personal world that was, first of all, his work, Mabel, his sons, and his home. Then there was a back-ground family in Montreal of two brothers and a sister. A mother was surviving at least until 1950. The father had been manager of a Montreal photo-engraving firm. Jack thrived on relationships and the humanity of those relationships. He always had a group of close friends in school, at work as a commercial artist, and in his fine-art avocational studies where he cultivated friendship with senior teachers as well as his peers and students. Another important pool of friendship for Mabel and Jack was the 'Supper Club' of neighbours and friends, few of them in the art world, who met regularly for many years at dinner parties. Jack was a very powerful and gifted human being and his capacity for strong affection and feeling flourished in all these relationships. A less obvious influence was his deeply religious nature and his upbringing as a High Church Anglican. This emerged in some of his 1947-51 paintings and in his struggles with church teaching and authority. His funeral service was a beautiful expression of his devout faith.

The pressures to comply with authoritative figures as they developed in his adult work became the source of his tensions. He needed to use his powers freely and in his own way. At the same time he feared to break the new ground of nonconformity and risk rejection or abandon-ment. By 1947 the challenges and constraints from his ethical background, from the business world of commer-cial art, and from the fine-art world of Toronto, beyond which he had not yet ventured, were building up pressures inside him that brought him to me. He was sent to me by his physician, in my capacity as a neurologist and psychiat-rist, for an opinion and treatment of a tension state. The problem resided almost entirely within his constraint to self-expression. I proceeded to treatment with general psychotherapy and counselling. At no time did I feel he needed psychoanalytical measures. He found my help supportive and it certainly produced results. It may have had a special force and power because of my appreciation of his unusual artistic powers and aesthetic sensibilities. At the first interview I was impressed with the force of his constrained powers and gifts. After three interviews I was sure of it. The immediate need was for him to embody his personal experience and pent-up feelings freely in his paintings. I advised him to paint in any way he felt inclined, about anything or any experience or any feelings that he might wish to represent, and to free himself from the constraints of Toronto conventions or artistic opinion.

After that it all just flowed. Since 1945 the new art books from Skira had opened the world of European art to him. In 1947 and for the next two years he let himself go in highly emotional paintings where his feelings were embodied and hung out in symbolic and abstracted human figures and scenes. This culminated in the watershed exhibition of October 1949 at the Gavin Henderson Galleries, Toronto. Here he exposed his break with local tradition and his adventures in creativity from within himself. The next ten years saw him moving to bigger and bigger canvases, shedding derivative influences and moving to colour-field painting without figures. By 1947, at the age of thirty-eight, he had mastered drawing and painting for commercial art, as can be seen in the wonderful series of drawings produced for the International Nickel Company of Canada Limited. They were published by INCO as a *Review of Institutional Advertising 1932 to 1947* and exemplify a powerful artistry already well developed. At the same time, he had won his place in the front rank of young Ontario painters.

By 1950 he had been to New York, and found Pollock, Gottlieb, and the big canvases. The Museum of Modern Art had opened doors to his resolve to work absolutely independently. He continued to grow and develop inside himself. The size of the canvases reflects his march to his later works in an expanded scale where he felt unfettered and at ease. By 1955 he was painting canvases up to 40" x 30". By 1961 with New York and Painters Eleven behind him, he was using canvases up to 95 3/4" x 81" – and thriving on the expansion.

In these years he developed the courage and ability to express himself in forms for which he alone took responsibility. This was the essential counsel I had given him: 'Never mind fussing about what you do – just do it and let it stand on its own merit.' From what Jack has told me I believe that Mr Clement Greenberg, when he came on the scene in the 50s, gave him similar advice – to be his own man, to have the courage to paint his own way and let the result earn its own place. I am quite sure that Mr Greenberg was not telling Jack how or what to paint but to paint his own way and avoid derivation.

By 1949 it was obvious that he could work masterfully in colour and symbols without conventional figures and imagery. In this freedom he glowed. After he found the New York scene, he seemed to settle down to the serious business of major creativity. The new scale of canvas increased his comfort and fired his daring to create and explore. Another fact that stimulated his growth was that in the crucial 1949 show in the Gavin Henderson Galleries

he was not rejected but won respect and some acclaim from Toronto art critics, in particular from Pearl McCarthy. Then came the sequence of exhibitions, including those of the Painters Eleven, and the growing purchases and the recognition that was at hand. These supports from the local art scene greatly strengthened his confidence to proceed into the 60s with a palette and a painterly style that was uniquely his. My impression was that he valued other people's work very much and could enjoy it as their mode of expression. His odyssey was aimed at expressive forms that fulfilled himself. He did not seem to be competing with others for rank, but within himself for authority to express his personal experiences in the most beautiful and most powerful creations he could devise.

He dressed like a banker or a business executive. He was neat, conventional in appearance, and lived within middle-class manners and mores. This conformity came from his upbringing and he would have to break out of it to express himself artistically. While in commercial art, he remained natty. Then when he went on his own his hair became longer, his moustache less trimmed, and his clothes less formal. He now looked comfortable and relaxed. He had long been good looking in the sense of a Ronald Coleman and by the 70s he had a handsome elegance.

Well, I never heard about 12-tone in advanced modern music from him but he loved jazz, could play the piano, and I heard a good deal about the Basin Street type of blues and emotional music, as well as classical and church music.

He loved sports. He loved the spectacle and the competition. I think he played games as a boy and he watched hockey and football on television. His metaphors were those of the ball park. He liked to be in his garden and his home and his studio. He had a studio right in his house. As a Sunday painter he produced and produced and produced. It had to be the best he could do. As he grew in confidence and had measured himself with Gottlieb, Hofmann, Olitski, and Noland, that's when he got to talking about the big league and 'knocking the ball out of the ball park.' He loved to score – not to beat others but to produce the most powerful and moving paintings that he could. Those were his home runs.

I can't look at a Bush painting without thinking of our relationship and friendship of some depth. It wasn't just that he was relying on me for counselling. I had the similar happiness that a teacher would have with a student. I was counselling him to express himself and to have no hesitation in revealing what was inside him. He was a powerful and compulsive worker – a 'workaholic' as they say nowadays. He couldn't be idle. This was something inside him, not psychopathic, but the gift of an incessant drive to create. He had such humanity! Wife, father, brothers, children – he worked all those relationships. Socially, he transacted with the other person and drew him out. He had a great heart and it was spread across jazz music, his loving nature, his social nature, his aesthetic nature, and his ability to use colour to communicate this power. Finally, there is Mabel – his wife – the central catalytic person in his life stream. They were well bonded within a fine marriage. She never doubted his ability, she backed him in the low spots, rejoiced and shared in the high moments, and loved him deeply. Without such a heavy fertilization of his emotional nature I doubt if he could have produced such beauty.

K.M. (Kate) Graham (b 1913), painter

I first met Jack Bush after the war. My husband had been in the navy, and when he came home we returned to Toronto. We had no place of our own to live and went to stay in the Cleeve Hornes' studio. When the Hornes came back after the war there was still no place for us to move, so we stayed on with them. Many artists came to the house. There were many meetings and parties, and we were just part of it. That's when I first met Jack. These people were all involved in the Ontario Society of Artists, the Water Colour Society, the Royal Canadian Academy, and all those things. Jack was one of their group and very much a part of it. I would have seen his paintings in those exhibitions. So, if I didn't know his work the day I met him, I knew it soon after.

Jack was always very gentle, very quiet at parties. He was never the life of the party, the great wit. He was not that kind of person. I always had a nice quiet conversation with Jack. As well as art, my great interest at that time was in literature and writing, but Jack wasn't interested in them. He wasn't a reader. What would we talk about? We'd talk about exhibitions, really. It was art talk.

In the 50s I was quite active on the Women's Committee of the Art Gallery of Toronto. I was on a committee to get people to look at Canadian art. Up until then they'd mostly been buying English art. It had to be English or Dutch art, possibly French, that sort of thing. There was little interest in anything Canadian – even the Group of Seven was suspect. The committee was really to get people to look at Canadian art and to begin to have a bit of confidence in it. We encouraged them to buy and to take a chance on things. I can remember having a difficult time in the beginning getting the Women's Committee to accept Jack for their exhibitions and sales. His work didn't look like anybody else's. It was much fresher. It was open.

It was full of colour. It wasn't cluttered. There was a lot of post-Cubist painting being done in Toronto at that time, and so his things looked quite unlike anybody else's. During the 50s Jack's things certainly stood out. And they'd usually be very badly hung in exhibitions – they'd be in a corner or by a doorway. You could tell people didn't know what to do with them.

Who were the people who bought his pictures? I'm going to have to say that I was one of the first. They just spoke to me very directly. My husband liked them too. It would be hard to put into words why. They have a universal quality, great directness, and depth of feeling. Sam and Ayala Zacks saw *Mute Beginning* (page 31), a painting we owned, in our house one day. They liked it, and I said, 'Would you like to meet Jack? I think he has done some wonderful paintings.' So I took the Zacks to his house, and they were very excited, and bought a number of things. Then they went back a few weeks later, and bought a whole lot more, which are the basis of the collection they gave to Queen's University. And I know they bought still other things which they gave to the Art Gallery of Ontario. I remember them saying to me after we left Jack's house after their first visit, 'You mean these paintings have been here, and nobody is buying them? Nobody is looking at these beautiful things?' They couldn't believe it. That was around May 1961, and they were his first big patrons in Canada.

My impression is that he didn't change at all with success. He was always the same: gentle, thoughtful, a family man. While I was always interested in art and painting, for many years I had family obligations that came first. I travelled a great deal with my husband, and spent time in art galleries in New York and Europe. During the early 60s, after my husband's death, I thought, 'Now's the time, if you really want to be a painter, begin now.' Jack came to the house one time and saw a lot of my paintings. He said, 'They're beautiful. There is nothing else being done like them. You've got to show them.' So, he selected some, and he arranged for my first show at the Carmen Lamanna Gallery. He even bought one from the show. That encouraged me. Also, one time, Jack said to me, 'Don't you know there aren't any rules?' Once that sank in, it freed me completely from the idea that I had missed something by never having gone to art school.

He didn't talk to me about the sudden leap in the size of his paintings. But he did mention once what a difficult thing it had been for him to change from working on a sized canvas to working on an unsized one, and how the brush would stick – I don't know whether he said it or I thought it – like a cat's tongue, that coarseness of the unsized canvas. That had been very difficult for him. He really had to persevere because he had been accustomed to a sized surface that had a nice smooth feeling about it. He did say that he had talked to Clem Greenberg, and had said, 'Oh, Clem, it's tough.' And Clem just said, 'Keep at it,' or something like that. Once I asked Jack about the rumours that Clem was telling him how to paint. I knew it wasn't true, but I wanted to hear it from Jack himself. He said that Clem had just encouraged him to keep working in this area that was rather unlike anything that was being done around him. Clem had never told him how to paint, or what to paint. It was just a question of encouraging him.

New York meant a great deal to him. There he met other painters he could talk to. He was showing with them, too. He had found his peers. That made him relax. He felt at home.

He never seemed rushed. He never seemed to be in a hurry. That's my one impression of him: he always had time. He used to laugh, and call himself a weekend painter. He was always putting himself down that way.

They had a band in the family basement. His sons would play various musical instruments and he would play the piano. I think he used his music the way he used colour – to express his feelings. After my first exhibition, which he arranged, we all came back to my house, and Jack just sat at the piano and played all evening.

I talked with Jack about a week before his death. We were sitting in the David Mirvish Gallery on the raised circular bit above the desks. We were preparing for the group exhibition at the Hirshhorn Museum in Washington. Suddenly he turned to me and said, quite out of the blue and out of context, 'David [Mirvish] has never been anything but good to me.' I wondered at the time why he said this to me, but now I realize he was under a great strain and wanted to put the facts straight.

Jack was profoundly religious. I think he sensed order in the universe, the sense of order behind it all. I never knew him well when he was attending St Thomas' Church – that's High Anglican. It has a very beautiful, a very elegant service. The colours, the music, aesthetically, it's a joy. I know he was involved but that was in the 50s and early 60s. I was troubled that he had requested at his funeral a very old-fashioned, depressing hymn, 'Now the Day is Over.' I couldn't understand how a man with deep Christian feelings could feel that everything was over. I was very puzzled by that. Then I began thinking, he was never interested in theology, he wasn't interested in the intellectual aspects of it. He had a deep sense of worship. He had a deep sense of the presence of God in the universe. But he didn't analyse it, just the way he didn't analyse a lot of other things. He was not an intellectual. He was a devout and good man and lived his life that way. For

me, his paintings are an expression of his religious convictions.

I feel at peace when I look at Jack's paintings. I feel a great sense of pleasure. I suppose it would be better if we took a specific painting like *Mute Beginning*. That has always said to me, 'In the end, everything works out for the good.' Now, if you want to tie that into his religious convictions, I think you may.

Walter Moos (b 1926), Gallery Moos

I opened the gallery in May 1959, and in 1962 we had our first Jack Bush show. Jack was a vital, affirmative, optimistic person who was very much interested in what was going on around him. I had seen an earlier show of his works at the Park Gallery. They were transitional paintings, and rather instructive. Jack came to the gallery because we were one of the first, if not the first, gallery to show contemporary art in a consistent way in Toronto. At the time, I was showing Jack Craig, Sorel Etrog, Yves Gaucher, Marcelle Ferron. I was also very friendly with Clement Greenberg, and he was impressed with Jack Bush's work. Since I liked his pictures, we decided to hold an exhibition. The first one was quite controversial, and so was the second. They were always controversial exhibitions in Jack's case. He was almost considered an oddball. People were not used to the kind of painting he was doing. People had not yet been exposed for very long to abstract pictures. The city had not yet woken up to any extent about contemporary art.

Jack visited exhibitions. He looked, even if it was not in the field he was pursuing. He would appreciate it if he thought it was good. He came around even after he left the gallery. We would talk about exhibitions, whether here or in New York or elsewhere. He would come back to town, and say I saw this show or that show. We would talk about other artists, and the great currents in art. Whenever he considered a painter that was very good, he would say 'That's what you have to do – be better than they are.' That was one of his statements. He would say that the people you admire it is very good to admire, but what you have to do is really out-do them. That was at the back of his mind, to make paintings of great importance. And I think he did do that.

In Jack's case, you can say in retrospect it was good that he stayed in Canada, because the pressure was off in a way. You could look at your neighbour from an independent scene without being so involved. You can speculate and say, I wonder what would have happened if ... But that's pointless to do. I think if Jack had moved somewhere else, he would still have been the person that he was, and the painter he became and wanted to be. You could really say that he was in the place where he wanted to be.

Robert Elkon (1928-1983), Robert Elkon Gallery, New York

We met in 1961. Our first show was in 1962. I had been very friendly with Clem Greenberg when I was a private dealer. In general, I was sympathetic and attuned, at the same time, to Clem's vision, but I exercised my own independent judgment. One day, after I opened my gallery, Clem talked to me about an artist who lived in Canada by the name of Jack Bush, and I saw some slides. I liked them. Did he come to New York, or did I go to Toronto? I don't recall the circumstances. The point is I did see his works, and I decided to show them.

I liked him as a person. He was a very warm person, and a handsome man. He was dashing, debonair. He looked like a British officer who had served in India for a year or two. Moustache, and blue eyes, pink cheeks. He was a kind man, and smiling, and he didn't have any chip on his shoulder. His wife was very nice, and we got along very well. He was a family man, and a painter. I wouldn't say he had a strong personality. He was a gregarious person – friendly, open, the sort of person you could meet in a bar somewhere, have a drink with, enter into conversation, and have a good time. He didn't give the impression of being introspective. His moods didn't seem to run the gamut from one extreme to another. He was a very stable person. And he treated his vocation just as any person would treat his own vocation as a carpenter or an art dealer. In other words, he did not, as some artists do, set himself aside as a creative person and act accordingly. In many ways, he was very much like Thomas Mann. Mann was a bourgeois writer who wrote by the clock from such time to such time. And this is the way that Jack Bush impressed me.

Noland and company believed in what Bush was doing. They incorporated him spiritually within their group. How the public reacted is really immaterial. It always takes time for people, for art lovers, to adjust themselves to become familiar with an unknown figure. And that was the case with Jack. The important thing was that he was integrated and regarded highly by the American painters at the time.

My own reaction was that I responded to his work because of the colours, the lightness, the freshness of all his canvases, the imagination in handling the colours. It made me think a great deal of Matisse. When I held a show recently, and whenever I pull out paintings from the racks, I am always amazed at the colours that he used, the relationships of the colours, the shapes that seemed to have evolved through colour, and the freshness of his painting.

Robert Murray (b 1936), sculptor, New York

I knew of Jack by reputation when be belonged to the Painters Eleven. He started showing originally with Bob Elkon, and I went to his openings there. We probably met in 1963 or 64. Our friendship, to a large extent, was based on the fact that we were, at one point, the only non-Americans Mirvish was showing, the only two Canadians, to put it the other way round. I started showing with Mirvish around 1965, and then I used to see quite a bit of Jack. He then became very active here in New York

Jack was still working as a commercial artist when I first met him. He was typical of a lot of older artists in Canada – they pretty much worked full time in order to support what little painting they were able to do. Jack had a house in north Toronto in the suburbs – 1 Eastview Crescent – and he had a 9-to-5 job; and that was a whole way of life. He's been called a late bloomer, but that's not such an unusual situation in Canada. It's literally only been in the last ten to fifteen years that you'll run into people who are able to pursue their work on a fulltime basis. When I met him, Jack's studio was a room which would have been a bedroom in the house where he lived. It didn't look so unusual to me for the reasons that I've just mentioned. It was typical of a lot of people that I knew when I was growing up. Later, Jack had a studio downtown. For Jack, that was a big jump in his life, and he didn't have it for many years. When he quit his job, which he seemed almost to feel guilty about, I knew that being home all day in that house and trying to work, he and Mabel would be hard pressed not to be bumping into each other all the time. It was inevitable that he was going to need an outside studio. I would tease him about that. In fact, he was very curious to know how I was making out in New York because I had a studio in my first apartment. Before the end of my first year here, though, I was helped to some extent when my wife got a job and was out of the house all day. I remember Jack and I used to talk about the problems of working at home. His studio downtown was the back half of a floor. It was a large, rectilinear room with an alcove, with windows along that side. That was the only source of natural light, I think. But Jack painted under artificial light. He'd been painting weekends and mostly evenings for so many years, anyway.

The first time I went to visit Jack, I remember, he had a Dave Brubeck record on that was one of my favourites – I'd had the same record. One time, when he and Mabel were down, they took me to a Brubeck concert at Lincoln

Center. It was fantastic. There was this huge stage and the quartet sitting in the middle of it, with a spotlight on them. It looked like a Dutch painting. It was when Brubeck was still going strong. They were in terrific shape. We went to hear jazz on a number of occasions. Jack really liked jazz and, particularly, people like Brubeck, Paul Desmond, and so on. There was the Five Spot, the Village Gate, and a couple of places on St Marks Place that were going pretty strong then. It got lively for jazz there again for a while. I went to hear Sonny Rollins with Jack and Mabel one night, and I went to hear him with Barney and Annalee Newman another night. Sonny Rollins had just made some sort of reappearance, and come out with a new sound. It was interesting.

Jack had an amazing, almost innocent take on everything. Some people used to think he was putting them on; but he had a kind of off-handed way of looking at things that could be quite disarming. He would want to talk about painting, want to talk about how somebody did their paintings, and so on. He had an endless fascination for this very direct, simple concern for painting. When I first met Jack, I saw him on the basis of work that was being shown for the first time in New York; but, you know, I had this notion of Jack, from talking to him and after I got to know him, that he was, in a sense, a frustrated artist. He still had a job and a family to worry about. He had that kind of enthusiasm where he wanted to get into it fully. That whole transformation in his life was kind of amazing, coming late as it did. But, hell, he was fresher than most people half his age, always. That kind of very direct attitude stood him in good stead. He was already trying things in his work. He was a very refreshing guy to talk to that way.

He talked about being a Canadian, and his hope for serious things to happen in Canada, in a very unashamed sort of way. Yet, at the same time, we used to talk mostly about what was happening in New York. Jack was full of curiosity whenever he came down, to know what was going on. Underneath all that, I think, was a concern on his part to see something happen there. Jack appreciated the idea that there be less of a provincial attitude in Canada. He and I used to talk about those things because, like trying to work a fulltime job, a lot of the people we knew in Canada were trying to escape a lot of other categorical hangups. What seldom ever gets mentioned is the fact that by exhibiting in London, he helped that situation. There was no question about it, Jack's importance as an artist was really finally made on the basis of not what he did in Canada, but what he did by showing abroad. He had an international reputation finally that, in time, registered in Canada. In a sense, he had two careers

in that he had been known and active in, say, the Painters Eleven and he also had friendships with guys who go back to the early Academy – the RCA – William Winter, Carl Shaeffer, those guys. He made himself known as a painter in a couple of different situations in Canada. His real blossoming as a painter was finally done on the strength of his own work as it was exhibited outside Canada at Emmerich in New York and Waddington in London. But he was very much interested in maintaining a Canadian identity. Mabel and Jack were quite happy in Toronto. I don't think Jack would have been happy living in New York. He would have blown his circuits out, really. He used to get so excited. He was like a kid when he was down here. Toronto was kind of staid. He lived in a very bourgeois neighbourhood. He had a nice stable influence that he could go back to. Besides which, people began to come to his door anyway.

It was pretty easy to look at his painting back in the early and mid 60s and see a kind of oddball, slightly off-kilter drawing quality — those asterisk sort of things floating around – that looked a bit like graphic symbols. There was this tendency to want to link a lot of this stuff to his background as a commercial artist. I always had this image of Jack at the drawing board with his magic markers making all kinds of doodles, and then rushing home to carry them out. But the thing is, in a certain way, they had a kind of lopsided uniqueness to them. It's just like a Matisse palm leaf. Everybody figures they can scribble out a Matisse palm leaf, but the minute somebody else tries it, it looks like Walt Disney, it gets cartoonish looking. Jack had the ability to fool around with odd little shapes, emblems, chevrons, slashes, and so on in his painting in a successful way. In the hands of most people, they could be rather trite, ornamental little devices. They were devices all right, but they worked. Jack had the most unsophisticated way of expressing himself about these things. It was refreshing. He was so unlike, say, the painters of his age or older in the States here who worried about all kinds of social and philosophical problems, and for good reason. Jack was basically uninvolved in that sort of thing. And, in the painting, there was a kind of light brightness. It runs all the risk of being superficial, and design-like, and all of those bad and evil things. Somehow, it overcomes it. And, I think, that's his uniqueness. There is a kind of lightness of spirit to them. Sometimes the colour combinations just put your teeth on edge. There are wonderful discordant notes in them. There was an expression Clem used during the years when I knew him: 'flat-footed.' Jack's paintings looked flat-footed, in a way, this kind of off-kilter drawing, and the relations of the contours to the shapes to the arrangement, and so on. Often, they surprised with the particular and somewhat unusual choices of colour, and the juxtapositions, and so on. They were paintings with good feelings.

Martha Baer (b 1939), senior vice-president, Christie's, New York

When I worked at the André Emmerich Gallery from 1968 through 1972, we had a lot of the early pictures in Santini's storage, and I was the one who went over to the warehouse with a client to show the work. When I started, Jack wasn't selling well; and then, there was a real flourish to buy. Everything was sold. These were pictures we had had down here for some time. It was great. All of a sudden he caught on, and there was a real interest among Americans. Jack, meanwhile, had become a friend. I would visit him quite a bit because he was a wonderful person, and I loved his art. And he was a supporter of mine, too. When I went on my own at Acquavella, he cleared it with André Emmerich so that he would be able to give me a painting every once in a while for sale. When he came down to New York while I was still at Emmerich, he always saw that I was taken out to dinner along with everybody else. He was very generous to the little guy. He always saw that all of us who were working at Emmerich were asked to the dinner, and he involved us all in looking at his new work.

He was a wonderful man, a terribly nice person – generous, ethical, and serious about his work. He was pleased when things went well. He was never unduly modest nor was he ever a braggart. He was a real gentleman. He was more formal than American artists for the most part, very polite, and never outrageous in his demands, firm about certain things, but never showy in his actions.

We'd talk about art and his paintings, for the most part, and personal things and mutual friends. He cared about people. He was not hung up on ego trips. He was a very generous person. He was very good about looking at young artists' work, and supporting their work. There was not a mean streak in him as far as I could tell. He was just a sweet, sweet person. He deserved what he got, and he got his fame late in life. He was *so* well liked by people. Everybody loved him.

Aaron Milrad (b 1935), lawyer, Milrad & Agnew

I first met Jack Bush when he was in the process of renting some studio space in the mid 1960s. Some time before, Sam Zacks had donated a painting he had bought to the Art Gallery of Toronto, but when I went to the Mirvish Gallery to buy one, all other sales seemed to have occurred to non-Canadians. I bought my first painting, a Funnel picture with pinks, blues, and beige, in 1965. I met him a short time after that. Gradually, I got involved with a number of concerns he had involving contracts, a will. We hit it off very well. And, as I got more and more involved with Jack's day-to-day affairs, it became pretty normal for us to speak at least two or three times a week, and Sunday night was reserved by the two of us – we spoke on the phone for at least an hour about what had happened and what would happen in the week to come.

Jack was a gentleman. He never second-guessed one. If he respected you, he took your advice. And there was an openness about him that was just special. I was like a son, but not like a son. I was close enough to him for my age to be of help to him in recognizing the feelings of collectors and of his own children. But he had enough respect for my ability to treat me as a lawyer rather than as a junior. I never ever got the feeling that he was distrustful of my advice, or not sure whether I could handle the matter. On the contrary, a great concern I had was that he put so much trust in me.

He rarely swore. The only word I ever heard him say was 'Hell.' He had a terrible drinking problem, which is not unusual in creative people. He loved Mabel, and always was concerned about her. He was very concerned about the boys and where they were going and what their futures were about. He wanted to be a father, and yet he wanted to make sure that he gave them the responsibility of growing up and learning on their own. He spent time talking to younger artists, and being supportive. He would not be so presumptive as to impose his own views, but, when asked, he would give opinions. Whenever you were in Jack's company, you felt warm.

He had an innocence about him. No matter whose company he was in, Jack was always sort of wide-eyed and listening. He enjoyed hearing good stories. He would sit there, and love to participate in conversations. He'd puff away on his Camel cigarette and tell stories of art collectors who came up to Toronto to see him or what he saw when he went on trips.

Jack was short and slight. He had the most beautiful white hair you ever saw – a full head of the most gorgeous white hair. A handsome man – he looked like Errol Flynn to me, only with white hair and with a moustache. He had twinkling eyes and wonderful eyebrows. He was just one of the most handsome men. He always looked happy. He obviously had turmoil. But, on the outside, he was warm, happy, twinkling – good company.

He always was an internationalist. He was proud of his heritage, but he looked world class. He wanted to be world class. He never thought art should be inhibited by

APRIL GROWTH acrylic on canvas, April 1972
58½" x 27¾" (148.6 x 70.5 cm)
Dr and Mrs Hilbert H. De Lawter, Charlottesville, Virginia

JUNE BUD acrylic on canvas, June 1972
75½" x 33¼" (191.8 x 85.7 cm)
André Fauteux and Carol Sutton, Toronto, Ontario

nationality or by geography or anything else. Great art could happen anywhere, and it shouldn't be restricted. People who paint should be painters who are Canadian, but not Canadian painters. He was very concerned about painters who were professional nationalists rather than professional painters. That was a real concern to him.

He kept a lot of ideas running around in his head, and he would take little pieces of white paper, and with watercolour or with pencil, sketch out a whole series of preliminary ideas or concepts. When I went to the studio, I would see some of these things in there as well as bits of canvas, where he tried out colours, hanging down like streamers. When he painted, he painted on a wall. He had a large sheet of plywood leaning against the wall, and he would tack his canvases up on the wall and paint against them. So, he had a wall against a wall. Then, he would roll up all his canvases and keep them there. When dealers would come in, he had a wonderful system of allowing them to pick out good work. He would always make certain that there were enough pictures there. Then, he would say to the dealer: 'You're going to have first choice; then, I'm going to have second choice. You'll have third choice, and I'll have fourth choice.' And they would go through, say, thirty pictures and pick out fifteen of thirty. Then, he would paint some more pictures and add to the pile, and bring in a second dealer a few months down the road. And he would go through the same exercise with him so that no one dealer ever got second choice as such. There were always good pictures available for everybody.

Yes, he lived and breathed art. He looked at a lot of art books, but he was not a deep reader. Jack was visual, and anything would stimulate him. Looking out on the garden was a wonderful thing for him. To walk in the garden would stimulate all kinds of art for him. Seeing clothes on a clothesline stimulated a whole series of pictures. Walking in front of a dressmaker's store with a dummy led to the Sash pictures. He was influenced that way. He could envision the way things would appear on canvas. And, he could abstract them.

When I hear the name Jack Bush, I see the man and the paintings in one because Jack's personality is in those paintings. The colour! The vibrancy! The sense of life! The sense of Mother Earth all comes out that way. I can't believe that such a man was able to give such strength on to canvas. I just can't believe it. He was modest and let his art speak for himself. He never felt the need to blow hard. The pictures did it. Jack let all the other artists do the talking. He did the painting.

PHYLLIS TUCHMAN teaches art history at Williams College, Williamstown, Mass, and writes regularly about twentieth-century American art.

SOFT LEFT acrylic on canvas, January 1967
72½" x 120" (184.2 x 304.8 cm)
Mr and Mrs H. Arnold Steinberg
Montreal, Quebec

ROSE CORNER acrylic on canvas, February 1967
46" x 59" (116.8 x 150.0 cm)
Private Collection

110

SKY LIGHT acrylic on canvas, May 1967
73" x 45½" (185.4 x 115.8 cm)
Mr and Mrs David Mirvish, Toronto, Ontario

STRIPED TOWER acrylic on canvas, August 1967
68" x 112" (172.7 x 284 cm)
Westburne Collection
Montreal, Quebec

GREY LAUGHTER acrylic on canvas, January 1968
68" x 94" (172.7 x 238.8 cm)
Debut Realty Ltd, Kitchener, Ontario

CROSS CUT acrylic on canvas, June 1968
55½" x 117½" (150.0 x 298.5 cm)
Private Collection

FLOATING BANNER acrylic on canvas, July 1968
87" x 81½" (220.9 x 207 cm)
Mr and Mrs David Mirvish, Toronto, Ontario

THIS TIME YELLOW acrylic on canvas, July 1968
86¾" x 68" (220.3 x 172.7 cm)
Private Collection

LIGHT GREY acrylic on canvas, July 1968
89" x 68" (226.1 x 172.7 cm)
Graham Gund
Cambridge, Massachusetts

COLOUR LADDER acrylic on canvas, August 1968
111" x 34" (281.9 x 86.4 cm)
Lois and Georges de Menil, Paris, France

118

BLUE STUDIO acrylic on canvas, October 1968
53" x 138" (134.6 x 350.5 cm)
Lewis Cabot
Boston, Massachusetts

BIG A acrylic on canvas, November 1968
90" x 57" (228.6 x 114.7 cm)
The National Gallery of Canada, Ottawa, Ontario

120

BURGUNDY acrylic on canvas, November-December 1968
84" x 68" (213.4 x 172.7 cm)
A.J. Pyrch
Victoria, British Columbia

SQUAWK acrylic on canvas, December 1968
44" x 98½" (111.8 x 250.2 cm)
Lewis Cabot
Boston, Massachusetts

WEDDING acrylic on canvas, 9-20 January 1969
114" x 28" (289.6 x 71.1 cm)
Mr and Mrs David Mirvish, Toronto, Ontario

SCOOP acrylic on canvas, 9-11 February 1969
29½" x 30½" (75 x 77.5 cm)
Mrs Jack Bush, Toronto, Ontario

SPLIT (DART) acrylic on canvas, March 1969
49⅛" x 133¾" (126 x 343 cm)
Bogislav and Elizabeth von Wentzel
Cologne, West Germany

SPASM #1 gouache, 10 April 1969
22¾" x 29¾" (57.8 x 75.8 cm)
Elizabeth L. Cabot
Boston, Massachusetts

SUDDEN acrylic on canvas, 13-17 April 1969
108" x 23" (274.3 x 58.4 cm)
Michael Steiner
New York, New York

TEST acrylic on canvas, 4 May 1969
12½" x 55½" (31.8 x 141.0 cm)
Jack Bush Estate

The Legacy

TERRY FENTON

ASSIGNING INFLUENCES ISN'T ALWAYS SIMPLE, NOR IS IT always fruitful. Sometimes a single master influences pupils or followers, but if they are slavish, the fact of his example matters little, whereas an influence used well is sometimes adapted and altered beyond recognition. For most artists, clear-cut influences are mingled with less obvious ones. These are the myriad of influences 'in the air' at any one time, and they in turn are mingled with that intangible called individual talent or personal style. Influence is usually transferred from the artists of one generation to those of a younger generation. In the past, when artists were taught under a system of apprenticeship, this chain of cause and effect was relatively easy to trace. Today it is more complex, but the same general principle applies. Young artists tend to look to the mature art being produced around them and at the artists who are producing it. Mature artists, of course, are not always available or accessible; sometimes they are only available at second hand, but their presence can be as important an influence as their art. A tradition is basically a vital chain of influence, and these influences must be picked up and passed on by producing artists. So the opinions, prejudices, and personalities of artists sometimes complement and sometimes, even, confound the influence of their art.

It is hard to separate the influence of Jack Bush's art from his personality, the two were so completely intermingled. If Bush stood apart from his art, he did not stand apart from other artists. However, a curious fact relating to his influence should be noted: his influence skipped a generation – primarily because his art matured late. He came into his own in his late forties rather than in his mid thirties. As a result, he was old enough to be the father of the young artists who came to admire his work. While the work of many senior artists is admired by the young, the possibility of personal contact is often remote. Bush relished that contact; his relation with the young tended to be a kind of active, open, and somewhat fatherly exchange.

His influence in Toronto may have come a bit later than it did in western Canada, where an exhibition in 1964 at Regina's Norman Mackenzie Gallery awakened an early interest. That exhibition was organized by Andrew Hudson, who was then living in Saskatoon. Hudson, himself, was painting abstract pictures at the time, although these, in retrospect, seem to owe more to Adolph Gottlieb and Helen Frankenthaler than to Bush. In fact, it is hard to assign a Bush influence to the work of any of the Saskatoon painters working then. Henry Bonli and William Perehudoff seem to have arrived at their similarities independently, as did Otto Rogers. In any case, all three of these artists were closer in age to Bush and all were part of the 'in-between' generation that his influence seems to have skipped. So were members of the Regina Five. Kenneth Lochhead was the only member of that group who embraced what came to be known as colour-field painting, and he, like the painters of his generation in Saskatoon, did so on his own. Some of the young painters in Regina, particularly Kenneth Peters, Simon de Jong, and Bruce Parsons, were impressed by Bush's work. Of these, Parsons was the one who drew upon Bush most directly, and he looked, as Bush did, to the drawing, as well as to the colour, of Matisse. Parsons' paintings from the mid 60s, which made use of flower motifs, remain some of the most adventurous and beautiful paintings produced in Canada at the time. Unfortunately, they failed to attract attention outside Regina. Perhaps they did not seem 'conceptual' enough for 60s taste.

Bush's own 'old-fashioned' look is another reason for

ABOVE Bush in 1976, during the installation of his retrospective exhibition at the Art Gallery of Ontario

his delayed influence in Toronto. During the 1960s Toronto experienced a cultural explosion, albeit one that had been in preparation for many years and which Bush, as a member of the Painters Eleven in the 50s, had helped to prepare. On the surface, this delayed reaction seems hard to explain. In many respects Bush was a quintessential Torontonian. He always reminded me of a character from a Morley Callaghan novel. Somehow, one does not expect a Morley Callaghan character to be a major artist, and, because in Toronto, Bush's art and personality were so mixed together, a confused reaction to both may have lingered into the 70s. His art and his personality may have offended or perplexed the artists of the in-between generation, but together they won over many younger artists.

Bush was a man of surprising personal charm, a charm of a peculiar kind. It had little to do with social skills, apart from good manners (something too seldom prized by artists). His charm stemmed more from his character, from his essential nature. At bottom it was a *moral* charm, a peculiar blend of unaffected humility and naïve candour. It was not simply that Bush was honest, as he unquestionably was, but that he never used his honesty against anyone. He gave everyone and everything the benefit of the doubt. He wasn't what you might call a 'thinker.' His intelligence was enormously practical, and it was reinforced by that unique, and sometimes confounding, charm.

As an example of his charm I recall a visit to his studio on Wolsley Street in late 1969, soon after he had hired Alex Cameron as an assistant. At one point, as we were unrolling pictures, he turned to me and said, 'Terry, I think I'm painted out. The ideas for pictures just won't come.' Then he added matter-of-factly, 'But Alex and I keep painting them.' I was taken aback by his comment in relation to the pictures we were looking at, early fringe pictures with calligraphic shapes drawn on the field, among them the beautiful *Irish Rock #1* (page 36) now in the collection of the Wellesley College Museum. How could he be so out of touch with his genius? And why, if he believed that he was painted out, would he risk being misconstrued about sharing production with an assistant? What impresses me in retrospect is that Bush restated, in his own terms, what Keats called 'negative capability.' Bush really *could* paint great pictures in the midst of doubt and confusion. But statements of that kind – and Bush was often disarmingly frank about himself and his art – could put some people off; they could be baffled and even angered by them.

That naïve frankness was in Bush's art, too, and it was there deliberately. Bush admitted to making his pictures difficult. He didn't want them to be admired by the wrong people or for the wrong reasons. If this was an expression

of prejudice that delayed his popularity, the prejudice, itself, was democratic. He let his art put philistines to the test. It found them, and found them wanting, in bohemia as much as in the middle classes and the establishment.

My reaction to the first Bush painting I saw bears this out. It was an oil painting of 1963 entitled *Black Velvet* (page 53), now in the collection of the Art Gallery of Hamilton. William Townsend had included it in the Sixth Biennial Exhibition of Canadian Painting, organized and circulated by the National Gallery of Canada in 1965. I helped unpack and install that exhibition at the Norman Mackenzie Gallery in Regina. It was a peculiar time in Regina. The Norman Mackenzie, as I have mentioned, had mounted a Bush exhibition in early 1964, and, when I arrived in mid-year, controversy raged about his work. But the controversy did not fully prepare me for the reality, and the reality threw me initially to the side of Bush's detractors. *Black Velvet* may not be the best Bush painting – as I recall it is dark and rather light absorbent, whereas his best pictures are frequently high keyed and radiant – but it is a quintessential Bush insofar as it embodies many of the difficulties of his art. It has a flat 'hourglass' layout that looks as if it should be symmetrical but isn't; it has shapes that look as if they should be bounded by gentle, regular curves, but aren't; and it has surfaces that seem to call for flat, even colour but have been painted sloppily with a brush. If it is not the best Bush, however, it was definitely the best picture in the Sixth Biennial. By the end of the exhibition it stood apart from the crowd. Clement Greenberg has observed that no matter how bad a Bush picture looks, it never gets worse. I had been puzzled by the observation when I heard it first. My subsequent exposure to Bush's art has confirmed it. And my experience with *Black Velvet* proved its corollary – that some Bush paintings 'come on' slowly; familiarity engenders appreciation.

The *Black Velvet* 'effect' – Bush's awkwardness, asymmetry, and loose handling of paint, when hard edges, clean, flat surfaces, and clear-cut 'conception' were expected – delayed Bush's reception. The 60s was an era when clear, flat design that fitted neatly inside the picture rectangle was thought by some – by too many, in my opinion – to be 'intellectual.' To those eyes, Bush's paintings probably looked inept.

By the early 70s, Toronto painters were turning increasingly to Bush for inspiration. These included younger painters like David Bolduc, Alex Cameron, Paul Fournier, Daniel Solomon, Milly Ristvedt, Carol Sutton, Joseph Drapell, and the older late starter, Kate Graham. Karen Wilkin has described Toronto abstraction as being characterized by eccentricity and high-key colour. How much this aspect of Toronto painting stems from the

DOWN AND ACROSS acrylic on canvas, June 1974
77½" x 90" (196.9 x 228.6 cm)
Lewis Cabot
Boston, Massachusetts

influence of Jack Bush is hard to say. To some extent, Bush himself may have participated in, and improved upon, a pre-existing tendency. Toronto's high-key colour may be a legacy from the Group of Seven, or it may stem from commercial art, which so many Toronto painters practised. The eccentricity is largely a matter of drawing. It, too, may have roots in the Group of Seven and in commercial art. For Bush, as for some other Toronto painters, that drawing was remarkably illustrative: again and again it referred to motifs outside the picture, to flowers, Christmas wrapping, neckties, dresses and costumes, paint splashes on the studio floor, totems, feathers, roadmarks, electrocardiogram blips, and musical notations. Such figuration is not common in abstract art these days, especially outside Toronto.

Bush's influence extended beyond Toronto. I suspect it carried farther than any Canadian painter's influence ever has. I know that his art is admired in London. In the early 70s some young Scottish painters living in London – John McLean, Douglas Abercrombie, Fred Pollock, and Alan Gouk – drew upon it. It was even more widely admired later in London, by artists including Geoffrey Rigden, Mali Morris, and Jennifer Durrant. And his painting won admirers in the United States as well. By the late 60s Dan Christensen was openly exploiting aspects of Bush's art, and subsequently other aspects were picked up by young painters such as Darryl Hughto, Sandi Slone, Kikuo Saito, and Harold Feist (who lived in western Canada, as well, and now lives in Toronto). In western Canada during the 70s, Bush influenced Robert Christie in Saskatoon, Bruce O'Neil in Calgary, and Douglas Haynes in Edmonton. The influence of his paintings

became extensive in the 70s and, in some ways, crucial.

All the painters I have mentioned were indebted in one way or another to the art of Jack Bush. Although this influence seems to be all that some of these artists have in common, Bush, I am convinced, was important to each of them. I think he pointed a way out of the 'classical' abstraction of the 60s. In this, his relation to American abstraction of the 60s is similar to that of Piero di Cosimo to the painters of the High Renaissance in Florence, particularly to Leonardo and to Fra Bartolommeo. I make no claim to be an authority on High Renaissance painting. I owe most of what I know of it to Vasari, to Wölfflin, and to Sydney Freedberg, as well as to the paintings I have seen. And I realize that, by implication, I am suggesting that American abstract painting must constitute a kind of classical style in its own right. I believe this to be true. I believe that from the late works of Jackson Pollock through Morris Louis and Kenneth Noland to Jules Olitski, a kind of classical manner prevailed. Symmetry, a harmonious balance between the subject and the enclosing picture shape, an easy and eloquent relation between formal means and expression, and an immediately perceived sense of wholeness characterized their art. Classical styles in any medium tend to close things off for subsequent artists. Classical equilibrium, it seems, cannot last. It gives way to manners that are inherently unsettled, to Schumann and Chopin after Haydn, Mozart, and Beethoven, to Mannerism after the High Renaissance. In the classical context of the early sixteenth century, Piero di Cosimo's art looked both forward and back. (So, I'm told, did Schubert's music.) It assumed classical postures, but set them in archaic trappings. But the very disequilibrium

---

GALA DAY watercolour, 1949
22⅛" x 29½" (56.2 x 74.9 cm)
Jack Bush Heritage Corporation Inc.

SUMMER DAY watercolour and pencil, 1952
18½" x 25¾" (47.0 x 65.4 cm)
Private Collection

WHITE HAT acrylic on canvas, June 1974
89" x 36¼" (226 x 92 cm)
José Luis F. de Castillejo
Stuttgart, West Germany

133

this produced offered a clue to the generation of artists which followed, to his one-time apprentice, Pontormo, and through Pontormo to Bronzino and others.

Bush certainly adopted classical attitudes himself, especially towards the end of the 60s when his Ladder and Fringe pictures nodded in the direction of Kenneth Noland. But even then he avoided symmetry and seldom aligned his drawing completely with the picture rectangle. There was always an eccentricity somewhere. And his archaism, throughout his career, constantly threatened the balance and harmony of 60s classicism. His love for the art of Matisse shows through again and again, in awkward contours, in loose brushwork, and in the 'cut-out' motifs he exploited during the 70s.

Bush's avoidance of equilibrium suggested new alternatives for many artists. It is apparent today in the asymmetrical layouts of painters like Darryl Hughto, Carol Sutton, Harold Feist, and Douglas Haynes. These artists and many others paint figure-ground paintings, as Bush did, but their figures and grounds are even more ambiguous, unsettled, and shifting than Bush's were; in their paintings, figure gives way continuously to ground and ground interchanges with figure.

Ultimately, however, perhaps Bush's character was even more influential than his paintings. Some time ago I asked Darryl Hughto whether Bush had influenced him; 'Certainly,' he replied, and went on to describe how important was the example Bush had set. 'He showed me the way,' he said, 'he showed me how to be an artist.' Bush proved that you did not have to be a social outcast to make art (in that respect he was so unlike Piero di Cosimo); he proved that you could be kind, concerned, decent, and neighbourly. Jack Bush radiated a sense of psychological well-being.

That was nowhere more evident than at the opening of his retrospective at the Edmonton Art Gallery a week before he died. The gallery was packed, crowded with students, collectors, artists, and even a smattering of 'beautiful people,' all of them admirers of Bush's art. Earlier that day, Bush had asked if he might speak at the opening. As I introduced him, the public address system failed and he had to speak to that enormous crowd without amplification. He moved in front of the microphone and spoke clearly and quietly for a few minutes. I was struck by how small and vulnerable he looked, but how, at the same time, he captivated the crowd. He seemed to make himself understood by everyone despite the lack of amplification. I cannot recall everything he said, but I do remember one thing, which summed it all up: 'Being an artist,' he said, 'is the greatest job in the world.'

TERRY FENTON is director of the Edmonton Art Gallery, Edmonton, Alberta. In 1976 he organized the Jack Bush retrospective which toured Canada. He is co-author, with Karen Wilkin, of *Modern Painting in Canada*.

POLYPHONIC FUGUE acrylic on canvas, March 1975
68¾" x 167½" (173.4 x 417.8 cm)
The Edmonton Art Gallery, Edmonton, Alberta

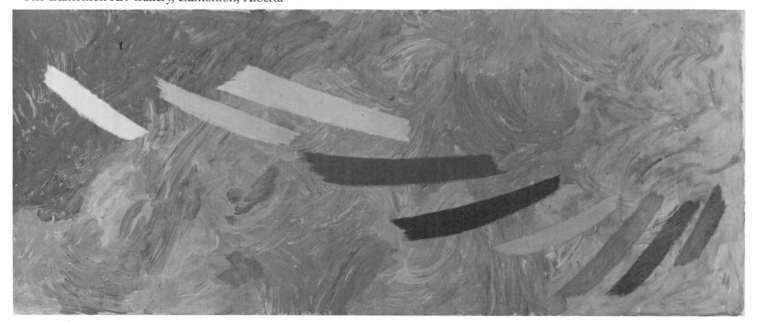

BULL FIDDLE acrylic on canvas, January 1976
68" x 106" (173 x 269 cm)
Elaine and David Kend
Boca Raton, Florida

Jack Bush and
European Modernism

JOHN ELDERFIELD

THE WHOLE ISSUE OF SOURCES IS AN EXTREMELY VEXED one, and before beginning to talk of Bush's European sources, three reminders are in order: one specific to Bush, one specific to the mechanics of artistic development, and one of very general application.

Specific to Bush is the reminder that his European sources did not constitute what David Smith once called the artist's filial heritage; American abstraction did. When Bush, for example, looked at Matisse, it was not of course through Kenneth Noland's eyes (to say that would be tantamount to saying that Bush, as an artist, was sheerly derivative: so intimately related is appreciation of the past and original addition to it), but it was, at least, after Noland's eyes; and Bush's Matisse was to a significant extent the one whose identity American painting had defined. Bush looked more specifically to European art than did those artists who constituted his filial heritage. He seems closer to Europe than they do. But he looked back to Europe through America. His status as an abstract painter is a curious one: he stands half way between the older European and the newer American kind of abstraction, and part at least – and possibly a large part – of the special character of his painting is to be discovered in his melding of these two strains.

The second reminder here is contained in another famous Canadian's well-put warning that in evaluating new works of art against their sources we should not be looking for a residual originality in such works. As Northrop Frye says, we should not think of the artist's real achievement as distinct from or contrasted with the achievement present in what he derived. Hence, the central importance of Bush's work is not to be found in those slide lectures that show (at always, it seems, exactly

the same size) a Bush next to a Matisse, or to a Noland for that matter, and point out how Bush's edges are harder or softer than his prototypes, his colours fewer or more ... Specific comparisons can be very useful (and I will be making some shortly), but only if it is clearly understood that the new work, if it is successful, reaches into its source to grasp and to preserve what gives it value and not to play stylistic games with it.

Bush, at his best, sees something in Matisse that had been central to one kind of great painting – a way of opening space that can be managed through a certain reticence of touch or a certain kind of irregular contour; or a way of stretching out the surface that certain colours at certain distances can achieve – and seeks to preserve that. He will not, if he is an original artist, do it in the same way exactly that Matisse did: 'derivation' is the copying of a style without grasping what that style serves. For what is important, and what is passed on (as Frye again says), is nothing so personal or so abstract as a style; rather, what an earlier style had itself been invented to preserve: namely, some of those primal conventions or 'possibilities' of painting – light of a certain kind; a particular sort of extension – that cannot, like styles, be inherited but that are, in the invention of original styles, constantly reinvented and thus kept alive.

The final, and most important, reminder has two parts; both, however, have to do with style. First, stylistic originality is not intrinsically important. We value it primarily as a reflection of artistic authenticity. Residual originality is not important at all: Frye is right in saying this. But originality itself is only important insofar as it allows the artist to speak frankly and directly and not in impersonation of the past. The past is challenged by truly original art not in some impossible dream of escaping from it; simply because authenticity (in Lionel Trilling's words) 'is implicitly a polemical concept, fulfilling its nature by

---

ABOVE Montreal Museum, Spring Show Jury, 1 March, 1962. *From left to right:* Jack Bush, John Fox, Paul Authur, Agnes Lefort, and Ron Bloore

TEXT CONTINUED ON PAGE 145

RED, BLUE #4 (Blue Red #4) acrylic on canvas, 28-30 May 1969
87½" x 55" (214.4 x 139.7 cm)
Private Collection

HOOK acrylic on canvas, December 1969
69½" x 42½" (220.3 x 107.3 cm)
Private Collection

BEND acrylic on canvas, March 1970
78" x 78" (198.1 x 198.1 cm)
Kathryn Silke Moffett
Cambridge, Massachusetts

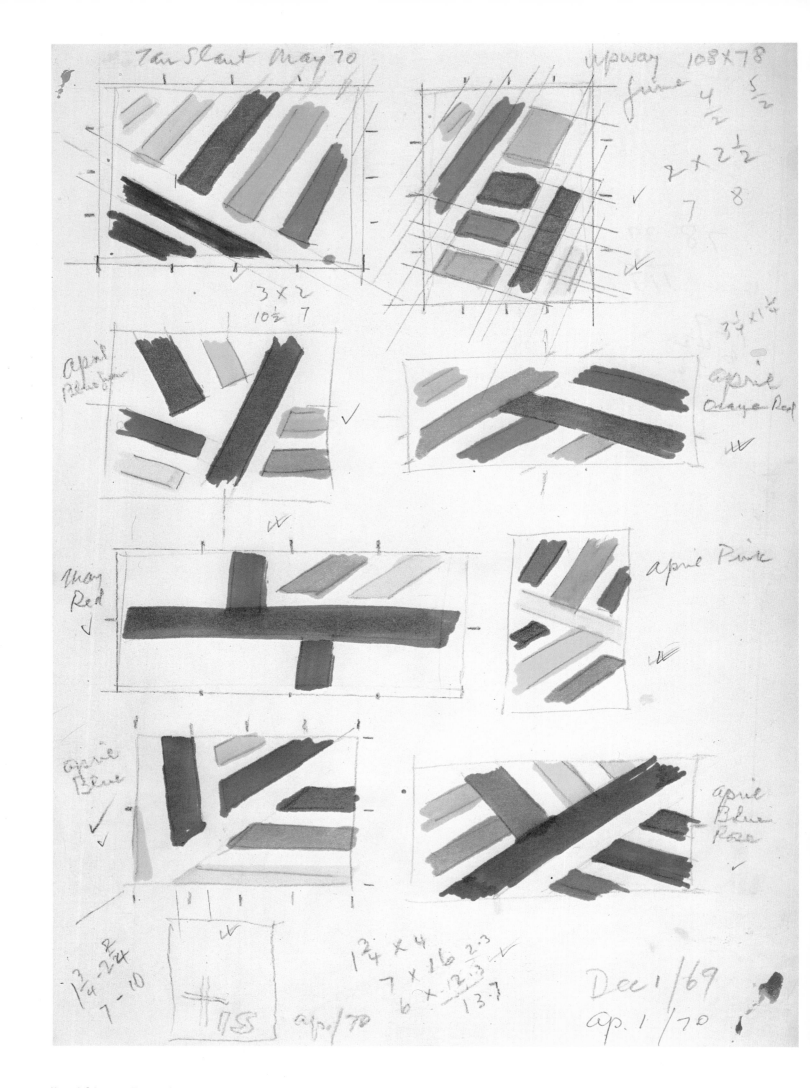

SKETCHES FOR SERIES D pencil and felt pen, December 1969
Jack Bush Heritage Corporation Inc.

APRIL BLUE ROSE acrylic on canvas, April 1970
78" x 167" (198.1 x 424.2 cm)
Steinberg Inc.
Montreal, Quebec

RISING acrylic on canvas, June 1970
65½" x 203½" (166.4 x 516.9 cm)
Lewis Cabot
Boston, Massachusetts

ROSE LOOP acrylic on canvas, June 1970
196½" x 67½" (499.1 x 171.5 cm)
Ontario Institute for Studies in Education
Toronto, Ontario

LEMON LOW acrylic on canvas, August 1970
36½" x 43" (93 x 109 cm)
Ruth H. Mitchell, Edmonton, Alberta

dealing aggressively with received and habitual opinion ...'

How Trilling continues takes us to the second part of this reminder. 'One topic of its polemic,' he says of authenticity, '... is the error of the view that beauty is the highest quality to which art may aspire.' Concentration on beauty, he argues, has historically been seen as tending to diminish the function of art to the desire to please, and therefore to dependence upon the taste and approval of its audience. The modern notion of authenticity opposes such delegation of authority. While the quality of a work of art is (obviously) accessible only through aesthetic intuition, through taste, this is not to say that the function of art is to create something pleasing to which taste can be applied. While it must be recognized that achieved art will, sooner or later, be seen to be beautiful and to give pleasure, its likelihood of producing other than counterfeited beauty and stale pleasure would seem to be diminished if it does not deal as aggressively with beauty (necessarily a matter of received taste) and pleasure (necessarily a matter of habitual sensibility) as with the past from which such taste and such sensibility derive.

Style – as the locus of an artist's own taste and own sensibility – is therefore the place in which this battle must need be fought. Style, then, or 'form' in general, is not subject to independent invention in art that is authentic and truly original, for to give to the operation of taste itself an unimpeded freedom in the creation of art is necessarily to defer, to greater or lesser extent, to received and habitual opinion. At worst, this means a merely derivative art; at best, one that addresses the more sensitive members of its audience with a particular intimacy, and seals its minority in consequence. One of the major changes between early and late modernism – between the period of Bush's European sources and the period in which he worked – was (as Trilling observes) the way in which the faculty of taste re-established itself at the centre of artistic experience. To the extent that specific sources are recognizable in a given work of art, that work of art demands qualitative as well as stylistic comparison with those sources. Both kinds of comparison are necessarily a part of what follows.

Bush's specific European sources are not difficult to decipher. Matisse and Miró seem to have been most important to him: especially the 'decorative' Matisse of around 1910, of the 1930s, and of the late *découpages* (although I sense the 'Cubist' Matisse in some of Bush's paintings of the mid 1960s), and the Miró of the later 1920s, the 1930s, and of the 1960s when he went back to his 1920s style. Also, at times, Bush drew upon the late Klee and late Braque; and, clearly, Monet's *Nympheas* pictures and even some of van Gogh's last landscapes had

their effect on Bush in the 1970s just as Mondrian had something to do with Bush's art of the previous decade. And those fray-ended bands of colour that virtually became Bush's trademark look ultimately back to Cézannist hatching as transmitted into the twentieth century through the arbitrary colour breaks in the trunks of Fauvist trees.

All this can be pointed to in Bush's pictures and in the pictures of those artists from whom he learned. But what was he learning? One thing only – a way of using imagery – I will refer to here: not only because one lesson can serve for all (for simple reason that in concentrating on a single 'problem,' the painter, knowingly or not, revises the formulation of every other), but also because this was the main thing that European art rather than American could teach Bush.

From the very beginning, Bush was an imagist painter. By around 1960, however, when he was making his first original paintings, advanced American art had reached a level of abstractness unknown to earlier modernism, and in so doing repudiated separable imagery as a threat to its holistic identity. Imagery as such – in the work of artists like Noland and Stella – was submitted to and controlled by the physical properties of the painting support (especially its shape and the porosity of its surface) to such an extent that the address to the observer made by imagery was not easily distinguished from that made by the painting as a whole. Bush, however, remained an imagist painter. Indeed, we can reasonably talk of his wanting to preserve imagery for painting despite what American art had achieved in its absence. But he did inherit from American art a holistic conception of painting that required, at very least, the firmest possible bonding of imagery to the picture surface, and we see its effect on him in the way he would, around 1960, attempt to fix imagery and ground, despite their contrasts of value, onto one plane: usually by painting imagery directly onto the bare canvas rather than on top of a ground and by carrying the then painted ground up to the edges of the imagery to hold it firmly in place. Imagery is so 'inserted' into the ground that its tendency to jump visually is opposed by the sensation that imagery constitutes an absence of ground. It therefore possesses a curiously ambiguous spatial hold on the surface, one that is highly reminiscent of the more thinly painted Matisses of around 1910, and of certain Mirós (like *The Song of the Vowels* of 1966), which fix imagery and ground coextensively to the surface in a similar way.

The reason, of course, that one thinks here of Matisse or Miró rather than, say, Noland or Olitski, both of whom used similar procedures, is the atavistic character of Bush's drawing. His drawing returns him to the early modernists, for like them Bush was unwilling to surrender painting's traditional iconic power. The more traditional (because more imagist) Americans, such as Gottlieb or Motherwell, were clearly helpful to Bush in showing him how such a return could be managed. It is interesting to note, however, that at this early stage in Bush's mature career he avoided the serial procedures that were gaining a hold in American painting, even among the imagists, and treated each picture separately after the European model. Bush separates himself, however, from the early European modernists in this respect: although he began painting 'modern' pictures by abstracting from nature and continued to use forms that were abstracted from specific elements of the external world – and in this regard followed older European procedures – he would never present these forms as ciphers. Their meaning is exclusively a function of the context in which they are used; they derive from the world but do not, as individual forms, return to it to tell us of their derivation, as is the case with even the most abstract Miró and (ultimately) with every Mondrian. From the older abstraction, that is to say, he accepted the idea that paintings have external sources, often a discernible iconography; after the model of the newer abstraction, however, he refused acknowledgement of meaning other than can be comprehended within the context of the painting itself – at least, insofar as such a thing is ever possible. His paintings, therefore, frequently have sources but these sources constitute their genesis rather than their meaning. (And this is true of his art-historical as well as his worldly sources.) This being so, the European conception of imagery as the container of inherited and invented meanings gives way to one in which imagery has more purely a functional or formal significance, and is conceived as iconographically neutral, intrinsically aesthetic form.

In the period 1963 through 1969, Bush carried this conception to such an extreme as to submit imagery to the American neutralizing device of modularity. He closely approaches Noland at this point, and his sources as such merely initiate a form of colour orchestration whose relationship to the visual world is an entirely abstract and generalized one. At least – and this is where Bush's concern with imagery continues to show itself – his sources become abstracted and generalized in their submission to colour orchestration, and as they do so they give to this orchestration unique and discordant accents of colouration and draftsmanship that refuse to be controlled by the holistic modular bias of the paintings and thus preserve for themselves a condensed form of separable imagist address. Only now, the gap, as it were, between imagery and painting is much closer than it was in the previous works. But the sense of there being some kind of distinction – and therefore tension – between imagery and painting continues to be crucial to Bush. Indeed, the success of his work seems importantly to depend upon the way in which this distinction is provided.

Of Bush's paintings between 1963 and 1969, the Sashes and Funnels are the more personal, and by and large the more successful, paintings precisely because we sense in them a wonderfully exhilarating tension between image and ground, but now spread out throughout the whole surface. There is something of this effect in the Ladders and Banners: in Bush's tendency to give dominance to one part of the colour spectrum and then throw off the harmony with an opposite contrast; in his fondness for bunching colours of similar value and then inserting a passage of strongly contrasting stripes (as Matisse would do around 1915-16); in his way of cooling in one area a basically warm picture; in his throwing off geometry by a fragment of eccentric drawing. All these things work against the modular all-overness that dominates the Ladders and Banners, and without them (or comparable 'distortions') the paintings become too harmoniously decorative. Bush seemed to be temperamentally uncomfortable with the idea of an evenly accented painting after the American model, and insofar as he approached that model his paintings seem not only derivative but also, for all their beauty, pleasing rather than affective.

I will return to this distinction later. For the present it is enough to say that Bush did tend too often to succumb to merely decorative effects when the jarring influence of imagery was not sufficiently present to enliven the surface: when he tried to be 'American.' At the same time, however, some paintings fail because they are too jarringly broken: his 'European' impulse to want to design the surface was finally incompatible with all-overness. He was not a painter like Noland who could spread out flatly a whole multicoloured surface of more or less even inflection and find there space enough to cohere it. Like Noland, he was a painter of juxtaposed, saturated (and usually warm) colours. But his notion of pictorial coherence was different from Noland's.

For Bush, cohesion was a function of placement, of the resolution of differences, of a dialectical interpretation of painting – which is why the Sashes and Funnels tend to be his best works of the 1960s. Not only are they full of internal tensions – of figure-ground contrasts frankly set up and as frankly cancelled; of obviously hand-drawn, irregular edges opposing the evenness of the colour areas they bound – they also as a whole seem to derive great power from the tension of their historical moment in Bush's career as he was beginning to submit imagery to all-overness (Europe to America, even) and, in balancing

SPRING BREEZE acrylic on canvas, June 1971
77½" x 128¾" (196.9 x 327.0 cm)
Private Collection

the two, created the specific internal drama that makes them such exhilarating works.

I am reminded at times of certain very late 1920s Mirós (like the *Portrait of Mistress Mills*) made when Miró turned from drawing on open fields to area composition and more compact design. This led, in the 1930s, to Miró's most achieved art. With Bush, however, the change in his art from the 1960s to the 1970s is exactly opposite to Miró's from the 1920s to the 1930s. He moved away from area composition towards drawing on open fields. As a result, his art aligns itself not to the greatest period of Miró but to the most audacious and original one. Bush, in effect, transformed in the 1970s Miró's calligraphic drawing of the 1920s into a broader, more painterly form. Late in the 1960s, explicit imagery returned to Bush's art.

Bush's first attempts to revive explicit imagery were not entirely successful. The pictures organized by means of little bleeps of colour are often dynamic and free in a way unlike any previous group of Bush paintings. They suggest familiarity with Monet's *Nympheas* as well as with Miró. But too many of the calligraphic and *Irish Rock* pictures (pages 36, 151) are flat and inert, their imagery simply 'presented' on the scumbled grounds. It was not until he began, in the early 1970s, actually to structure (rather than decorate) his new prepared surfaces with bands and areas of superimposed drawing that he found himself again. He returned to explicit composing, and in so doing finally found a way of using imagery so that it retained its iconic vitality yet actually composed pictures rather than simply being contained by them. This was, in effect, to return imagery to the very service of painting in an active and expressive way such as purely abstract art – art, that is to say, of iconographical neutrality – had rarely seen. It tended to separate Bush from American abstraction; only, however, to carry him closer to Europe (and especially to Miró) than ever before. In the 1970s, Bush's is a European conception of painting, of painting as an art of placement, of drawing in colour, and it depends (as John McLean has observed) upon inspired drawing to an extent that is unusual in American abstract art, which usually depends far more on treating the surface as a single unbroken continuum. The work of Abstract Expressionist 'imagists' like Gottlieb and Motherwell (and Hofmann to a certain extent), and later of Frankenthaler and Dzubas, represents important exceptions to this generalization: they too have found ways of reopening older options. Bush's principal achievement must, I think, be considered his returning to painting some of the freedom, eccentricity, and multiplicity of effects that it possessed before being submitted to the kind of all-overness that Pollock established as the model for post-war abstraction – which is, of course, a descriptive, not a qualitative evaluation of Bush's achievement.

It was in the 1970s that Bush learned most from European painting, or at least most originally. In the 1960s, Matisse was obviously very important to him. We see, as I have noted, Matisse of circa 1910 in Bush of 1960 (also something of Matisse's *découpages*); possibly Matisse of paintings like the Chicago *Bathers* of 1916-17 in the give-and-take spacing of a number of the striped paintings; and, more generally, the influence of Matisse's tinting technique and post-Fauvist colour, especially his tendency to set off and dramatize prismatic hues by earth tones and neutrals. Bush could have taken all of these things through the mediation of American sources. The same is true of those other instances where one seems to detect European sources in the 1960s: the Klee of paintings like the 1929 *Highways and Byways* in the Funnels; certain tall vertical Mondrians of 1935-42 in the Ladders; even a 1915 Malevich like *Supremus No. 50* in the Series D paintings (pages 47, 140, 141); and so on. Whether some of these sources can be proven to have had a direct influence on Bush, and others not, seems curiously beside the point when we look at his 1960s paintings. We know that whatever he was taking from Europe, whether through America or directly so, was established artistic currency in that decade. His borrowings from these sources is derivative, not original, borrowing and tells of his susceptibility to received opinion. Again this is a descriptive not a qualitative evaluation of Bush's work of the 1960s, although it does carry with it implications that finally do form part of our evaluation of that decade of his work, and which I touched on above.

The three-stage development of Bush's career from paintings with an obdurate imagist force, to paintings which submit that force to a sense of modular order learned from his filial heritage, to paintings which escape stylistic dependence on that heritage and achieve a sense of release that recaptures in a newly modern form the original imagist emphasis: this development recalls Cézanne. This comparison, while throwing into relief the minority of Bush's art, does serve to remind us of the hard-won liberation of his late style. It was achieved by setting aside a highly topical style that had brought him international recognition and by looking beyond the topical to the styles of the early modernist past.

Bush's fray-ended bands ultimately derive, I said earlier, from Cézannist hatching. The serrated ends of these elongated colour units share with Cézannist hatching, and especially with the Fauve painters' polychromatic expansion of this technique, the function of allowing an easy sense of gradation – or *passage* – between two positive pictorial elements, in Bush's case between figure and ground. By bringing his colour units to a slow stop in this way, Bush insinuates them into the flatness of the surface at those crucial narrow ends of the units which would (and do, in some paintings) lift off visually from the surface if cut off sharp. (Lateral edges that are sharp pose far less of a problem in this respect since the eye tends to sweep along their length, and if they do seem to billow off the surface at times, this may indeed add drama to a picture, especially if the frayed terminal edges succeed in snapping them flat again.) But figure-ground cohesion is not the only reason for these frayed edges: they also imply (but without quite specifying) directional movement when they are made into pointing shapes, and perspective recession when (as frequently happens) the ends of a single band are sloped in opposite directions. Bush is thus able to animate his colour forces in a suggestive rather than specific way and to twist, bend, and direct them sufficiently away from the flatness of the surface to give a sense of air and space around them, and to twist, bend, and direct by proxy the flatness of the surface as well. In effect, Bush uses the different ways of drawing his imagery as a way of providing in his paintings a new form of traditional modelling in space.

Cézannist and Fauvist colour hatching was developed not merely to assist *passage*. *Passage* itself was needed because continuous volumetric modelling had been sacrificed in favour of the schematic division of volume into a series of flat planes that could better be aligned to the flat painting surface. Bush's colour units are the descendants of separate units of volume in early modernist paintings. At times, their original function reasserts itself. This is especially so when the units abut each other. In one group of paintings of 1973-4 – where lengthy bands are created from abutted sequences of different colours – it becomes specific. In this case, the comparison with Fauvist painting is so evident that one wonders whether Bush was familiar with Derain's impressive *Three Trees, L'Estaque* of 1906 in the Zacks Collection of the Art Gallery of Ontario. The colour breaks in the trees that effect their spatial and extensive movement, and the juxtaposition of flat colour columns and more loosely treated background, are mirrored in Bush's paintings.

If the drawing and disposition of Bush's image units do present themselves as the abstracted fragments of early modernist modelling sequences, then like their prototypes they read individually as being flat, and do so despite the spatial inflections provided by their edges. The flatness of their colour guarantees that effect (as also, at times, does their scumbled or translucent treatment which exhibits through them the flatness of the underlying ground, thus demonstrating their own flatness, despite their drawing to

the contrary – and the more perspectival their drawing, the more such treatment is needed). And insofar as these image units are flat, they function against their scumbled grounds like those other descendants of Cézanne's planes: the collage and especially the typographical elements in Analytical Cubist paintings.

Like stencilling in Cubist paintings, Bush's images set themselves positively forward as the connotative (in Cubism, denotative) parts of the paintings, while also reinforcing the flatness of the surface they cover (just as it, on occasion, reinforces theirs). With Bush, as in Cubism of this kind, we see a reversal of traditional figure-ground relationships. The denotative or connotative figure is flat and purged of most of its volume, that being transferred in generalized illusionist form to the ground, which accrues to itself a sense of 'body' traditional to figures in premodernist art. This is another reason why Bush's images read almost as negatives at times: the grounds of his paintings come increasingly to possess a moody and meditative sense of *gravitas* in their ever more modelled monochromy, so that the images often seem to be weightless spirits in contrast. At the very end, in 1976, the surface is often so expressionistically worked, and lights and darks within the surface given such free rein, that one is tempted to look beyond Cubism, to paintings like the tragic July 1890 van Gogh landscapes, to find the source for the unusual abstracted animism such paintings seem to possess. Even the imagery of some of these paintings supports such a comparison.

Since Bush's image units look back ultimately to Cézanne, they bear comparison with features in the work of any number of post-Cézanne artists – from Klee's mobile, directional arrows to the silhouetted birds in late Braques; from the casually cut rectangles in Arp's Dada collages to those in the late *découpages* of Matisse – as well as with certain earlier artists' compositional devices, such as the scumbled, foreshortened ovals of Monet's *Nympheas* series. Rather, however, than present Bush's work as a kind of chrestomathy of the modernist past, let me close this discussion of specific sources with some comment on the placement of Bush's images, with specific reference to what he learned in this regard from the single artist who had certainly the greatest impact on his work of the 1970s: Miró. Of course, the whole notion of painting as placement – as balancing across the rectangular canvas – goes back to Synthetic Cubism. Bush's art of the 1970s derives ultimately from the 'constructional' approach to painting made possible by the invention of collage. But it does so through the mediation of Miró's art, and through what Miró himself learned from Cubism about the use of images as units of pictorial construction.

For example, Bush's 'bleep' paintings recall Miró's *Birdsong in Autumn* (1937) and similar works; his regular use, in the early 1970s, of cut-off long bands looks back to Mirós like the 1935 *Animated Forms*; his use in 1967 of irregularly flapping or windblown rectangles bears explicit comparison with such famous Mirós as the 1927 *Painting (The Toreador)*; his use, that same year, of dense, irregular circles contrasted with primarily linear forms has multiple precedents in Miró's art. The basic affinity, however, between these two artists is to be found in the adjustment to the surface and the composition of their respective imagist forms. It is also to be found in their very conception of painting, but there we find dissimilarity too.

Bush is a disciple of Miró in the way he develops a colour area away from a firmly drawn contour until it finds, as if of its own accord, its own particular limits, and shades off then, dissolving against the prepared ground. We see this often in Miró's work of the 1920s. For both artists, it was a way of preventing visual separation of figure and ground. So was their use of colour areas that are lighter in value than that of the ground, and often more thinly applied too, so that they sit in the ground and float across it at one and the same time. Both of these techniques (and there are others that serve the same end) speak of a desire to use images not simply as separate units of signification but as a way of pictorially altering the surfaces on which they are placed. More than the integration of figure and ground is involved here.

Bush's paintings of around 1960 were successful in achieving such integration. They were conceived, however, as containers of imagery, as vehicles for its presentation. What distinguishes his best work of the 1970s is the way in which imagery, by revealing the format of the picture, reveals itself. By first establishing the size and the character of the surface and then by using imagery to bring it pictorially alive, Bush makes the precise form of his imagery (its shape, colour, area, contour, its implied direction, its relation to other images, its degree of covering power) so integral to the success of his paintings that it cannot, when he is successful, be imagined apart from them. The frequent repetition (in Bush as in Miró) of elements of similar size and shape so as to provide a kind of narrative or conversational flow across the surface is one way in which these artists use imagery to fix the format of the picture and in so doing fix imagery to that format. Bush's use of a crossed axial format (in the paintings of 1973-4) to mark out the limits of the picture surface – a compositional device that looks directly back to Miró's Catalan Peasant paintings of the mid 1920s – serves the same purpose. So does his virtual framing by drawn elements of the perimeters of the rectangle, and his cantil-

evering of the surface away from drawn elements that push into it from one edge of that huddle into one of its corners (extremely frequent in Miró): both of these devices warp the flatness of the picture and open pictorial space, but do so in such a way that recalls its flatness in the drawn elements themselves.

Basic to all of this is the idea of discovering through drawing the generating forces of the canvas surface, forces that find their expression by means of the colour and shape the drawing assumes. Also, a conception of painting itself as an additive, constructive one; and as a kind of extended and accumulative drawing (even writing) on prepared grounds, a form of drawing in colour that calls attention to itself for its intrinsic splendour and emotive power, yet finally surrenders its inscriptive meaning to the service of a surface it is there to make visible as possessed of a pictorial energy far greater in significance than any of its own.

Bush's closeness to Miró, however, is finally more than a technical or a compositional one. Miró was the greatest and the most original of the Surrealist painters in part because he was a synthesist. He combined the formal stability of the Cubist tradition with a freedom of invention made possible by the kind of subject matter that he used. He thus found a way of breathing new life into Cubism that was finally more open and flexible than that provided by those who developed Cubism in ever more generalized and geometric forms. Bush shares Miró's playfulness (and stubborn awkwardness that controls this playfulness) and also benefits from the eclecticism of his approach. Although far less volatile, and substantial, an artist than Miró, Bush too found a way of extending his filial heritage, which was also a geometric one, in a more inventive way than most of the other artists whose starting points were the works of Noland and Stella. That he did so by looking back to modern art much earlier than that of his filial heritage gives to his painting a kind of complexity – in feeling as well as in form – that distinguishes it from a great deal of recent modernism. It is its attraction and merit as well as its modesty and its limitation. Again like Miró, it may well have been Bush's position as an outsider and latecomer to his own particular mainstream that allowed him to find so individual a voice.

One of the very few axiomatic things that can be said about the aims of art is a negative one: art cannot safely pursue beauty, only something else that may produce beauty. As Northrop Frye observes, to aim at producing beauty (or ugliness, for that matter) is inevitably to rely upon received opinion and to end up by producing a merely pleasing rather than affective art. If art pursues something other than beauty, that something is not easily defined: if only

IRISH ROCK #2 acrylic on canvas, 4-9 October 1969
65½" x 54½" (166.3 x 140 cm)
Jack Bush Heritage Corporation Inc.

because a measure of art's success is (as Frye says) the extent to which it is its own object and refuses to allow us usefully to treat it as descriptive of something else. It is clear, I think, that even if Miró's and Bush's pursuits both do involve a similarly specific concern with imagery, then Miró's differs from Bush's in that revelation of the intrinsic power and attributed meaning of imagery would seem to be the decided object of his pursuit. To say this is necessarily hypothetical, despite Miró's own confirmation of it, for all statements of intention are necessarily suspect, and, as Frye notes, if intention is still thought to be apparent in a work of art itself, the work is being regarded as incomplete. However, to compare Miró's work to Bush's is to see in Miró's (and not in Bush's, at least not in so clear a way) imagery that our attention fixes on because it interests it more, and it would be foolish to suppose that Miró did not want it that way. To look at Miró's work is also to see that each of his images is also (to borrow a Bergsonian phrase) 'only the best illuminated point of a moving zone' and is carried by the stream of the surface of which they are all, at their different moments, its defining representatives. That is to say, images function in Miró's art as they do in Bush's: as agents of space, extension, pictorial tension, and so on. But they do so if not obliquely (because these functions are integral to the form and placement of the imagery), then not exclusively. They are also there for 'something else.'

Neither Miró nor Bush is (I presume) concerned with beauty itself. Miró's concerns, however (and this is true of pioneering European modernism as a whole), are one step further away from a concern with beauty than are Bush's, and pure abstract painters' as a whole. The freedom of purely abstract art is often celebrated: its freedom to concentrate on problems internal to itself; its freedom to find its inspiration purely in its own medium and in the pictorial possibilities of that medium. It is a freedom that brings its own risks. Roger Fry can explain, writing to G.L. Dickinson in 1913, how he had been thinking of the function of content in painting and had come to the conclusion that content 'is merely directive of form and that all the essential aesthetic quality has to do with pure form.' Insofar as art becomes more intense, he insisted, 'the content is entirely remade by the form and has no separate value at all.' Regardless of an artist's involvement with what he painted, form or structure was what finally mattered aesthetically. But then a caution: 'The odd thing is that apparently it is dangerous for the artist to know about this.'

Late modernism is an extremely knowing period. The danger to which Fry alludes is that when form is known separately as the locus of aesthetic value, this can lead to concentration on the pursuit of aesthetic value, and hence on the reactionary pursuit of beauty itself: because the artist's pursuit is now much closer to the pursuit of beauty itself. The risk is obvious: an art of 'effect rather than of cause, of choice rather than necessity,' to borrow Clement Greenberg's characterization of the later Picasso.

When Bush fails it is for this very reason: because he succumbs to the notion of what Greenberg calls the 'finished and self-contained object,' a notion which rests painting 'on a set of conventions that restrict, rather than liberate, inventiveness,' turning all difficulties into 'difficulties of craft, to be solved by craftsmanship' – in effect, by the creation of a beautifully finished object. The early modernists themselves were not by any means immune to failure on these same grounds, but to the extent that form is known separately and especially to the extent that form is inherited, not invented, the risk of failure would seem to increase. This is not of course to say that an art knowingly composed from inherited forms cannot attain a level of achievement that goes far beyond the pleasure principle, for no art entirely escapes this description; it is merely to say that Bush's late modernist relationship to his early modernist sources was an especially taxing one, of which he was a victim as well as victor. Those who more abruptly cut themselves off from the European past avoided some of the problems, and comparisons, that Bush faced. Bush, however, chose to paint with remembrance of a tradition that produced the most sublime works of art this century has seen. The integrity with which he sought to preserve that tradition, and to extend it, cannot be demonstrated with reference to his art, any more than can its quality, but it is conspicuous just the same.

JOHN ELDERFIELD is director, Department of Drawings, and curator, Department of Painting and Sculpture, at the Museum of Modern Art, New York. He is the author of many publications on twentieth-century art.

NOTES
In the text above, I have referred by name of author to the following works: Northrop Frye, *Anatomy of Criticism* (Princeton: Princeton University Press, 1967); Clement Greenberg, 'Picasso at Seventy-Five,' *Art and Culture* (Boston: Beacon Press, 1961); John McLean, 'Jack Bush: Recent Paintings,' *Studio International*, July-August 1974; Lionel Trilling, *Sincerity and Authenticity* (Cambridge, Mass.: Harvard University Press, 1974). My indebtedness to the works by Frye and Trilling extends beyond the passages quoted. My reference to Roger Fry's letter to G.L. Dickinson comes from Virginia Woolf, *Roger Fry: A Biography* (New York and London: Harcourt Brace Jovanovich, 1940).

TOWARD BLUE acrylic on canvas, November 1970
79¾" x 44¾" (202.6 x 113.7 cm)
Mrs John Cosgriff
New York, New York

RIGHT TO LEFT acrylic on canvas, March 1971
75¼" x 112⅜" (191 x 285.5 cm)
Montreal Museum of Fine Arts, purchase, Horsley and Annie Townsend Bequest
Montreal, Quebec

154

SIX STACK acrylic on canvas, March 1971
75" x 112¾" (190.5 x 286.4 cm)
Private Collection

TWO GREENS acrylic on canvas, December 1971
76¾" x 85" (195 x 216 cm)
Private Collection

156

JANUARY #6 acrylic on canvas, January 1972
78" x 126½" (198.1 x 321.3 cm)
Lewis Cabot
Boston, Massachusetts

JUMP UP #2 acrylic on canvas, July 1972
32⅛" x 43½" (81.6 x 110.5 cm)
Private Collection

DOROTHY'S COAT acrylic on canvas, October 1972
67¼" x 180" (171.5 x 441.0 cm)
Labelad Inc., Toronto, Ontario

SUNSOUT acrylic on canvas, January 1973
66½" x 93½" (168.9 x 237.5 cm)
Private Collection

Jack Bush: His Imagery

KAREN WILKIN

EVERY STUDENT OF ART HISTORY LEARNS HOW INDIVI-
dual artists declare themselves by apparently unavoidable
preferences for certain facial and figure types. We readily
come to recognize Titian's voluptuous blondes and have
no trouble distinguishing them from their sisters painted
by Tintoretto or Veronese; Memling's wizened infants are
totally different from solemn Christ children by van Eyck
or van der Weyden, and so on. These types are as
distinctive as signatures, as characteristic as brush strokes
or choices of colour. They are often more reliable than a
signature in identifying the hand of a particular artist –
especially 'unimportant' bits such as ears or nostrils – so
that debates over authenticity frequently hinge upon
whether an eyesocket or a hand or the swell of a neck is
typical of a given artist.

The phenomenon is not restricted to figurative art.
There are equivalent ways in which an abstract artist
makes his unique presence felt. I am not speaking of a
signature format, arrived at to some degree in a conscious
way, but rather of unconscious preferences, the result of an
individual's 'will to form,' in the German art historian
Wilhelm Worringer's phrase. The abstract painter betrays
himself by peculiarities of touch, habits of composition,
and characteristic shapes no less distinctive than the types
of his ancestors. In the radically emptied-out paintings of
the past two or three decades, purged as they are of
narrative, spatial illusion, or overt subject matter, these
particularities are more important than ever in establishing
the presence of the individual. A special kind of tremulous
edge drawing, for example, reveals the hand of Jules
Olitski, while crabbed scrubbings and jagged patches of
paint announce Clyfford Still, and fluid, expansive calligraphy, Adolph Gottlieb.

With an artist such as Jack Bush, whose work evolved

from figuration to abstraction, it is often possible to find
identical habits of construction and invention throughout
his entire career. These repetitions are probably involunt-
ary, but the record shows that the best painters and
sculptors usually managed to make use of them – as Bush
did – and employ them as marks of individuality, without
allowing them to become predictable, pat solutions. It is
unlikely that even this process is entirely conscious. It has
something to do with recognition of what seems peculiarly
one's own, with remaining alert to what looks like no one
else's work, but ultimately, it is probably like the development of an individual handwriting.

It is easier, of course, to spot these constants in retrospect, to look back at early pictures, informed by the
characteristics of mature works, and draw conclusions
about preferred ways of putting paintings together. The
conclusions are none the less true, and for Bush, at least,
can be illuminating. Since his career is popularly seen as
broken into several very different phases – an early figurative period, followed by a brief exploration of Abstract
Expressionist ideas, and a sudden shift to a stripped-down
kind of abstraction – it is particularly informative to
identify the unchanging aspects of his art.

Bush's mature paintings are unmistakeable. They have
highly recognizable formats, strokes or bands of intense
and varied colour, idiosyncratic drawing, and a spontaneous touch. Yet no matter how simplified the image, Bush's
pictures are never reductive. They never seem deduced
from the established givens of the canvas – that is to say, its
vertical and horizontal edges, its proportions. Instead,
there is a sense of pictorial events having been wilfully
forced on to the canvas, so that the picture seems a
container for incident rather than a subdivided surface.
This does not mean that there is any suggestion of illusion
or of enterable space; on the contrary, Bush often risks
compositions which come dangerously close to being

ABOVE Jack Bush about 1975

merely effective two-dimensional layouts and cause his detractors to deplore his years spent as a commercial artist. In Bush's best pictures, though, the dangers of knowing placement are counteracted by deliberate awkwardness, eccentricities of drawing and touch, and above all, by a taut play of colour.

A curious sense of *anima* further tempers and enlivens these paintings. Each colour bar or stroke or calligraphic shape functions as a lively individual, not just as an optical phenomenon, even though it exists chiefly as a painted, *made* mark. The vigour of these colour strokes owes something to Bush's quirky drawing, and something, as well, to his habit of appropriating fragments of his surroundings as starting points for pictorial invention. These undertones inform Bush's art, even though the resulting images remain self-sufficient and largely non-allusive. The colours, shapes, and even the general layout of a picture such as *Lilac* (1966, page 90), for example, may have been suggested by Bush's actual experience of his garden, but it is definitely not a painting about looking out a window at a lilac tree in bloom. It is about the relation of particular shapes to the shape of their support and to each other, and about the juxtapositioning of particular colours. Yet Bush was never shy about acknowledging his often unprepossessing visual sources, and even left clues in many titles. *Tight Sash* (page 52), *School Tie* (page 75), *Dorothy's Coat* (page 159), *Christmas Present*, and *Off the Wall*, among many others, point unequivocally to his unexpected perceptions of the visual possibilities of women's clothing, giftwrap, and wallpaper. Other paintings were spurred by flags, road signs, and even, on one occasion, Celtic boundary marks (*Irish Rock #1* and *#2*, pages 36, 151). Frequently, Bush's garden was the main stimulus for imagery.

It is common enough practice for artists to mine everyday experience for the materials of formal invention, and to say that Bush was dependent upon these visual triggers in no way detracts from the potency of the result. If anything, it should enhance our awareness of his achievement. It takes nothing away from Matisse, for example, to point out the essential ordinariness of his literal subject manner – bourgeois interiors, pretty women, traditional studio set-ups. These unremarkable, frequently explored themes are utterly transformed by Matisse's powerful formal intelligence. The banality of his subject matter serves, in part, to heighten our perception of his invention. Bush admired Matisse greatly, and I suspect that he was as interested in this kind of transformation as he was in the French painter's astonishing composition, colour, and touch. Nevertheless, in Bush's own work, as in Matisse's, it is formal inspiration that determines the success of the pictures. Bush's compelling shapes, ravish-

ing colour, and audacious placements force our attention, not the possible sources of some of his images.

Bush's habitual configurations resist easy identification with specific sources, as though particular shapes and structures exist independently of whatever may have generated them in the first place. A constellation of floating shapes, for example, appears sporadically in early works, such as *Tulips* (page 162) and *Floating Spirit* (page 163), with varying degrees of stylization. Then in 1960 it appears as a fairly recognizable floral image. It turns up again in the Garden pictures of 1972, and yet again in 1974, in a painting suggested by a physician's description of diseased liver cells. And the drawings for a last series of pictures, left unrealized by Bush's death, show floating discs in similar arrangements, independent of any specific source. The Thrust pictures of 1961, with their 'stalks' and 'bursts,' undoubtedly owe something to Adolph Gottlieb, but their configuration has precedents within Bush's own work. They can be rationalized as deriving from 1959 paintings of a single long-stemmed rose, but their general layout can be seen as early as 1948 in a watercolour of a weeping boy, and in 1951, in pictures of a stylized, spiky tree.

Similarly, a recurring fat comma shape and distorted frayed-off disc can be seen as early as 1950, in the backgrounds of several figurative expressionist works. They reappear as flower and leaf-like stains in the abstract Garden pictures of 1960, and then again as the fluttering 'heart throbs' in a remarkable series of 1969. The heart throbs, Bush said, were how he visualized his spasms of pain during a severe attack of angina. He was perfectly forthright about the origin of the floating shapes of the

TULIPS oil on masonite, 1945
17" x 22" (43.2 x 55.9 cm)
Jack Bush Heritage Corporation Inc.

'heart attack' pictures, but it is obvious that the image already existed for him, as a characteristic Bush shape.

Even a casual survey of Bush's work reveals a lexicon of related motifs – loops, scribbles, unnameable gestures – sometimes as minor elements, sometimes as dominant images. Bush certainly did not repeat shapes and motifs consciously, but he recognized recurrences, after the fact, and referred to them as his 'handwriting.' In retrospect, we can quite easily zero in on these repetitions and see Bush's development as a deliberate attempt to isolate characteristic elements in his pictures, but this is altogether too cerebral an interpretation. Bush was a very intelligent painter, but he was primarily an intuitive one. His intuition led him to clarify and simplify his pictures, in the interest of making better art. Extraneous things disappeared, allowing potent elements to declare themselves more readily. They had been there all along, although they had often been disguised or subordinated to other concerns.

In early works, these habitual motifs and structures were rationalized by Bush's choice of subject matter, or relegated to background areas. The gradual ascendancy of characteristic motifs corresponds with the development of Bush's mature painting. It seems, at least in part, a process of growing self-reliance, of trusting his own ability to invent imagery which satisfied him. He began by selecting, or perhaps recognizing, 'Bush' images in existing reality, in a rational way. Then, as his work became more abstract, he made use of fragments of the existing world, both as springboards for specific pictures and as general suggestions for picture types. (It is obvious, of course, that the various paintings of Bush's mature series derive as

FLOATING SPIRIT oil on masonite, 1948
17" x 22" (43 x 56 cm)
Private Collection

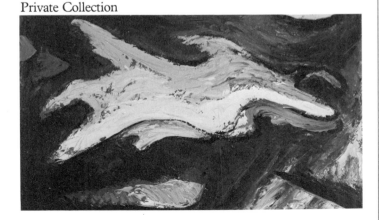

much from one another as from a particular ur-image.) His way of using found images is analogous to the way collage sculptors such as David Smith and Bush's friend Anthony Caro used found objects. Like his sculptor colleagues, Bush isolated his chosen motifs from their normal context, altered them, and reassembled them within the boundaries of his new construction. In this new context, the selected fragments were subordinate to a new whole, and when the picture succeeded best (like sculpture of the collage tradition) the previous identity of the found object became irrelevant.

After about 1972, Bush's characteristic motifs are very much present, but they are no longer attached to – nor, apparently, generated by – pre-existing images. They are set free and used as a personal visual language. In the Garden gouaches of 1971, for example, there are none of the recognizable, albeit isolated and abstracted, floral references of earlier garden pictures. Instead, there is a varied vocabulary of marks, scribbles, and typical strokes, used almost symbolically, as non-specific painterly equivalents of Bush's delight in his spring garden. Pictures such as *Spring Blossoms* (page 196) and *Falling Blossoms* (pate 198) are autonomous inventions, no matter what their stimulus, not simplifications or abstractions of garden motifs. Bush was a knowledgeable, fervent lover of jazz, so it is perhaps not far-fetched to compare this kind of free, loosely thematic improvisation to the solos and runs of the jazz musicians he admired.

There are instances of this kind of free improvisation in earlier works as well. It is present in one of the crucial paintings of 1958, *Chanson d'Amour* (page 23), one of the first canvases in which Bush was able to achieve the sparseness and economy of his late 50s watercolours. Bush was fond of explaining how the picture had been suggested by a visit to the dining-room of the Hotel St Moritz in New York. The floating patches of red, blue, brown, and gold, he said, came from the menu's French flags and the room's mahogany walls and gold silk curtains. These rather specific references, though, are presented as nonallusive strokes and scumbles of fairly dry paint, in a typical Bush configuration, without any sense even of the opulent materials of their origins.

By 1973 Bush's characteristic colour strokes and patches were completely autonomous. In the Totems, the London series, and the late paintings with musical titles, colour itself seems to have been the generating force of the pictures. Bush appears to have used his strokes and patches as neutral carriers of colour, but there are a few late drawings, studies for future paintings, whose annotations suggest that he was thinking about some sort of correlation between the sounds and rhythms of various instruments and the placement of visual elements.

No matter what the source or stimulus of Bush's imagery, particularities of shape and drawing are usually subsumed by larger issues of composition and colour. It is virtually impossible and probably fruitless to try to separate colour from structure from drawing in Bush's pictures, since each seems to have determined the other, but it is none the less possible to recognize recurring habits of composition as well as recurring motifs. Bush was a master of a kind of spreading, decentralized composition in which elements are forced to the peripheral areas of the canvas. This expansive structure is already present in some of his earliest landscapes and cityscapes of the 1920s and 30s, but it is clear that Bush learned a great deal about centrifugal composition from the helpful example of Matisse's art. As well, Bush was at home with the notion of organizing a painting around a single dominant axis, a generating spine.

Henri Matisse **THE ROSE MARBLE TABLE** oil on canvas, 1917
57½" x 38¼" (146.1 x 97.2 cm)
The Museum of Modern Art, New York,
Mrs Simon Guggenheim Fund

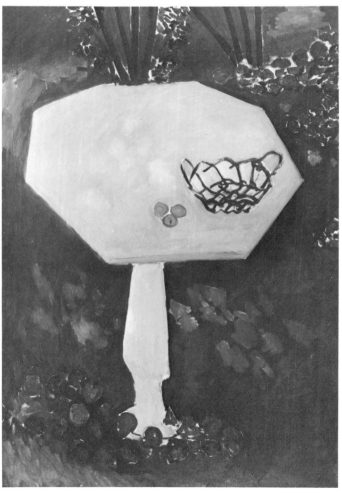

It can be seen in the long-stemmed rose pictures which preceded the Thrusts, and in the Thrusts themselves. Its permutations include the Bilaterals, the Sashes of the 60s with their vertical stacks of colours, the linear motifs of a series of 'walkway' pictures of 1969 and 1970, and the stacked Totems of 1973. There are, in addition, individual 'spine' pictures at various times throughout Bush's production, including the heraldic *Red, Blue #4* (1969, page 137), the severe *Up To* (1969, page 45), and *Zip Red* (1971, page 61), which resembles a diagrammed Thrust. This type of simplified, flat, centralized structure also owes something to Matisse, who created a paradigmatic version in *The Rose Marble Table* (1917, page 164), now in the collection of the Museum of Modern Art, NY. Like Matisse, Bush counteracts the dominant central element by astutely placed peripheral incidents, and, above all, by the variety and richness of his colour.

Colour, of course, is the single most conspicuous constant in Bush's art. The pursuit of variations of hue – chromatic improvisation which also provokes analogies with jazz – occupied him for most of his life as a painter. Except for a brief period in the late 40s and 50s when he painted tonally, first in a struggle with an intense, personal symbolism and later, under the influence of Abstract Expressionism, Bush's colour was relatively unmodulated. He was fascinated not by gradations, but by discrete hues placed side by side. Again, we think of Matisse's influence, but Bush had an example, closer to home, of a Canadian painter with similar concerns in the person of Goodridge Roberts. While there seems little overt similarity in their work, Bush is known to have admired Roberts' painting and to have attended his Toronto exhibitions in the 50s and 60s, although he must have been aware of his work as early as the 1940s. Roberts may have stood, for Bush, as an example of a good Canadian painter who did not conform to official standards, but more importantly, he must have found some aspects of Roberts' use of colour sympathetic. In many pictures, Roberts tended to strew a neutral, brushy ground with a great variety of unrepeated, distinct areas of colour – as Bush did. As with Matisse and Bush, the relationship between Roberts and Bush is not one of simple influence, but rather of affinity. Bush used colour in similar ways in his earliest work, although he always chose subject matter which not only allowed him scope for his sense of colour, but permitted him to rationalize the use of a brilliant range of hues. In the background of a 1931 *Ward Sketch*, colour is carried by washing on a line, while the sky of a 1927 view of the Laurentians is unusually intense and varied. *Eastern Townships, Quebec* (1929) is remarkable chiefly for a hot-pink steeple and the rendering of grasses, in the lower part of the panel, as a series of loose,

TOP SPIN Magna on canvas, December 1961
64¼” x 43¾” (163 x 106 cm)
Museum of Fine Arts, Boston, anonymous gift, Boston, Massachusetts

multicolour strokes.

Even in these early works, colour is never simply decorative. It is what builds the picture, so that a 1934 panel, *Ward Sketch, Toronto*, seems to anticipate many of Bush's later concerns. The drawing is rather awkward, the relationship to the framing rectangle curious (as it often was in Bush's later pictures), but the little painting is held together by its inventive colour. The mauve roof and blue façade of one house is framed by the ochre of its own side and the intense yellow of an adjoining house, while a range of reds and greens provides counterpoint in window and door frames, fences, and foliage. On the left, the view

ROSE #2 oil on canvas, 1959
61⅜" x 34" (155.9 x 86.4 cm)
Jack Bush Heritage Corporation Inc.

between two buildings is rendered clumsily, not very convincingly, but with the luxury of hindsight it can be seen as a startling prefiguration of the kind of colour stacking that preoccupied Bush in the late 60s: blocks of colour are trapped between the ochres of the flanking buildings. It is hard to read in a rational way, but it is fascinating to see in relation to Bush's later Sashes.

Similarly, in a fine small panel of 1934, *Children Playing* (page 9), Bush assigns a different colour to the clothing of each of the figures scattered across the canvas, while the row of houses behind them provides excuses for still more, equally varied hues. Again, with the perspective offered by Bush's later work, it is impossible not to think about the colour stacks of his 60s pictures and the floating strokes of colour in his paintings of the 70s.

The colour and structure of these early pictures are the very qualities that set them apart from the work of artists Bush was trying to emulate at the time. The Group of Seven set standards for Canadian painting in the late 20s and 30s, when Bush painted his small oils, and it is likely that his choice of working on small panels was a response to the Group's example (as well as a result of economy) as was his broad, post-impressionist paint handling. But the paintings remained resolutely Bush, despite his best efforts. He never achieved the sense of flat patterning, of observations having been forced into orderly design, nor the accomplished, sinuous drawing so typical of the Group. (Bush learned to draw with great facility, of course, but after the 1940s he excluded that kind of expertise from his painting, reserving it for his work as a commercial artist.) When Bush reminisced about his early years, he always mentioned his desire to have painted like the Group of Seven and his distress, at the time, at not being able to. Predilections we can now recognize as peculiarly 'Bush' happily prevented him from doing so.

By the 40s and 50s, 'Bush' motifs had become so dominant in his watercolours that literal subject matter (which had provided justification for the images in the first place) is almost overwhelmed by suggestive, typical configurations. A 1949 watercolour, *Road to Orillia* (page 11), has as its ostensible subject the hills and roads of Ontario's Lake Simcoe region. But landscape elements seem to have been chosen primarily for their likeness to Bush's preferred forms, so that their identity as radiating wedges of colour is almost stronger than their connection with existing geography. A similar construction of flat bars of varied colour, radiating from a dominant spine, appears in the Series D pictures of 1969 and 1970 (pages 47, 140, 141). It is as though the naturalistic references of *Road to Orillia* had been erased, leaving the abstract structure of the painting bare.

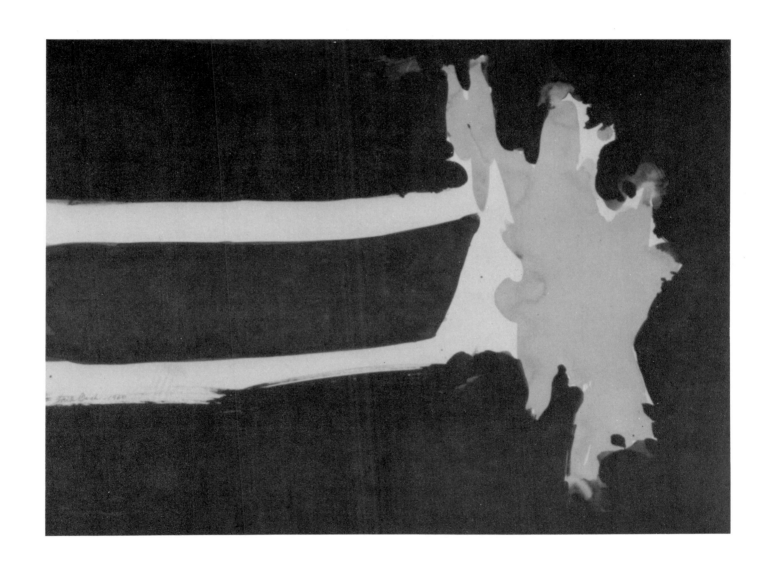

BLUE THRUST TO YELLOW watercolour 1960
15¼" x 20⅜" (38.7 x 51.6 cm)
Jack Bush Heritage Corporation Inc.

A similar harbinger of later abstract work in early figurative pictures can be seen in watercolours of the early 50s. *Summer Day* (1952, page 132) and *Red Sky, White Suns* (1952, page 12) have as their point of departure a holiday spent by the Bush family at Lake of Bays, north of Toronto. They are spirited pictures, reminiscent of John Marin's marine watercolours in their angular, prismatic rendering of nature and their free handling of the medium. The works are especially notable for their stacks of floating, varied geometric shapes, each with its own colour, strung vertically down the page, like nautical flags. They anticipate both the stacked colour patches of the Totems and the clean-edged fluttering 'handkerchiefs' of some of Bush's last paintings, even though the Totems and the Handkerchiefs cannot be rationalized or even assigned a visual source.

These examples of what might be described as the

typology of Bush's images are simply that – examples – drawn more or less at random to illustrate their continuity. Any attentive observer of Bush's art will be aware of these recurrences at almost any point in his career, with the conspicuous exception of the years during the 50s when he was deeply impressed by American Abstract Expressionism.

Like his colleagues in what became known as Painters Eleven, and unlike most other Toronto painters at the time, Bush had abandoned even cursory representation by about 1953. He often spoke of the impact of seeing reproductions of advanced New York painting in magazines of the period, of the excitement of finally seeing Abstract Expressionist works during later visits to New York, and of his deliberate efforts to achieve the intensity and up-to-date quality of these works in his own painting. These attempts did not always have happy results. Ambitious as Bush's works of the the mid 50s were, they appear to ape the manner rather than the substance of the art he admired at the time. The fact that they are curiously devoid of many of the 'Bushisms' we easily identify at other times seems to confirm this impression. This is not to say that Bush suddenly began painting in a manner foreign to him. His typical gestures and strokes are very much present, if not obviously so. It is not so much a question of his having abandoned his characteristic handwriting; rather, it is obscured by the layering and overloading of many of the canvases in his efforts to achieve the *look* of the New York school. In the simpler watercolours of the period, and in the best, least clotted paintings, this is less true and, not surprisingly, Bush's own manner seems more evident.

What we now refer to as Bush's first mature paintings – those from 1958 – are characterized by greater economy and a new clarity which, in the light of his later work, seem like the 'real Bush' emerging at last. It is very much to Bush's credit that he was able to recognize this authenticity. He began to rely on his ability to convey emotion through means which had at first appeared to him 'too simple,' but which he came to realize were particularly his own. He had encouragement, of course, from perceptive people whose eyes and opinions he trusted, but ultimately he depended upon his own visual intelligence, intuition, and probity. The continuity of images and structures throughout Bush's art is no less than we expect from a painter whose work is as notable for its integrity as it is for its individuality.

CHELSEA HOTEL, BLACK SPOT gouache, 10 October 1962
35½" x 23" (90.2 x 58.4 cm)
Private Collection

KAREN WILKIN is an independent curator and critic who writes about twentieth-century art, currently preparing the Jack Bush *catalogue raisonné*. She is the author of *David Smith* (in the Abbeville Press series Modern Masters).

ISLAND acrylic on canvas, February 1973
44½" x 113" (113 x 287 cm)
Private Collection

LAST DAY BEFORE acrylic on canvas, February-March 1973
76" x 123½" (193.0 x 313.7 cm)
The Shawmut Bank of Boston
Boston, Massachusetts

CRISS CROSS acrylic on canvas, March 1973
78" x 119½" (198.1 x 303.5 cm)
Mr and Mrs David Mirvish, Toronto, Ontario

RED PINK CROSS acrylic on canvas, April 1973
66¼" x 89" (168.3 x 226.1 cm)
Artcounsel Inc., Boston, Massachusetts

LONDON #13 acrylic on canvas, September 1973
37½" x 67" (95.3 x 170.2 cm)
Mrs Natalie Schacter
Toronto, Ontario

BLUE TEE acrylic on canvas, October 1973
43" x 66¾" (109.2 x 169.6 cm)
Private Collection

TOTEMSPREAD acrylic on canvas, October 1973
65½" x 172⅛" (166 x 437 cm)
Lewis Cabot
Boston, Massachusetts

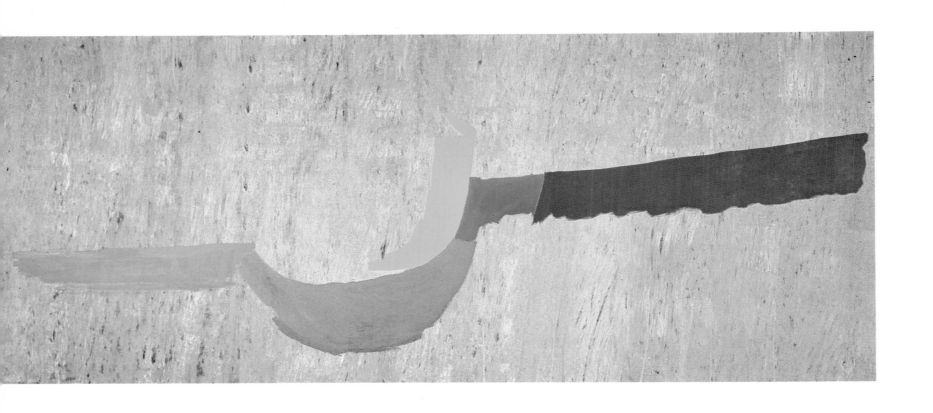

GREY SCOOP acrylic on canvas, January 1974
66¼" x 152" (168.3 x 386.1 cm)
Mr and Mrs David Mirvish, Toronto, Ontario

176

JAY TOTEM acrylic on canvas, January 1974
87" x 43¾" (221.0 x 110.5 cm)
Mr and Mrs Joseph Henderson
Washington, D.C.

JUNE GARDEN acrylic on canvas, June 1974
25" x 25" (63.5 x 63.5 cm)
Woltjen-Udell Gallery, Edmonton, Alberta

178

SLIVER DIPPER acrylic on canvas, June 1974
48" x 28³/₄" (121.9 x 73.0 cm)
Jack Bush Heritage Corporation Inc.

ON THE LEFT acrylic on canvas, July 1974
78" x 65" (198.1 x 165.1 cm)
Collection Lavalin Inc.
Montreal, Quebec

180

ARABESQUE acrylic on canvas, February 1975
80" x 116" (223.5 x 294.5 cm)
The Hirshhorn Museum and Sculpture Garden, Smithsonian Institution, Washington, DC

TROMBONE GLISSANDO acrylic on canvas, April 1975
53" x 114" (134.6 x 289.6 cm)
Woltjen-Udell Gallery, Edmonton, Alberta

BASIN STREET BLUES acrylic on canvas, June 1975
68¼" x 86¼" (173.4 x 219.1 cm)
Mr and Mrs H. Konopny
Thornhill, Ontario

SALMON CONCERTO acrylic on canvas, August 1975
56" x 201" (142.2 x 510.5 cm)
Art Gallery of Ontario, Toronto, Ontario

CONCERTO FOR TWO VIOLINS acrylic on canvas, April 1976
88" x 145½" (223.5 x 369.6 cm)
Jack Bush Heritage Corporation Inc.

SKETCH FOR CONCERTO FOR TWO VIOLINS pencil and chalk
Jack Bush Heritage Corporation Inc.

DAY SPIN acrylic on canvas, May 1976
80" x 80" (203.2 x 203.2 cm)
Lois and Georges de Menil, Paris, France

OCTOBER GOLD acrylic on canvas, October-November 1976
diamond 77" high, 54½" each side (diamond 195.6 cm high, 138.4 cm each side)
Private Collection

MOOD INDIGO acrylic on canvas, November 1976
77¾" x 77¾" (197.5 x 197.5 cm)
Jack Bush Inc.

MIDDAY SCATTER acrylic on canvas, November-December 1976
54" x 54½" (137.2 x 138.4 cm)
Private Collection

WOODWIND acrylic on canvas, December 1976
63" x 78" (155 x 198 cm)
Private Collection

CHOPSTICKS acrylic on canvas, January 1977
55⅜" x 163⅜" (140.7 x 415.2 cm)
Jack Bush Inc.

Wendy Brunelle talks with Jack Bush

ALBERTA ACCESS TELEVISION, EDMONTON,
JANUARY 1977

WB Welcome to the show, Jack.

JB Thank you.

WB I wonder when you hear me saying that you are, according to various people, Canada's best painter, how that makes you feel?

JB Well, I will answer that by saying the same thing I said to an interviewer, a nice young lady, in Montreal last June. She asked me the same question and I said I found it very embarrassing, which I still do. But then I thought a bit. I answered her and said, 'Well, it's not up to me to say that one way or another.' And I said, 'I look at everybody's paintings in Canada and I can't find anybody that is any better.' Well, that was all right with me, but the way she printed it in the paper, in the *Gazette*, was that I look around in Canada and can't find anybody 'as good as,' and, that was in print.

WB You are not going to say anything about it any more. We know very well, though, that some critics highly praise you and, at the same time, some critics damn you and I wonder what you think of art criticism generally, and of art critics and how different their opinions can be.

JB Well, I sometimes think, Wendy, that one thing a lot of them try to do is to get controversy going. They love it if somebody hates me and they'll needle it and try to get me, to get a rise out of me. But that doesn't bother me in the slightest because I don't expect art critics any more than I expect the general public to like what I do.

WB You don't?

JB No, I don't expect them to, and I don't mind if they don't like it either.

WB So good art criticism or bad art criticism has no effect on you at all?

JB It's nice if it's good. It gives you a nice feeling, but the bad criticism sometimes makes me, at any rate, think

about it, so I have to look at the work again. If it's the best I know how to do and if it looks OK, I can't do anything about it.

WB I have to bring up Clement Greenberg because, of course, he has had some influence on your life.

JB A little bit.

WB 'A little bit,' he said smilingly! Terry Fenton said something to me that I found very surprising, that there are as many opponents of Clem Greenberg's attitudes as there are proponents. Have you found that in your career?

JB Oh yes, it's terrible. So that I have to watch myself. What I would like to do is to rave about Mr Greenberg. His helpfulness, and his knowledge, and the trouble he takes with young artists, old artists, as long as he feels that they are trying to be better. If I talk glowingly about him, for instance, his opponents will say 'Aha, there's Bush, another Greenberg guy. Greenberg just picks up the phone and tells him which colour to put here,' and all that jazz, which is all a lot of phoney nonsense. So I've sort of stopped doing it. But the part about Mr Greenberg that I like, coming out here for the first time, is that all the artists here know all about it. They have met him and he has talked to them so I don't have to say anything about Greenberg at all.

WB There is a sort of general adulation out here for him.

JB Well, and maybe opponents too.

WB There may be, I don't know if anyone here is even aware enough to be opponents.

JB Well, in Toronto they are well aware and New York too, and there is a strong element against the man. There is no doubt of that.

WB Let's change the focus a little now. Often young artists who I have met feel very strongly about what happens to their work. It is almost like a mother feels towards her child. Do you any longer feel that way about your paintings?

JB I don't think I ever did. Certainly they're your chil-

ABOVE Bush in his Wolsley Street studio, 1975

dren, no doubt of that, but you've got to eat and you've got to earn your bread. And if you are going to sell your paintings you've got to be hard-nosed enough to let them go. You don't own them any more.

WB This is something I wasn't aware of. Can you tell me a little about that?

JB About what?

WB Well, your paintings, when you give them to the gallery, they are not yours?

JB No, if they buy them, they are not mine at all. If I give them to the gallery, they are not mine. They are out of the house. They're bought and sold – and get on with the next one.

WB So you don't have to think about whether or not it is going to a loving home?

JB No. There's only one thing that I don't do very much of, but I am very conscious of. I found that if I see my paintings in somebody's home, if they look happy, I am pleased, and they can change a whole room, you know – which brings up a story about Adolph Gottlieb in New York that I heard some years ago. Adolph was painting very big canvases, you see, and this one canvas he heard

---

FRIGHTENED BOY watercolour, 1947
23¾" x 19¼" (57.8 x 48.9 cm)
Jack Bush Heritage Corporation Inc.

had been sold to such-and-such a collector. His dealer told him that. So Adolph said, 'Well, I would like to see it in the house before I let it go. I always follow my paintings around where they are going to make sure they are happy where they are.' Well, that's the story. I don't think anybody can really do that, but that would be the feeling, I would think, with good painters. They would like the paintings to be in a happy home, but they have no control over it. I think that if we make our paintings good enough, strong enough, and tough enough, they can battle a bad home.

WB And the people will grow to love them, in spite of it?

JB Maybe not. If they don't, they will go out in the ashcan. We can't control it.

WB But your paintings now are almost a commodity, like stocks. Some people buy them that way, you must admit. What sort of response do you have to that?

JB Well, I am old enough, I think, to feel that in competitive society, anyway, this stock market attitude is a fact of life. It's supply and demand. It's just fortunate for me that my paintings are being bought. There are lots of other good painters who aren't selling. Well, I can't give the answer to that. Maybe it's fashion. All I can do, Wendy, is to make those canvases as good as I can make them. After that, it's up to who buys them and who owns them.

WB This commodity business, and the possibility of your work being fashionable, it wasn't always that way, was it?

JB Oh no, it only started ten years ago.

WB Or even less. It was only in 1968 that you gave up your work as a commercial artist. Up to that time, did you feel that you were sort of prostituting yourself in your art?

JB Not in the least, no!

WB How did you defend yourself from the kind of criticism people make, 'if he really thinks he's good he should be staying home and painting?'

JB I don't happen to think that painting is so precious a thing at all. It is not that ivory tower thing. It is funny at this retrospective how often this topic of working commercially has come out. I had forgotten all about the commercial aspect of earning a living. But if you look at it, from a client you get the size of the advertisement to design, how many colours. He'll tell you how many colours. You may pick the colours, except you'll find that if you want to use a black and two other nice colours you'll find that the publication doesn't have those colours, so you have got to use the colours they have. That means you'll find all the limitations and you do the best job you can within those limitations, and make it work as well as you can. It looks beautiful and its purpose is to sell a commodity. Sell something, you see. But to look good is to sell it, all right? The only difference, when I stopped doing that and started to paint full-time, I'm the one who decides how big it is going to be, how many colours, when its going to be done. It's almost the same thing.

WB Just with the different perspective because you make the decisions?

JB Yes, then you're responsible for that decision.

WB Well, the change from working part-time as an artist to working full-time, was it a matter of financial success or was there … ?

JB Yes.

WB Just that? A question of money?

JB It wasn't a matter of commitment in any way, just dollars and cents. What happened to me probably won't happen to anybody else ever, but I worked commercially, Wendy, and I liked it and I was good at it. I married Mabel and we raised the kids and paid all the bills from that, so that I figured I bought my free time – nights and weekends and holidays – and I didn't have to please anybody with what I painted, and I didn't have to sell anything to get a nickel out of it.

WB Let's talk a little bit now about the creative process. I know a lot of people wonder about where you get your ideas from – can you tell us anything about that at all?

JB It's amazing where they come from. I don't look for anything. It comes to me. I may be walking along a road and I see a mark on the road; it looks interesting, so I try it out as a painting. Or looking at some flowers in the garden – how can I get the feel of those colours, of the flower colours, the nice smell and everything? That's all. It starts from a little note. I'm not painting flowers. I'm painting the essence, the feeling to me only, not how somebody else feels about those flowers, only me. Then I forget the flowers and make a good painting of it if I can. The people who look at it won't appreciate the flowers, but they may get a feeling of those flowers out of it.

WB As you stood in front of these huge canvases that were bare, have you ever felt defeated by the empty expanse of canvas?

JB Before I start? Oh no, that is a thrill of a lifetime.

WB You never really felt that – my God! what am I going to do next?

JB Yes, I often feel that, but if you don't press it, something will come along.

WB Is that right? So how do you work? Let's talk a little bit about that.

JB Just by intuition mainly, plus a discipline, like policing the freedom.

WB You actually …

JB I just let it go as it feels inside, and I think I might illustrate it. The toughest thing in the world, on that bare canvas, is to put the first colour on, the first mark.

Everybody's afraid of that. That's the big frightening thing, and you have to have enough nerve to put the first thing on. Once you put one or two things more, then it gets fascinating because, to me, the painting starts to grow then like a flower almost. And I have said this to other people: I'll put on a yellow to start with. I am safe with that one. 'Well now, Mr Yellow, what would you like next door?' (I am just thinking to myself). If the answer isn't sure, I will put a piece of colour over here. Let it take care of itself. It starts to almost tell me sort of what to put next. So if you just let this flow, at least, that's the way I do, just let it flow, and you are often very very surprised at the crazy results. For instance, you might think you can get a nice mauve down there. Well, you can't possibly put an orange there. It would be frightful. Well, let's see, I am all alone painting this thing. Let's see what does happen when you put that down there. Zoop! I say, it works. You see, without trying it you never know. If it doesn't work, it will scream. OK, you can tear it up, change it, scrape it off.

WB So you don't work in miniature first?

JB Only in a slight pencil form, just like a rectangle, a square, a diamond, and just sort of break it up, use your ad layout business, laying it out, designing it. In the old days,

TENSION watercolour, 1947
22¾" x 19¼" (57.8 x 48.9 cm)
Jack Bush Heritage Corporation Inc.

the painters used to talk about composing the picture. The composition is such-and-such. We don't use that term again, it is all gone. It is a question of layout, which is just a dividing of space, this flat rectangular space is being divided up into sections.

WB If you don't use miniatures and you just hit that canvas with yellow – Mr Yellow right off the bat – then what about backgrounds? It looks to me as if those backgrounds were painted before Mr Yellow did his thing.

JB Yes, that is the safe thing to do, you see, when I said that big canvas scares you. All right, you're frightened, but at least I can put a ground colour on. I don't have to worry about that, so you just hang loose and put it on. When it's dry, then you start the Mr Yellow business from there.

WB Oh, I see. Now the backgrounds, that brings us to how you actually work, and not everyone is fortunate enough to be able to go to your studio to visit you and see you in action. What happens? Is it on the floor that you do that sponging?

JB No, it is stapled on a false wall, like a plywood wall, slight slant on it. With a lot of modernist art, back in the 50s and 60s, it was painted on the floor. The painters broke a lot of rules and painted on the floor, they dribbled on and they worked all the way around the thing. Well, I've got a bad back through lifting heavy bags or something, so I can't work on the floor. My canvas goes almost on an easel, but it is not on an easel, and there's lots of canvas. I don't decide the cropping or anything until the painting is all finished.

WB And what about the cropping? There have been comments that people make now about art by consensus. Do you have anyone who comes in and gives you an idea … Why did you crop it there? Or ..

SPRING BLOSSOMS gouache, May 1971
22½" x 30" (57.2 x 76.2 cm)
Private Collection

JB It happens sometimes, sure. I listen, and I'll try it and see. There is a great fashion right now in turning paintings sideways or upside down and the art public is just horrified at this. If you are painting a landscape with a barn and a sky, you don't turn that upside down at all. You can't. But in this modernist art there isn't any top or bottom, really, especially when Jackson Pollock worked all around his canvas and dribbled. He couldn't think about top and bottom until it was finished.

WB And then he decided which side was which?

JB Which looks better …

WB And signed his name in the appropriate corner after that?

JB The object there, if the people will be patient enough to follow the process – the object there is to get the painting, finally, to be the best thing that's on that wall – that's all. It seems to work better if it's turned upside down or sideways. Well, that's our business as to how we decide to do that.

WB After the fact?

JB After the fact.

WB What about destroying canvases? You say that you put it on and Mr Yellow might not like Mrs Orange or something. Then, do you say to yourself, if you can't rip that part off, do you say, well, that goes in the garbage?

JB The best thing to do is to cut it up and put it in the garbage and start all over again and not to try to save it.

WB And you do that?

JB Fortunately, I haven't had to lately much, but that's a process that a lot of young artists have trouble with because of the actual cost. You are frightened of the cost of that piece of canvas or the lovely watercolour paper or something. But you have to learn to defeat that even though you can't afford the next piece of canvas. If it is bad, destroy it, or even better, I think, is to put the canvas away, turn it around – don't destroy it, put it away for a couple of months, then come back and see it. Often times it looks pretty good when you bring it out again.

WB Is that right? Your colours are obviously the thing that people know you for. You're considered a supreme colourist. Some of your critics have said things like, your colours are merely decorative, they are commercial, they are child-like. I wonder, I don't want you to try to justify yourself, but I am wondering about the association you may have with specific colours. I can see a certain pink and I know that is Jack Bush. Do you have any associations with colours?

JB No, because that pink is the same pink that many other artists use – same pink. You've only got so many colours. Everybody can buy them, use them the same way. It is how each artist uses them for some strange reason. I don't know why.

WB Certain colours don't mean certain things to you or some kind of a joy to you? They are colours for their own sake?

JB I mean, if you put that yellow on again related to something that's over here on the canvas, that reflects something but it has also got to reflect what's over here, that balance going on. The next painting may be a very high-key light painting with the yellow and these other colours, that's a happy thing. Then we get into a cloudy day and the same yellow takes on a different role altogether.

WB Many of your paintings have musical titles. What about that? Do you start with the title and work? I loved *Basin Street Blues*, and I couldn't help wondering if I played 'Basin Street Blues,' would I begin to see the rhythm? Were you playing it when you were painting it?

JB No, *Basin Street Blues* came from a recording by the great trombone player, Jack Teagarden, I think, who is now dead. He was marvellous, soft singing. His slide trombone was very tender and not brassy or anything. If you remember the background in that thing it is kind of dull, a softly dull thing, and Jackson used to sit on the left-hand side of the group with the orchestra playing there. I kept my colours on the right-hand side – he would be on my right-hand side, you see. And sort of the way he played the trombone or sang his 'Basin Street Blues' – 'Coming along with me' – I tried to get the colours to sort of feel like that music. That's a completely personal thing that may not mean anything to anybody else, and they do not have to know about Jack Teagarden either, but that is where it came from.

WB I like it all.

APPLE BLOSSOM BURST gouache, May 1971
22½" x 30" (57.2 x 76.2 cm)
Mr and Mrs David Mirvish, Toronto, Ontario

JB I like it, too.

WB Have any essayists or critics, in your mind, actually captured in words what you do?

JB No, I am surprised at what they say. Again, it's a very private thing, and a lot of art dealers think if they only knew how I felt when I was painting, then they could understand it. And Wendy, the way I felt painting, I might have been feeling awful. This has happened over and over. I might have a hangover or something, and why it comes out like that I don't know. It is a discipline, it has nothing to do with people outside anyway. It is the painting they should look at, not how I felt.

WB I see. So you want people to examine not Jack Bush the person, but Jack Bush's painting.

JB I would like people to do that – to try to understand it, that's the main thing. Just allow themselves to look at it, react to it, which they have to do. They can't help but react. And if they feel bad about it, admit it. If they don't like it, say so, walk on. If they like it, tell us 'I like this.' It's like music again, we are back to there. We listen to music and it pleases us or it doesn't, it's that simple. We don't mind saying we don't like that piece of music. I like this one. Why not do that with painting?

WB It doesn't have to be a great esoteric exercise?

JB Hell, no!

WB It's amazing, you know; adults who are uninitiated very often find your work very difficult. They can't understand it. They can't cope with it. Yet, I have found children don't seem to have any problem at all. Do you think your work is basically, perhaps, very simple?

JB I work very hard to get it back and childlike, as innocent as I possibly can.

WB I wondered at the opening. You made a comment about the emperor's new clothes and the kind of illusion that goes with that. Jack Bush really can't – you know – that's the transference you would make. Do you ever feel that maybe there is some kind of …?

JB I wasn't fooling when I said that.

WB You weren't?

JB No. Everybody has doubts about what they do, or most everybody. See, because it's not a real world. Painting is only for a small group of people that really love it. It always has been through the centuries. I say to my assistant many times when we're working on the canvas alone there, 'What a crazy way to make a living doing this jazz.' But then, like I said the other night, go and see what someone else has done. It's real, it just moves me. All I can hope is that what I do may please somebody else and move them, and obviously it has. It's upset a lot of people, too, but I can't control that.

WB You will just have to keep painting who you are. But

who you are has to have come from somewhere. If I wanted to find out the sort of influence in your life, can you just tell us? I know it is very difficult and perhaps tedious to do this. I presume Clement Greenberg has had some influence. But what about other artists whose work has influenced you, or did you come straight from yourself?

JB Oh no, no, I don't think any artist does.

WB So I would like to know …

JB I think the big trick there is that you are obviously going to be influenced by somebody else, if you are a hero-worshipper at all, or maybe it is an artist that does a better job. If you are a musician you will want to play a trombone like Teagarden, who was probably the best at that time. Well, you are not going to play like him, but you are inspired by him, to play your way as well as he can play, if you follow me. So a painter doing that is obviously going to show influences from time to time, *but* if he is lucky and if he has a handwriting of himself, if he is honest and open and forthright, the influence from people will show. The influence is there – but you admit it. There is a

lot of yourself, too, that counterbalances that influence, and hopefully sooner or later you get to a spot where that influence doesn't show any more.

WB Are you influenced though by the old masters that you are aware of?

JB Certainly, absolutely.

WB Can you name a couple of favourite painters that we might hang on to?

JB What, any of the old masters?

WB It is just as easy as that?

JB Goya, Velazquez, Rembrandt.

WB Greatness is greatness.

JB Yes, the wonderful thing with them is that a lot of their work, if you checked art history, wasn't popular at the time. A lot of the artists and the critics said, 'that's no good.' But the reason they're so great right now is that their painting has held up, has stood up to the test of time and all the criticism available. People find out the best thing that is there, this guy 200 years ago has got that and a little more. That's why they are old masters. And that's why they are so valuable.

WB In the two minutes that we have left, Jack, my goodness – what does Jack Bush do when it is not painting day, when it is not his four hours in the studio?

JB Watch television, cops and robbers and things, nice relief.

WB You like Kojak?

JB Oh, sure.

WB What else? You have a wife and …

JB We go to movies and things.

WB What kind of movies? I want to get a feel of what kind of person you are.

JB Well, like television, for instance. I don't watch good television, I want ordinary television. Good television is too demanding. The art world is demanding enough. You want a release from it. It's like the old days, when doctors evidently read cops and robbers novels going to sleep, just to get your mind off.

WB So basically you are a very simple person.

JB I hope so.

WB A really delightful man. Thank you very much for joining me on the program tonight. Goodnight.

FALLING BLOSSOMS gouache, June 1971
30" x 22½" (76.2 x 55.1 cm)
Mr and Mrs David Mirvish, Toronto, Ontario

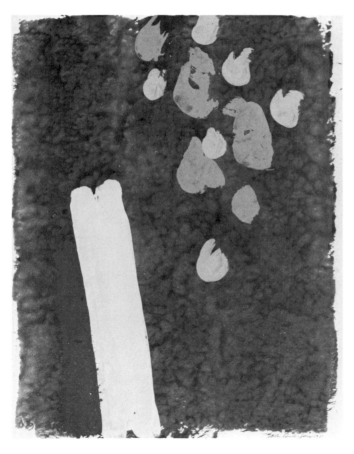

YELLOW TO RED SCRIBBLE gouache, September 1970
22½" x 30" (57.2 x 76.2 cm)
Private Collection

Chronology

PREPARED BY JENNIFER MURRAY

1909

March 20
Born in Toronto family home in Beach area. Father, William Charles Bush, was the manager of a photo-engraving business. Bush was the third of four children, Maxwell, William, Jack, Constance.

1911
Family moved to London, Ontario. By this time, father had his own business, Charles Bush Ink Company.

1918
Family moved to Montreal, where Bush attended Westhill High School.

1926
Graduated from Westhill High School. Began working as an apprentice commercial artist at the Rapid Electro Type Company, of which his father was the manager. The firm was later to become the Rapid Grip Company.

1926-7
Studied with Edmond Dyonnet and Adam Sherriff Scott in night classes.

1927-40
Worked on small-scale paintings aspiring to the standards set by the Group of Seven and the Canadian Group of Painters.

1928
Moved to Toronto office of the Rapid Grip Company.

1929-39
Studied in night classes at the Ontario College of Art with Frederick Challener, John Alfsen, and Charles Comfort.

1934

September 3
Married Mabel Mills Teakle, a family friend from Montreal.

1936

October 30
First son, Jack, Jr, born.

1937
Collaborated with Charles Comfort on illustrations for the International Nickel Company of Canada advertising account.

1938

June 28
Second son, Robert, born.

1939-41
Illustrated the International Nickel Company of Canada advertising account.

1942

April 30
Third son, Terry, born.

Became a member of the Canadian Society of Painters in Water Colour.

November 6-December 6
Participated as a guest artist in the 63rd annual exhibition of the Royal Canadian Academy of Arts at the Art Gallery of Toronto.

Formed Wookey, Bush and Winter, 9 Adelaide St East, Toronto, with Leslie Wookey and William Winter. The firm's motto was 'Design and Illustration for Discriminating Art Directors.'

1943
Joined the Ontario Society of Artists.

March 5-29
Participated in the 71st annual spring exhibition of the Ontario Society of Artists held at the Art Gallery of Toronto. Exhibited *Trees in Autumn* (1942) and *September 1939* (1939).

1943-4
Vice-president and treasurer of the Canadian Society of Painters in Water Colour.

1944

March 18-April 9
Participated in the 72nd annual exhibition, 'Artists Paint Artists,' of the Ontario Society of Artists at the Art Gallery of Toronto. Exhibited *Portrait of W.A. Winter* (1944), *Engine House* (1942), and *Spring Landscape*. Bush saw a Picasso painting, *Boy Leading a Horse* (1906), for the first time. He later commented on being excited and interested by the painting.

April 21-May 14
Participated in the 18th annual exhibition of the Canadian Society of Painters in Water Colour at the Art Galley of Toronto. Exhibited *Testing Trucks – Camp Borden* (1943), *Camp Borden School House* (1943), and *Army Hitch-Hiker* (1943).

1944-45
Life and *Time* magazines and Skira Books available in Canada, giving Bush his first opportunity to see advanced European and American painting.

1945

February
Participated in the 19th annual exhibition of the Canadian Society of Painters in Water Colour at the Art Gallery of Toronto. Exhibited *Winding Road* (1945), *The Bridge* (1945), *The Gateway*, and *Market Place*.

One-man exhibition in Sudbury, Ontario.

March 3-April 1
Participated in the 73rd annual spring exhibition of the Ontario Society of Artists at the Art Gallery of Toronto. Exhibited *The 10:29* (c 1945), *Procession* (c 1945), and *Landscape* (1945).

April
Exhibition at the Arts and Letters Club, Toronto.

'Jack Bush and William Winter,' a two-man exhibition at Hart House, University of Toronto.

1945-6
President of the Canadian Society of Painters in Water Colour.

1945-8
Paintings became more personal and expressionist. Evolved a simplified figurative style totally unlike the Group of Seven approach. Religious subjects and themes of struggle and release frequent, especially toward the end of this period.

1946
Vice-president and treasurer of the Ontario Society of Artists.

Elected an associate of the Royal Canadian Academy of the Arts.

January
Participated in the 20th annual exhibition of the Canadian Society of Painters in Water Colour at the Art Gallery of Toronto. Exhibited *At the Window* (1946), *Haunted House* (1945), *Pine Tree*, and *Summer Cottage* (1942).

One-man exhibition at Trinity College, University of Toronto.

March 9-April 13
Participated in the 74th annual spring exhibition of the Ontario Society of Artists at the Art Gallery of Toronto. Exhibited *The Old Couch* (1946), *Mountain Stream*, and *Village Procession* (1946). Won the Rolph, Clarke, Stone Award for *Village Procession*.

Participated in an exhibition with Jacques de Tonnancour, Paul-Emile Borduas, and Oscar Cahén at the Public Library and Art Museum, London, Ontario. Bush and Cahén gave lectures.

1946-7
Exhibited *Ditch Diggers* (1945) in an exhibition of the Canadian Group of Painters and the Art Association of Montreal at the Art Gallery of Toronto. In the catalogue Bush is listed as an invited artist, since he was not yet a member.

1947
First referred by Dr Wallace Graham to Dr Allan Walters for treatment of a tension state. At Dr Walters' encouragement, he began experimental work, to paint more freely and express himself. Professional consultation between Bush and Walters was brief, but they became life-long friends.

January 10-February 2
Participated in the 21st annual exhibition of the Canadian Society of Painters in Water Colour at the Art Gallery of Toronto. Bush exhibited *The Red Boat* (1946) and *Across the Valley* (1946). The latter picture was purchased by the Art Gallery of Toronto in that year.

February 8
Participated in a two-man exhibition with William Winter at Adelaide House, YWCA, Oshawa, Ontario.

March 7-30
Participated in the 75th annual exhibition of the Ontario Society of Artists at the Art Gallery of Toronto. Exhibited *Yesterday* (1947) and *The Red Wheel*. *Yesterday* was featured on the cover of *Saturday Night*.

November 6-30
Participated in the 68th annual exhibition of the Royal Canadian Academy of the Arts at the Art Association of Montreal. Exhibited *Winding Road* (1945) and *Market Place*.

1947-8
Participated in an exhibition of the Canadian Group of Painters as an invited contributor. Exhibited *Lonely Land* and *(Old) Man with a Rose* (c 1947). The exhibition was at the Art Gallery of Toronto and the Art Association of Montreal.

1948
Became a member of the Canadian Group of Painters and the Art Directors' Club.

February
Participated in the 23rd annual exhibition of the Canadian Society of Painters in Water Colour at the Art Gallery of Toronto. Exhibited *The Meeting* (1947) and *House of Doors* (1947).

March 6-28
Participated in the 76th annual spring exhibition of the Ontario Society of Artists at the Art Gallery of Toronto. Exhibited *Adventure* (1948; later called *Exploration*) and *Acceleration*.

1948-9
Painted some biblical scenes. Work was becoming more abstract, though still expressionist, and contained some symbolism, showing influence of Borduas.

1949
Art Gallery of Toronto, 'Contemporary Art: Great Britain, United States, France.' The exhibition included works by Jackson Pollock and Robert Motherwell.

October 17-29
'New Paintings by Jack Bush,' one-man exhibition at Gavin Henderson Galleries, Toronto. Bush designed the cover for the exhibition catalogue. Dr Allan Walters bought several paintings to encourage Bush, including *Flute Player in Shadow* (1949) and *Floating Spirit* (c 1948).

November 11-30
Participated in the 70th annual exhibition of the Royal Canadian Academy of Arts at the Montreal Museum of Fine Arts. Exhibited *The New Road*.

1950

March 3-April 16

Participated in 'Exhibition of Contemporary Arts' at the Art Gallery of Toronto. Exhibited *Spring Song*.

Travelled to New York for an Art Directors' Club meeting and visited the Museum of Modern Art. Bush was encouraged by what he saw, feeling it was a confirmation of the direction he was taking with his own work.

November-December

Participated in an exhibition of the Canadian Group of Painters at the Art Gallery of Toronto. Exhibited *Summer Afternoon* (c 1950) and *The Thirsty Man*.

1951

January 26-March 4

Participated in the 'Silver Jubilee Exhibition' of the Canadian Society of Painters in Water Colour at the Art Gallery of Toronto. Exhibited *Gala Day* (1949) and *Journey*.

March 10-April 5

Participated in the 79th annual exhibition of the Ontario Society of Artists at the Art Gallery of Toronto. Exhibited *Release* (1950) and *The Tree*. Also participated in a special section entitled 'Ways of Painting,' which comprised twenty works, including one by Bush.

Awarded the Art Directors' Club Medal in Toronto.

1951-2

November 23, 1951-January 6, 1952

Participated in the 72nd annual exhibition of the Royal Canadian Academy of the Arts at the Art Gallery of Toronto. Exhibited *Summer, Deer Lake*.

1952

February

Participated in the 26th annual exhibition of the Canadian Society of Painters in Water Colour. Exhibited *Scarecrow* (1951) and *Composition with Birds* (1950).

February 16-March 1

One-man exhibition at the Roberts Gallery in Toronto. Bush designed the cover of the exhibition catalogue. Included in the show was *The Old Tree* (1951).

March 8-April 13

Participated in the 80th annual exhibition of the Ontario Society of Artists at the Art Gallery of Toronto. Exhibited *The Good Samaritan* (1951).

Participated in the 'First Canadian All Abstract Exhibition,' Oshawa, Ontario. Exhibited *Summer* (1952).

November 14-December 7

Participated in the 73rd annual exhibition of the Royal Canadian Academy of Arts at the Montreal Museum of Fine Art. Exhibited *Summer Afternoon* (1950).

1952-3

November-January

Participated in an exhibition with the Canadian Group of Painters at the Art Gallery of Toronto and the Montreal Museum of Fine Art. Exhibited *Summer* (1952).

1953

January 9-February 22

Participated in the 27th annual exhibition of the Canadian Society of Painters in Water Colour at the Art Gallery of Toronto. Exhibited *Melon on Red Table* (1952), *Red Sky and White Suns* (1952), and *Pine Tree and Island*.

February 28-March 30

Participated in the 81st annual exhibition of the Ontario Society of Artists at the Art Gallery of Toronto. Exhibited *July*.

Awarded the J.W.L. Forster Award by the Ontario Society of Artists.

Painting in a fully developed gestural, abstract mode, strongly influenced by New York Abstract Expressionism.

October

The Robert Simpson Company, 'Abstracts at Home.' Exhibited *Painting* (1953) and *Square Pattern*. William Ronald was working as a display artist at the Robert Simpson Company and at his suggestion the exhibition was mounted in the windows of the department store, along with furniture displays. Included were William Ronald, Jack Bush, Oscar Cahén, Tom Hodgson, Alexandra Luke, Ray Mead, and Kazuo Nakamura. The artists gathered for a publicity photograph and thereupon decided to form a group. Later the group met at Alexandra Luke's studio, along with Jock Macdonald, Harold Town, Walter Yarwood, and Hortense Gordon, and formed Painters Eleven. Continued to exhibit as a group until 1959.

1953-4

November 27-January 10

Participated in the 74th annual exhibition of the Royal Canadian Academy of Arts at the Art Gallery of Toronto. Exhibited *Before Spring*.

1954

January 15-February 21

Participated in the 28th annual exhibition of the Canadian Society of Painters in Water Colour at the Art Gallery of Toronto. Exhibited *Indian Summer* (1953) and *Summer Day*.

Awarded the Art Directors' Club Medal, Toronto. Exhibition held at the Art Gallery of Toronto.

February 13-27

'Painters Eleven,' Roberts Gallery, Toronto. Late March and early April the same exhibition was shown at Robertson Galleries, Ottawa. Bush exhibited *The Prisoner*, purchased by T.D.F. Advertising Ltd, Toronto, and *Moonlight over the Water*, purchased by Mr M.F. Feheley of T.D.F. Advertising Ltd.

November 19-December 19
Participated in the 75th annual exhibition of the Royal Canadian Academy of Arts at the Montreal Museum of Fine Art. Exhibited *The Sleeper* (1953).

November-December
Participated in an exhibition of the Canadian Group of Painters. The exhibition travelled from the Art Gallery of Toronto to the Public Library and Art Museum, London, Ontario, the Art Gallery of Hamilton, and the National Gallery of Canada, Ottawa. Exhibited *Festive Confusion* (1954).

1955

January 7-February 9
Participated in the 83rd annual exhibition of the Ontario Society of Artists at the Art Gallery of Toronto. Exhibited *Holiday* (1954).

February 11-26
'Painters 11,' Roberts Gallery, Toronto.

March 5-31
'Painters 11,' Adelaide House, YWCA, Oshawa, Ontario. *The Amazed One* was sold to Cooper and Beatty Typesetting.

May
Bush spent six days in New York. Again he was excited and encouraged in his own direction by what he saw in the galleries, especially the Guggenheim, and at the theatres and jazz clubs.

May 6-June 5
Participated in the 29th annual exhibition of the Canadian Society of Painters in Water Colour at the Art Gallery of Toronto. Exhibited *Construction with Red* (1955) and *Early Spring*.

1955-6

December-February
Exhibited *Hymn to the Sun* (1955) with the Canadian Group of Painters. Exhibition travelled to the Montreal Museum of Fine Arts, Queen's University, Kingston, and the National Gallery of Canada, Ottawa.

December 7, 1955-May 1956
'Painters 11 Exhibition' travelled to the St Catharines Public Library and Art Gallery (December 7, 1955-January 1956), Hart House, University of Toronto (January), London Public Library and Art Museum (February 27-March 4), McLaughlin Public Library (March 22-April 5), Willistead Art Gallery of Windsor (April 6-May 2), Art Gallery of Hamilton (from May 16). Exhibited *Deep Dark*, (1955), *May* (1955), and *Painting* (1954).

1956

February 28-March 7
'Small Pictures by Painters Eleven,' Roberts Gallery, Toronto.

March 23-April 22
Participated in the 30th annual exhibition of the Canadian Society of Painters in Water Colour at the Art Gallery of Toronto. Exhibited *Theme Variation #1* and *Theme Variation #2* (1955).

April 8-May 20
'20th Annual Exhibition of American Abstract Artists with Painters Eleven of Canada,' Riverside Museum, New York. Exhibited *Reflection* (1955) and *Culmination* (1955), and attended the opening as a guest artist. It was then that he first met Kenneth Noland, Jules Olitski, and Barnett Newman.

c May 30
'Painters Eleven, Small Originals,' Pauline's Giftland, Oshawa.

Participated in an exhibition at the Canadian National Exhibition, Fine Art Gallery, Toronto. Exhibited *Reflection* (1955).

September 15-October 30
'Painters Eleven,' Arts and Letters Club, Toronto.

November 4
Death of Oscar Cahén. In response to this event, Bush painted a series of watercolours and coloured inks on paper.

November 16-December 23
Participated in the 77th annual exhibition of the Royal Canadian Academy of the Arts at the Montreal Museum of Fine Arts. Exhibited *Desert Dream* and *Quiet Day – Desert*.

1956-7
Exhibited with the Canadian Group of Painters at the Art Gallery of Toronto and the Vancouver Art Gallery. Showed *New York 55* (1955).

1957

February 8-March 3
Participated in the 31st annual exhibition of the Canadian Society of Painters in Water Colour in Hamilton. Bush exhibited *Theme Variation #6*.

March 9-April 7
Participated in the 85th annual exhibition of the Ontario Society of Artists at the Art Gallery of Toronto. Exhibited *Encounter* (1955).

June
At William Ronald's suggestion, Clement Greenberg visited Toronto, sponsored by the Painters Eleven. Harold Town and Walter Yarwood were opposed to the visit and refused to see Greenberg. He spent half a day with each of the other artists looking at their paintings and offering his comments. He advised Bush to continue with thinner paints, as he had already done in a recent watercolour series. Greenberg became a life-long friend, and through him Bush met many of his American colleagues.

Awarded First Prize, Canadian Sports Hall of Fame, Canadian National Exhibition, Toronto (football painting).

October 30-November 16
'Painters Eleven 1957,' Park Gallery, Toronto. Bush and Yarwood designed the catalogue to the exhibition containing text by Paul Duval. Exhibited *Coup-de-Main with Red* (1957), *French Facade* (1957), and *Strong Burst*.

November 7-December 8
Exhibited with the Canadian Group of Painters at the Montreal Museum of Fine Art. Showed *Coup-de-Main with Red* (1957).

1958

January 8-18
One-man exhibition at the Park Gallery, Toronto. Alexandra Luke bought *November #9* (1956).

Art Gallery of Hamilton, Ninth Annual Exhibition. Exhibited *Coup-de-Main with Red* (1957).

May 3-23
'Painters Eleven 1958' at the Ecole des beaux-arts, Montreal. Exhibited *Painting with Red* (1957), *Coup-de-Main with Red* (1957), *Upsurge* (1957, possibly destroyed), and *November #11* (1956).

May 30-June 19
'Painters Eleven,' The Alan Gallery, Hamilton. Exhibited *Bitter Sweet* (1957) and *November #6* (1956).

September 9-October 5
Exhibited with the Canadian Group of Painters at the Art Gallery of Vancouver. Showed *Dagger, Painting with Red* (1957), and *The Blue Cloud* (1957).

October 31-November 15
'Painters Eleven with Ten Distinguished Artists from Quebec,' Park Gallery, Toronto. Exhibited *Mute Beginning* (1958), *Mood with Yellow* (1958, later destroyed), and *White on a Red Ground*.

November 7-December 7
Participated in the 79th annual exhibition of the Royal Canadian Academy of the Arts at the Montreal Museum of Fine Arts and the Vancouver Art Gallery. Exhibited *Summer #4*.

1958-9
'Painters Eleven,' circulating exhibition through the National Gallery of Canada, Ottawa. Travelled to the Winnipeg Art Gallery (September 5-21), Fine Arts Gallery, University of British Columbia (September 26-October 8), Calgary Allied Arts Council (November 7-23), The Norman Mackenzie Art Gallery, Regina (November 28-December 28), The Edmonton Art Gallery (January 2-18), Agnes Etherington Art Centre, Kingston (February 13-March 1), and the Mount Allison School of Fine and Applied Arts, NB (March 6-22). Exhibited *Upsurge* (1957, possibly destroyed), *Coup-de-Main with Red* (1957), and *November #11* (1957).

'Points of View' (circulating exhibition), London Public Library and Art Museum (October 17-November 26, 1958), Art Gallery of Hamilton (December 1958), Hart House, University of Toronto (January 5-25), and Willistead Art Gallery of Windsor (March 1959). Exhibited *Chanson d'Amour* (1958).

During this period Bush's painting became more simple, with large thin floating areas of colour replacing the thick paint and dense gestural layers of the New York Abstract Expressionist manner.

1959

January 14-18
One-man exhibition at the Park Gallery, Toronto. Among paintings exhibited were *Red Vision* (1958), *Breakthrough* (1958), and *White On Red*. Bush designed the exhibition catalogue cover.

March 21-April 19
Participated in the 87th annual exhibition of the Ontario Society of Artists at the Art Gallery of Toronto. Exhibited *Painting*.

Began working in the art department of T.D.F. Advertising Ltd.

November 6-30
Participated in the 80th annual exhibition of the Royal Canadian Academy of the Arts at the Musée du Québec and the Municipal Auditorium, Winnipeg. Exhibited *Fire*.

November 7-29
Participated in the 34th annual exhibition of the Canadian Society of Painters in Water Colour at the Montreal Museum of Fine Arts and in Edmonton. Exhibited *Mulligan and Monk*.

1959-60
Exhibited with the Canadian Group of Painters, November-December 1959 at the Art Gallery of Toronto, February 1960 at the Lord Beaverbrook Art Gallery, Fredericton, NB. Showed *Hanging Figure* (1959), though it was not included in NB.

1960

March 26-April 24
Participated in the 88th annual exhibition of the Ontario Society of Artists at the Art Gallery of Toronto. Exhibited *Rose #3* (1959).

April 18-30
'Painters Eleven,' The Stable Gallery, Montreal Museum of Fine Arts. Exhibited *Let Them All Fall* (1959), *Early Summer* (1959), *Downflow on Green*, and *Mute Beginning* (1958).

Bush painted a series of garden pictures: *Bouquet, Bougainvillia, Snowball, Peony and Iris, Rose White, Flowers in a Glass*, and *Pink with Wild Violets*, but decided not to exhibit them. Mabel prevented him from destroying them.

October 19
The Painters Eleven decided to disband, realizing they had achieved their original aims and were going in their own directions.

Bush began to paint Thrust and Flag pictures.

November
Participated in the 35th annual exhibition of the Canadian Society of Painters in Water Colour at the London Public Library and Art Museum and the Vancouver Art Gallery. Exhibited *Green Field and Sun*.

1960-1

December 2, 1960-January 15, 1961
'Painters Eleven Exhibition,' Kitchener-Waterloo Art Gallery. Exhibited *Early Summer* (1959), *Storm #3* (1958), and *Downflow on Green*.

During this period Bush was working on geometric paintings such as *Three Circles* (1960).

1961

January 10-28
One-man exhibition at the Park Gallery, Toronto. Among works exhibited was *On a Green Ground* (1960).

'Toronto '61,' Toronto. Exhibit travelled to New Design Gallery, Vancouver, Seattle, San Francisco, and the Stable Gallery, Montreal.

Bush began a series of Thrust paintings which he continued to develop with variations until 1963. The image of a broad 'bar' and expanding 'burst' is first seen in a watercolour of 1960, *Blue Thrust to Yellow*.

March 18-April 16
Participated in the 89th annual exhibition of the Ontario Society of Artists at the Art Gallery of Toronto. Exhibited *Bouquet on Yellow*.

Kate Graham introduced Bush to Ayala and Sam Zacks, important Toronto collectors who later bought a number of pictures now in the Art Gallery of Ontario and the Agnes Etherington Art Centre, Kingston, Ontario.

Robert Elkon offered Bush his first one-man exhibition in New York for the following spring.

November 8-December 4
Exhibited with the Canadian Group of Painters at the Vancouver Art Gallery and in London. Exhibited *Red Rising* and *R#3*.

1961-2

November 24-January 1
Participated in the 36th annual exhibition of the Canadian Society of Painters in Water Colour at the Art Gallery of Toronto. Exhibited *Late Summer #1* (1961).

November 26-January 2
Participated in the 81st annual exhibition of the Royal Canadian Academy of the Arts at the Art Gallery of Toronto and the National Gallery of Canada, Ottawa. Exhibited *Rose #2* (1959).

1962

April 11-May 20
Participated in the 'Sixteenth Annual Exhibition and Sale of Contemporary Canadian Painting, Sculpture and Graphics' at the Art Gallery of Toronto sponsored by the Women's Committee of the Art Gallery of Toronto. Exhibited *White on Red* and *Signal on Green*.

Participated in the annual spring exhibition at the Montreal Museum of Fine Arts. Exhibited *Green on White* (1961). Acted as a juror for the exhibition.

Bush began to keep a written record with sketches of finished paintings. During this time he began to use Magna, a turpentine-soluble plastic paint.

April 17-May 5
One-man exhibition at Robert Elkon Gallery, New York. Paintings exhibited include *Bilateral with Blue* (1961), *Top Spin* (1961), *Zing Green* (1961), and *Zoom* (1961), which was bought by Mrs John David Eaton. *Zing Green* was bought by Gifford Phillips of California.

Awarded a Canada Council Senior Fellowship for study in New York and Europe.

May-June
Bush and Mabel travelled to England and Europe, including St Ives, Basel, Paris, Nice, Rome, Florence, Venice, and Madrid. In Europe, Bush saw Matisse's cutouts and was greatly impressed by them. In London, after viewing the Academy annual exhibition and finding it extremely depressing, Bush met with Anthony Caro, arranged through a letter of introduction from Greenberg. He was excited by the work Caro was producing.

October
Bush spent the month of October in New York at the Chelsea Hotel. He made 25 gouaches and left 5 of them with Elkon.

'Canadian Industries Limited: Art Collection, Contemporary Canadian,' at the Montreal Museum of Fine Arts, Montreal.

November 1-14
One-man exhibition at Gallery Moos, Toronto. Among the works exhibited were *Bilateral with Blue* (1961), *Ascension #1* (1962), and *Red on Pink* (1962). From the exhibition Mr and Mrs Sam Zacks purchased four paintings and Mrs John David Eaton bought two paintings.

1963

Participated in the 83rd annual exhibition of the Royal Canadian Academy of the Arts at the Art Gallery of Toronto. The exhibition travelled to Memorial University, St John's, Newfoundland, and the Agnes Etherington Arts Centre, Kingston, Ontario. Bush exhibited *Spain #1* (1962).

'Fifth Biennial Exhibition of Canadian Painting' at the Tate Gallery, London, England. A touring exhibition was organized by the National Gallery of Canada, Ottawa.

'Fifteen Canadian Artists,' a touring exhibition circulated under the auspices of the International Council of the Museum of Modern Art, New York, organized by the Canadian Advisory Committee with the assistance of the Canada Council. Exhibited *St Ives* (1962) and *Spain #1* (1962).

Participated in the annual spring exhibition at the Montreal Museum of Fine Arts.

'Jack Bush and Françoise Sullivan' at the Montreal Museum of Fine Arts.

April 9-27
'Jack Bush, New Paintings,' a one-man exhibition at Robert Elkon Gallery, New York. Among paintings exhibited were *Green on White* (1961) and *Red on Pink* (1962).

During this period Bush began to develop Sash paintings, the first was perhaps *Tight Sash* (1963). In the summer he painted a small group of 'fish tail' pictures such as *Green Fin* (1963). He returned to oil paint with the Sash series that he continued with until 1965.

In late 1963 Vincent Melzac, a collector from Washington, DC, visited Bush on the advice and introduction of Clement Greenberg. He purchased 14 paintings from Bush, the first major American collector to buy his works.

1964
In 1964 Bush began working as the art director for Paul, Phelan and Perry Advertising agency.

February 3-25
One-man exhibition at the Norman Mackenzie Art Gallery, University of Regina, Saskatchewan, curated by Andrew Hudson.

February 20-March 4
One-man exhibition at Gallery Moos, Toronto. Sold *Purple, Red on Green* (1963) to Mrs John David Eaton. Also included were *Green Fin* (1963) and *Black Velvet* (1963).

Participated in the annual spring exhibition at the Montreal Museum of Fine Arts. Exhibited *Blue Spot on Green* (1963).

April 23-June 7
'Post Painterly Abstraction' at the Los Angeles County Museum of Art. The exhibition travelled to the Walker Art Center, Minneapolis (July 13-August 16) and the Art Gallery of Toronto (November 20-December 20). Exhibited *Blue, Red, Orange* (1964), *Color Column* (1964), and *Orange, Pink, Green* (1964).

Resigned from all societies and organizations.

September 14-October 2
One-man exhibition at New Bennington Gallery, Bennington College, Bennington, Vermont. Works exhibited include *Green Apron* (1964), *Tall Column* (1964), *Orange Centre* (1964), *On Purple* (1964), and *Striped Column* (1964).

October 20-November 4
One-man exhibition at Robert Elkon Gallery, New York. Among works included were *Striped Column* (1964), *On Purple* (1964), and *Orange Centre* (1964).

1964-5
Participated in the 'The 1964 Pittsburgh International Exhibition of Contemporary Painting and Sculpture' at the Museum of Art, Carnegie Institute, Pittsburgh. Exhibited *Pink Orange* (1963).

1965
Participated in the annual spring exhibition at the Montreal Museum of Fine Arts. Bush was awarded the Grand Award (for *Colour Coat*, 1964), along with Guido Molinari.

Participated in the Sixth Biennial Exhibition of Canadian Painting, a touring exhibition organized by the National Gallery of Canada, Ottawa. Exhibited *Black Velvet* (1963).

'Colorists 1960-1966' at the San Francisco Museum of Art, San Francisco. Exhibited *Column in Browns* (1965).

During this period Bush was visiting artist at Michigan State University.

October 5-10
One-man exhibition at the Waddington Galleries, London, England.

December
Produced a portfolio of five prints, in an edition of 100, for David Mirvish, with an introduction by Andrew Hudson. The prints relate to five gouaches painted in 1962.

1966
Bush began variations in the Sash format (which he continued in 1968, after the 'stripe' paintings of 1967) by moving the centralized stack of colour bars to one edge of the canvas. He began to use acrylic water-soluble polymer paint during this period.

In 1966 Bush paintings were bought by the art Gallery of Toronto and by Aaron Milrad.

February 1-20
One-man exhibition at André Emmerich Gallery in New York.

Participated in a group exhibition at Scarborough College, University of Toronto.

'Images of a Canadian Heritage,' Vancouver Art Gallery.

'Jack Bush, Ina Meares, James Gordaneer,' Trinity College, University of Toronto.

Tate Gallery, London, purchased *Color Column on Suède* (1965).

Art Gallery of Toronto purchased *Dazzle Red* (1966).

November 17-December 7
One-man exhibition at the David Mirvish Gallery, Toronto. Among works exhibited were *Tall Spread* (1966), *Sway #1* (1966), and *Two Yellows* (1966).

Bush took a studio downtown at 115 Wolseley St. This large space allowed him to make larger scale pictures that he had previously, when he worked in a room in his Eastview Crescent house.

In late 1966, Bush's paintings began to be more densely packed with broad bars of colour, juxtaposed and stacked to fill the entire canvas. Bush said they were in response to seeing a group of Frank Stella's 'polyhedron' paintings at the David Mirvish Gallery.

1967

January
'Jacques Hurtubise and Jack Bush, Canada at Sao Paulo,' IX Biennial 1967, Brazil. Bush showed 15 canvases from 1965 to 1967, including *Sea Deep* (1965), *School Tie* [listed as *School Tree*] (1965), *Rose Red and Red* (1966), and *Awning* (1966).

February 7-March 4
One-man exhibition at the Waddington Galleries, London, England.

May 19-June 21
'Nine Canadians' at the Institute of Contemporary Art, Boston. Bush exhibited *Rose Corner* (1967).

'Prize Award Winners 1908-1965 Spring Exhibition,' Montreal Museum of Fine Arts.

Given the Albert H. Robinson Award by the Montreal Museum of Fine Arts.

May-September
'Three Hundred Years of Canadian Painting,' National Gallery of Canada, Ottawa.

May-October
'Painting in Canada,' Canadian Government Pavilion, Expo 67, Montreal. Exhibited *Two Reds, Two Greens #2* (1966).

'Ten Decades 1867-1967, Ten Painters,' an exhibition organized by Paul Russell and Barry Lord for the Rothman's Art Gallery, Stratford, and the New Brunswick Museum, Saint John, a Centennial project of the New Brunswick Department of Art.

September 23-October 19
One-man exhibition at André Emmerich Gallery, New York.

November 17-December 7
One-man exhibition at David Mirvish Gallery, Toronto.

November
'Statements: 18 Canadian Artists' at the Norman Mackenzie Art Gallery, University of Regina, Saskatchewan.

1967-8
Participated in 'The 1967 Pittsburgh International Exhibition of Contemporary Painting and Sculpture' at the Museum of Art, Carnegie Institute, Pittsburgh.

1968
Bush resigned as a commercial artist in advertising to devote himself full time to his painting.

'Canada 101' at the International Festival, Edinburgh, organized by the Canada Council.

January 15-February 16
'Canada – art d'aujord'hui' at the National Gallery of Canada, Ottawa. The exhibition travelled to the Musée national d'art moderne, Paris, to Brussels (September 15-October 15), Rome (May 15-June 15), and Lausanne. Exhibited *Tall Spread* (1966).

'Jack Bush, Helen Frankenthaler, Morris Louis, Kenneth Noland, Jules Olitski, Frank Stella, Robert Murray' at the Galerie du Siècle, Montreal.

'Seventh Biennial Exhibition of Canadian Painting' at the National Gallery of Canada, Ottawa. Exhibited *Yellow Pink* (1967).

Participated in an exhibition at Scarborough College, University of Toronto. Participants included Noland, Olitski, Louis, and Stella. Exhibited *Striped Tower* (1967).

Awarded the John Simon Guggenheim Memorial Foundation Fellowship.

Late September
Visiting artist at Cranbrook Academy of Art, Bloomfield Hills, Michigan, for two years. Among Bush's students were Joseph Drapell and Darryl Hughto.

November 8-December 4
One-man exhibition at the David Mirvish Gallery, Toronto.

1969
February 18-March 8
One-man exhibition at Galerie Godard Lefort, Montreal. Works exhibited include *Big A* (1968) and *Cross Cut* (1968).

April
Bush suffered an attack of angina.

Began a series of Spasm paintings using 'heart throb' motifs which he said was how he visualized his pain.

Bush and Mabel took a holiday in Ireland.

'The Canada Council Collection,' a touring exhibition organized by the National Gallery of Canada, Ottawa.

September 4-27
One-man exhibition at the Waddington Galleries, London, England. Works exhibited include *Light Grey* (1968).

September
Began the first two Series D pictures, *Spread Out* and *Walkway*.

October
Began the *Irish Rock* paintings.

1970

January and February
Working on 'Roadmark' paintings.

April
Began to work on Series D paintings again. He had abandoned the series in 1969 because he felt the results were 'too pat,' but then reworked them. Included in the series are *April Blue Rose*, *May Red*, and *Upway* (June, last of the series).

March 5-April 5
'Ten Year Retrospective' curated by Terry Fenton at the Norman Mackenzie Art Gallery, University of Regina, Saskatchewan. The exhibition travelled to the Edmonton Art Gallery, Edmonton (May 12-June 10). Works exhibited include *Blue, Green Split* (1964), *Floating Banner* (1968), *Rose Red and Red* (1966), and *Up To* (1969).

'Color and Field' at the Albright-Knox Gallery, Buffalo. The exhibition travelled to the Dayton Art Institute, Cleveland Museum. Bush represented by *School Tie* (1965), listed in the catalogue as *School Tree* and reproduced upside down.

'The Opening,' first exhibition at the newly renovated and enlarged David Mirvish Gallery, Toronto.

May 9-June 13
One-man exhibition at Harcus-Krakow Gallery, Boston. Among works included were *Squawk* (1968), *Soft Left* (1967), *Across and Down* (1966), *Burgundy* (1968), and *Color Ladder* (1968).

July
'Seventeen for Summer' at Galerie Godard Lefort, Montreal. Exhibited *Rain* (1969).

'Masters of the Sixties' at the Edmonton Art Gallery and the Winnipeg Art Gallery. Exhibited *May Red* (1970).

Bush worked on a series of gouaches.

October 24-November 12
One-man exhibition at André Emmerich Gallery, New York. Among paintings exhibited were *Bend* (1970), *Brown Roadmark* (1970), *Strawberry* (1970), *Rising* (1970), *Double Roadmark* (1970), *Red Hook* (1970), and *Off the Wall* (1970).

'Form and Color' at the Toledo Modern Art Group in co-operation with the Everson Museum of Art, Syracuse, New York.

Participated in 'The 1970 Pittsburgh International Exhibition of Contemporary Painting and Sculpture' at the Museum of Art, Carnegie Institute, Pittsburgh.

1971
During this period Bush was using rollered grounds in his paintings. He had first used the technique in the *Irish Rock* pictures, but not consistently.

January 16-February 13
One-man exhibition at the Nicholas Wilder Gallery, Los Angeles.

February 14-March 21
'49th Parallels – New Canadian Art' at the John and Mabel Ringling Museum, Sarasota, Florida. The exhibition travelled to the Museum of Contemporary Art, Chicago. Bush showed *Big A* (1968) and *Tall Spread* (1966).

February 23-March 14
'Painters Eleven: 1953-1960' at the Robert McLaughlin Gallery, Oshawa. Exhibited *Reflection* (1955), *Painting with Red* (1957), *November #9* (1956), *Breakthrough* (1958), *Storm #3*, and *Coup-de-Main with Red* (1957).

March 6-April 3
One-man exhibition at the David Mirvish Gallery, Toronto. Exhibited the Series D paintings.

Bush worked on a series of gouaches using garden motifs, such as *Apple Blossom Burst* (1971), returning to a notion already present in the 1960 Garden series.

September
'Twentieth Anniversary Exhibition' at Galerie Godard Lefort, Montreal. Exhibited *Spread Out* (1969-70).

Participated in 'Works from 1960-1963: Bush, Caro, Frankenthaler, Noland, Olitski, Stella' at the David Mirvish Gallery, Toronto.

October 6-30
One-man exhibition at the Waddington Galleries, London, England. Among the works exhibited were *Six Stack* (1971), *Right to Left* (1971), and *Across and Back* (1970).

1972
During this period Bush began to develop large-scale canvases.

From the 1970 gouaches Bush began a series of garden pictures using freely invented shapes and colours from his Eastview Crescent garden.

February 17-March 26
One-man exhibition at the Museum of Fine Arts, Boston. The exhibition, 'The Inauguration of the New Contemporary Gallery,' was curated by Kenworth Moffett. The paintings exhibited include *This Time Yellow* (1968), *Zip Red* (1971), *Striped Column* (1964), *School Tie* (1965, listed as *School Tree*), *Seven Colors* (1965), *Lilac* (1967), *Bend* (1971), *Toward Blue* (1971), *Rising* (1970), *Red Hook* (1970), and *Brown Roadmark* (1970).

March 11-29
One-man exhibition at André Emmerich Gallery, New York.

April 14-May 21
'Abstract Paintings in the 70s: A Selection' at the Museum of Fine Arts, Boston, curated by Kenworth Moffett. Exhibited *Spread Out* (1969-70), *April Pink* (1970), *Olive Loop* (1971), *Two Greens* (1971).

'Toronto Painting: 1953-1965,' a touring exhibition organized by the National Gallery of Canada, Ottawa. Exhibited *Painting with Red* (1957), *Breakthrough* (1958), *Paris #1* (1962), *Color Column* (1964, listed as *Color Columnal*), *Dazzle Red* (1965).

1972–73

December 2, 1972-January 2, 1973
One-man exhibition at the David Mirvish Gallery, Toronto.

'Painters Eleven 1953-1959' circulating exhibition at the Robert McLaughlin Gallery. Exhibited *Coup-de-Main with Red* (1957).

1973

May 17-June 29
One-man exhibition at André Emmerich Gallery, New York.

During this period Bush was working on the London series, for exhibition at the Waddington Galleries in London. Floating colour strokes against mottled grounds anticipate imagery of the paintings of 1975 and 1976.

June 8-July 11
'Jack Bush: Works on Paper,' one-man exhibition at the Edmonton Art Gallery, Edmonton, organized in collaboration with the David Mirvish Gallery, Toronto, and curated by Karen Wilkin. Works exhibited include *Yellow to Red Scribble* (1970), *Spring Blossoms* (1971), *Apple Blossom Burst* (1971), and *Falling Blossoms* (1971).

June 19-August 31
'Selection des œuvres de la Banque d'œuvres d'art du Conseil des Arts du Canada' at the Centre culturel canadien, Paris.

1973-4
Bush was developing the Totem series.

1974

February 9-March 5
Participated in 'Ten Years Ago' at the David Mirvish Gallery, Toronto.

March 30-April 27
One-man exhibition at André Emmerich Gallery, Zurich, Switzerland.

Participated in 'The Great Decade of American Abstraction: Modernist Art 1960-1970' at the Museum of Fine Arts, Houston, Texas.

May 21-June 15
One-man exhibition at the Waddington Galleries II, London, England.

June
Bush was working on three large-scale works on paper, one of which was chosen for a poster for the Lincoln Center 'Mostly Mozart' Festival, July 22-August 21, 1974.

October 19-24
Participated in the Cologne Art Fair, Germany.

November 16-December 4
One-man exhibition at the André Emmerich Gallery, New York.

1975

January 9-February 2
'Works of Art – Old Masters, New Masters,' Alberta College of Art Gallery, Calgary.

January 16-February 16
Participated in 'Peintres Canadiens Actuels' at the Musée d'art contemporain, Montreal.

January
'Jack Bush Print Retrospective,' a one-man exhibition of prints at the Jack Pollock Gallery, Toronto.

April 16-May 15
One-man exhibition at the Waddington Galleries, Montreal.

October 10-19
'Painters Eleven,' Sudbury Arts Festival Spectrum '75. Exhibited *Coup-de-Main with Red* (1957).

'Painters Eleven,' Tom Thomson Memorial Gallery and Museum of Fine Art, Owen Sound. Exhibited *Coup-de-Main with Red* (1957).

November 8-December 3
One-man exhibition at the David Mirvish Gallery, Toronto.

November 7-30
One-man exhibition at Prints on Prince Street, New York.

Participated in a group exhibition at Galerie Alen, Vancouver, BC.

Basel Art Fair, Switzerland.

During this time Bush was given a dictionary of musical terms. He began to title paintings with allusions to specific compositions and musical instructions. He was beginning to apply his grounds with sponges, instead of rollers, for a more gestural effect. Colour bars were applied as loose gestural strokes against sponged background.

1975-6

December 12, 1975-January 31, 1976
Participated in 'Fifty Years: The Canadian Society of Painters in Water Colour 1925-1975' at the Art Gallery of Ontario. Exhibited *Green Field and Sun* (1960).

Participated in 'Canadian Canvas' exhibition, a national touring exhibition sponsored by Time Canada. Exhibited *Thunderbird Totem* (1973) and *Dipper* (1974). Travelled to Musée d'art contemporain, Montreal, January 16-February 16, 1975; Musée du Québec, Quebec, March 6-30, 1975; Edmonton Art Gallery, April 24-May 22, 1975; Vancouver Art Gallery, June 12-July 10, 1975; Mendel Art Gallery, Saskatoon, July 24-August 21, 1975; Art Gallery of Ontario, September 6-October 11, 1975; Anna Leonowens Gallery and Dalhousie Art Gallery, Halifax, November 6-December 4, 1975; Alberta College of Art, Calgary, January 10-February 7, 1976; Winnipeg Art Gallery, February 21-March 21, 1976.

January 10-February 4
Participated in a group exhibition at the David Mirvish Gallery, Toronto, 'A Selection of Painting in Toronto.'

February 10-March 6
'Jack Bush, Recent Paintings,' a one-man exhibition at the Waddington Galleries II, London, England.

Made an Officer of the Order of Canada.

March

The National Ballet of Canada selected one of Bush's works, *Jeté en l'air* (1975), for a print.

Made a Fellow of the Ontario College of Art.

June 5-July 3

One-man exhibition at the Waddington Galleries, Montreal.

Participated in 'Changing Visions: The Canadian Landscape,' a touring exhibition organized by the Edmonton Art Gallery and the Art Gallery of Ontario. Exhibited *Lilac* (1966). The exhibition travelled to the Art Gallery of Ontario, February 13-March 21, 1976; Art Gallery of Windsor, April 7-May 9, 1976; Saidye Bronfman Centre, Montreal, May 26-June 27, 1976; De Cordova and Dana Museum, Lincoln, Mass., July 7-August 8, 1976; Edmonton Art Gallery, September 1-October 3, 1976; Winnipeg Art Gallery, October 20-November 28, 1976; Glenbow-Alberta Institute, Calgary, December 16, 1976-January 23, 1977; Burnaby Art Gallery and Simon Fraser University Art Gallery, February 5-25, 1977; and the Public Library and Art Museum, London, Ontario, March 18-April 17, 1977.

Participated in a group exhibition at Acquavella Gallery, New York.

October 2-20

One-man exhibition at André Emmerich Gallery, New York.

November 4-28

'Painters Eleven,' Kitchener-Waterloo Art Gallery. Exhibited *Coup-de-Main with Red* (1957).

During this time Bush had begun to develop the Handkerchief series of paintings, replacing the loose colour strokes of previous works with more geometric floating shapes. Continued sponged grounds.

1976-7

September 17-October 24, 1976

'Jack Bush: A Retrospective' at the Art Gallery of Ontario, Toronto, a travelling exhibition organized by the Art Gallery of Ontario and curated by Terry Fenton. The exhibition travelled to Vancouver Art Gallery, November 15-December 16, 1976; Edmonton Art Gallery, January 8-February 15, 1977; Musée d'art contemporain, Montreal, March 17-April 17, 1977; National Gallery of Canada, Ottawa, May 13-July 31, 1977. Included paintings from 1958 to 1975.

1977

January

Bush and Mabel attended the opening of 'Jack Bush: A Retrospective' at the Edmonton Art Gallery. Lectured at University of Alberta. Last interview of his life given to Wendy Brunelle for Alberta Access Television. On the way back to Toronto they stopped in Saskatoon to visit William Perehudoff and Dorothy Knowles.

January 24

Bush died suddenly of a heart attack. Last paintings left in studio include *Woodwind* (December 1976), in which he returned to a rolled ground, and *Chopsticks* (1977).

One-man exhibition at Downstairs Gallery, Edmonton. Included *Striped Tower* (1967) and *Rose Corner* (1967).

February 3-April 10

'14 Canadians: A Critic's Choice,' Hirshhorn Museum and Sculpture Garden, Smithsonian Institution, Washington, DC, curated by Andrew Hudson. *Concerto for Two Violins* (1976), *Passe Pied* (1976), and *Two Part Sonata* (1976) were shown.

November

'Eighteen Contemporary Masters,' United States Embassy, Ottawa. *Blue Arc* (1974) was shown.

1978

'Twentieth Century Masters' at the Waddington Galleries, Toronto.

'A Canadian Survey: Selected works from the Collection of Imperial Oil Limited,' a travelling exhibition. *White Over Red* (1956) was exhibited.

Summer

'Modern Painting in Canada' at the Edmonton Art Gallery. *Breakthrough* (1958) was exhibited.

July 6-August 11

'Painters Eleven 1953-1960' at Glendon Art Gallery, York University, Toronto. *Coup-de-Main with Red* (1957) was exhibited.

One-man exhibition at the Waddington Galleries, Toronto.

October 7-25

One-man exhibition at André Emmerich Gallery, New York. Works exhibited include *Summer Tan* (1961), *Blue Green Thrust* (1959), *White Thrust* (1961), *White and Blue Thrust* (1962), and *Hi Lo* (1974).

1979

March 29

One-man exhibition at the Equinox Gallery, Vancouver.

'Jack Bush,' a one-hour documentary film, was released by the National Film Board of Canada. The film, produced by Cinema Productions for the National Film Board, was produced by Rudy Buttignol and directed by Murray Battle.

October 6-31

'Jack Bush Paintings,' a one-man exhibition at the Waddington Galleries, Montreal.

November 3-28

'Jack Bush Paintings, 1929-1939,' a one-man exhibition at the Waddington Galleries, Toronto.

1979-80

November 2, 1979-January 31, 1980
'Color Abstractions, Selections from the Museum of Fine Arts, Boston,' Federal Reserve Bank Display Area, Boston. *Striped Column* (1964) was exhibited.

October 30, 1979-November 30, 1981
'Painters Eleven in Retrospect,' a travelling exhibition organized by the Robert McLaughlin Gallery, Oshawa. *Reflection* (1955), *November #9* (1956), *November #24* (1956), *Coup-de-Main with Red* (1957), *Storm #2* (1959), *Breakthrough* (1958), and *Painting with Red* (1957) were exhibited. The exhibition travelled to Stratford, Windsor, London, Kingston, Toronto, Montreal, Fredericton, Halifax, Saskatoon, Kitchener, and Guelph.

1980

'L'Amérique aux Indépendants,' Société des Artistes Indépendants, Grand Palais, Paris.

One-man exhibition at the Waddington Galleries, Toronto.

One-man exhibition at the Waddington Galleries, Montreal.

August-December
'Jack Bush Paintings and Drawings 1955-1976,' a one-man exhibition curated by Duncan Macmillan and organized by the Arts Council of Great Britain at the Edinburgh Festival. Works exhibited include *Culmination* (1955), *Painting with Red* (1957), *Mute Beginning* (1958), and *Sharp Flats* (1976). The exhibition travelled to London and Birmingham.

September 2-October 18
One-man exhibition at Downstairs Gallery, Edmonton.

September 6-October 19
'10 Canadian Artists in the 1970s,' organized by the Art Gallery of Ontario (toured Europe in 1981). Works exhibited include *Basin Street Blues* (1974), *Hot Time* (1976), *Sundance* (1976), *Teeter* (1976), and *Flyaway* (1976).

October 11-November 19
'Jack Bush: A Selection 1961-65,' a one-man exhibition at Robert Elkon Gallery, New York. The introduction to the exhibition catalogue was written by Clement Greenberg. Works exhibited included *Green on White* (1961) and *Zing Green* (1961).

November 29-December 31
One-man exhibition at Klonaridis Gallery, Toronto.

1981

February 5-28
'Jack Bush Paintings 1973 to 1976,' a one-man exhibition at André Emmerich Gallery, New York. Works exhibited include *Totem Spread* (1973), *Mood Indigo* (1976), *Woodwind* (1976), and *London #4* (1973).

March 18-April 9
'Jack Bush, Works on Paper 1958-1962,' a one-man exhibition at Theo Waddington Galleries, Toronto. Works exhibited include *Chelsea Hotel – Black Spot* (1962), *Red Centre* (1957), *November #10* (1956), *Study* (1958), *Four in Summer* (1960), and *Blue Thrust to Yellow* (1960).

1981-2
'The Heritage of Jack Bush: A Tribute,' curated by Ken Carpenter and organized by the Robert McLaughlin Gallery, Oshawa. Among the Bush works exhibited were *Red Hook* (1971), *Spring Breeze* (1971), and *Upway* (1970). The exhibition travelled from July 1981 to January 1983.

1982-3

December 5, 1982-January 30, 1983
'Canada at the Akademie der Kunste of Berlin,' a major multidisciplinary presentation organized by Akademie der Kunste, the Canada Council, and the Department of External Affairs. 'OKanada,' Historical Canadian Painting curated by Dennis Reid. *Village Procession* (1946), *Scarecrow* (1951), *Theme Variation #2* (1955), *November #24* (1956), *Painting with Red* (1957), *Awning* (1966), *Green Fin* (1963), and *Basie Blues* (1975) were exhibited.

1983

October 1-20
'Jack Bush, A Survey: 1959-1976,' a one-man exhibition at Gallery One, Toronto. Works exhibited include *Let Them All Fall* (1959), *Split Circle #2* (1961), and *Dorothy's Coat* (1972).

Selected Bibliography

1951

'In the Editor's Confidence.' *Maclean's*, 15 March 1951, 29

1952

'Jack Bush Exhibit.' *Saturday Night*, 29 March 1952, 20 (review: Roberts Gallery)

1962

Harper, J.R. 'Three Centuries of Canadian Painting.' *Canadian Art*, November/December 1962, 440

1963

Fried, Michael. 'New York Letter.' *Art International*, 25 May 1963, 71 (review: Robert Elkon Gallery)

Hudson, Andrew, 'Canada Letter: A Report Looks at Toronto Painting.' *Canadian Art*, November/December 1963, 339

McPherson, Hugo. 'Jack Bush at the Gallery Moos, Toronto.' *Canadian Art*, January/February 1963, 8

Munro, E.C. *Art News*, summer 1963, 17 (review: Robert Elkon Gallery)

1964

Campbell, L. *Art News*, December 1964, 15 (review: Robert Elkon Gallery)

Hudson, Andrew. 'Canada Letter: a Report from Saskatchewan.' *Art International*, 25 April 1964, 83-4 (review: Fifth Biennial of Canada Painting at the Norman Mackenzie Art Gallery)

Hudson, Andrew. 'Canada's Place in Abstract Art Today: Thoughts from an Exhibition at the Jewish Museum, N.Y.' *Canadian Forum*, May 1964, 27-8

Hudson, Andrew. 'Some Saskatchewan Painters.' *Art International*, May 1964, 27

Hudson, Andrew. 'Correspondence to the Editor.' *Canadian Forum*, November 1964, 177-8 (reply to letters by J.B. Lord and R.D. Mathews on Hudson's article 'Canada's Place in Abstract Art Today')

Langsner, Jules. 'What's Next after Abstract Expressionism?' *Canadian Art*, September/October 1964, 283

Los Angeles County Museum of Art. *Post Painterly Abstraction*, 1964. Foreword by James Elliott, text by Clement Greenberg. Reprinted *Art International*, summer 1964, 63-5

Phillipson, Don. 'Arts: Of Painting and Painters.' *Quest*, November/December 1964, 18-20

Rose, Barbara. 'New York Letter.' *Art International*, December 1964, 50 (review: Robert Elkon Gallery)

1965

Burr, J. *Apollo*, October 1965 (review: Waddington Galleries, London)

Hudson, Andrew. 'Jack Bush: A Traditional Modern.' *Art International*, February 1965, 17-19

Lynton, Norbert. 'London Letter.' *Art International*, 20 November 1965, 33 (review: Waddington Galleries)

Russell, John. 'Art News from London.' *Art News*, December 1965, 55 (review: Waddington Galleries)

San Francisco Museum of Art. *Colorists* 1950-1965, 15 October-21 November 1965. Foreword by Anita Ventura

Wolfram, Eddie. 'Jack Bush: Waddington Galleries.' *The Arts Review*, 16 October 1965

1966

Campbell, L. *Art News*, March 1966, 11-12 (review: André Emmerich Gallery)

Hudson, Andrew. 'Jack Bush: Five Color Prints.' *Art International*, April 1966, 2. Foreword to portfolio published by David Mirvish Gallery, Toronto, December 1965

Krauss, Rosalind. *Artforum*, May 1966, 49 (review: André Emmerich Gallery)

Lippard, Lucy R. 'New York Letter: Off Colour.' *Art International*, April 1966, 74-5 (review: André Emmerich Gallery)

Zimmerman, Sidney. 'In the Galleries: Jack Bush.' *Arts Magazine*, April 1966, 60 (review: André Emmerich Gallery, New York)

1967

Ashton, Dore. 'ıx Biennal de Sao Paulo: Notes from an Innocent Abroad.' *Arts Magazine*, November 1967, 29

Blakeston, Oswell. *Arts Review*, 18 February 1967 (review: Waddington Galleries)

Boston Institute of Contemporary Art. *Nine Canadians*, 19 May-21 June 1967. Statement by Sue M. Thurman, artists' biographies by Barry Lord

Bowness, Alan. 'Sao Paulo: Impressions of the Biennial.' *Studio International*, November 1967, 218

Brunelle, A. *Art News*, November 1967, 11 (review: André Emmerich Gallery)

Hudson, Andrew. 'The 1967 Pittsburgh International.' *Art International*, Christmas 1967, 57-64

Lord, Barry. 'Discover Canada.' *Art in America*, May-June 1967, 82

Lucie-Smith, Edward. 'London Commentary.' *Studio International*, April 1967, 198 (review: Waddington Galleries)

Lynton, Norbert. 'London Letter.' *Art International*, 20 April 1967, 49 (review: Waddington Galleries)

MacDonald, C.S. *A Dictionary of Canadian Artists*, ı (Ottawa 1967), 108

Malcolmson, Harry. 'Painting: A retrospective to forget.' *Saturday Night*, December 1967, 51 (review: Sao Paulo)

Mellow, James. 'New York.' *Art International*, 20 November 1967, 61 (review: André Emmerich Gallery)

Sao Paulo, Brazil. *Jacques Hurtubise and Jack Bush*. Canada at Sao Paulo, ıx, Biennial 1967. Introduction by Jean-René Ostiguy

Stratford, Rothman's Art Gallery; Saint John, New Brunswick Museum. *Ten Decades 1867-1967 Ten Painters*, 1967

Regina, Norman Mackenzie Art Gallery. *Statements* 18 *Canadian Artists*, 16 November-17 December 1967. Introduction by Avrom Isaacs

Wasserman, E. *Artforum*, November 1967, 60 (review: André Emmerich Gallery)

Whittet, G.S. 'The Biennial of Sao Paulo.' *Art International*, 20 November 1967, 36-42

1968

Aarons, Anita. 'Servicing the Arts for Architecture.' *Architecture Canada*, November 1968, 25–7

Edinburgh International Festival *Canada* 101, 18 August-7 September 1968. Introduction by David P. Silcox

Fenton, Terry. 'Looking at Canadian Art.' *Artforum*, September 1968, 55-60

Henault, Gilles. 'L'art contemporain à son musée.' *Culture Vivante*, August 1968, 14-21

'Jack Bush.' *Allied Arts Catalogue*, October 1968, 21

Kennedy, R.C. 'Paris.' *Art International*, 20 March 1968, 68-9 (review: 'Canadian Art' at Musée national d'art moderne)

Lord, Barry. 'Jack Bush: David Mirvish Gallery.' *Artscanada*, April 1968, 46-7

Paris, Musée national d'art moderne. *Canada: art d'aujourd'hui*, 12 January-18 February 1968. Introduction by Jean Sutherland Boggs

Silcox, David P. 'First-hand Familiarity with Canadian Art; at the Edinburgh Festival.' *Connoisseur*, August 1968, 273-9

'The Arts: Coming of Age in Edinburgh.' *Time* (Canada Edition), 30 August 1968, 77 (review: *Canada* 101)

'The Arts: Late Starter.' *Time* (Canada Edition), 22 November 1968, 22-3

Thompson, David. 'A Canadian Scene: 2.' *Studio International*, November 1968, 181-5

1969

Barker, John. 'Canadian Critics and the Season.' *Arts Magazine*, April 1969, 53-4 (review: Galerie Godard-Lefort)

Burr, J. 'London Galleries: Barbaric Beasts.' *Apollo*, September 1969, 255 (review: Waddington Galleries)

Bush, Jack. 'Letter to the editor.' *Artscanada*, June 1969, 55

Fenton, Terry. 'In Terms of Colour: Jack Bush.' *Artforum*, May 1969, 36-9

Lord, Barry. 'Jack Bush.' *Artscanada*, February 1969, 41 (review: David Mirvish Gallery)

Malcolmson, Harry. 'Art: Jack Bush's excellence as a painter is any one of two reasons why he's given Canadian art a new sense of confidence.' *Saturday Night*, March 1969, 46

Reid, Dennis. 'Jack Bush.' *Artscanada*, April 1969, 42-3 (review: Galerie Godard-Lefort)

Swartz, Burrell. 'Letter to the editor.' *Saturday Night*, 17 May 1969

1970

Buffalo, Albright-Knox Gallery, *Color and Field*, 1970. Introduction by Priscilla Colt

Fenton, Terry. 'Jack Bush.' *Artscanada*, June 1970, 42-3

Fenton, Terry. 'The David Mirvish Opening Show.' *Artscanada*, December 1970, 57-8 (review: David Mirvish Gallery)

Hale, Barrie. 'Canada.' *Arts Magazine*, February 1970, 52

'Huge American Abstracts Open the Expanded Mirvish Gallery.' *Toronto Calendar Magazine*, September 1970

Malcolmson, Harry. 'Art: What exactly is people's art?' *Saturday Night*, November 1970, 52, 57

Pittsburgh, Museum of Art, Carnegie Institute. *Pittsburgh International Exhibition of Contemporary Art*, 1970. Statement by artists

Ratcliff, Carter. 'New York Letter.' *Art International*, December 1970, 65-6 (review: André Emmerich Gallery)

Ratcliff, Carter. 'Jack Bush.' *Art News*, December 1970, 12 (review: André Emmerich Gallery)

Regina, Norman Mackenzie Art Gallery. *Jack Bush*, spring 1970. Text by Terry Fenton, reprinted and amended for *Artscanada*, June 1970, 42-3

Townsend, William, ed. 'Canadian Art Today.' *Studio International*, 1970, 33, 42, 85, 108

1971

Burr, J. 'A Balanced Judgement.' *Apollo*, October 1971, 309 (review: Waddington Galleries)

Domingo, Willis. 'Color Abstractionism: A Survey of Recent American Painting.' *Arts Magazine*, December/January 1971, 34-40

Greenwood, Michael. 'Jack Bush.' *Artscanada*, June/July 1971, 71

Millard, Charles. 'Jack Bush.' *Hudson Review*, spring 1971, 145-52

Moffett, Kenworth. 'Jack Bush: Illusions of Transparency.' *Art News*, March 1971, 42-5

Plagens, Peter. 'Los Angeles.' *Artforum*, April 1971, 84 (review: Nicholas Wilder Gallery)

Sarasota, Florida, John and Mabel Ringling Museum of Art. *49th Parallels: New Canadian Art*, 1971. Introduction by Dennis Young

1972

Belz, Carl. 'Deliberating with Color, Drawing with Light.' *Art in America*, May-June 1972, 114-16 (review: Museum of Fine Arts, Boston)

Bordon, Lizzie. *Artforum*, June 1972, 83-4 (review: André Emmerich Gallery)

Boston, Museum of Fine Arts. *Abstract Painting in the 70s: A Selection*, 4 April-21 May 1972. Introduction by Kenworth Moffett

Elderfield, John. 'Abstract Painting in the 70s: A Selection.' *Art International*, summer 1972, 92-4 (review: exhibition Museum of Fine Arts, Boston)

Fenton, Terry. 'Jack Bush's Recent Paintings.' *Art International*, summer 1972, 26-8

Hudson, Andrew. 'Boston Letter.' *Studio International*, April 1972, 162-3 (review: Museum of Fine Arts, Boston)

Marshall, W. Neil. 'Toronto Letter.' *Art International*, November 1972, 59-60

Ottawa, National Gallery of Canada. *Toronto Painting: 1953-1965* (Ottawa 1972). Introduction by Barrie Hale

Rose, Barbara. 'Homage to the Sixties: The Green Gallery Revisited.' *New York*, 20 March 1972, 72-3

Smith, Alvin. 'New York Letter.' *Art International*, May 1972, 58 (review: André Emmerich Gallery)

Withrow, William. *Contemporary Canadian Painting* (Toronto 1972), 49-56

1973

Baker, Kenneth. 'Toronto: Notes from an Exploratory Expedition.' *Art in America*, March/April 1973, 88-93

Elderfield, John. 'Painterliness Redefined: Jules Olitski and Recent Abstract Art, Pt. II.' *Art International*, April 1973, 36-41

Frank, Peter. *Art News*, September 1973, 85 (review: André Emmerich Gallery)

Marshall, W. Neil. 'Toronto Letter.' *Art International*, summer 1973, 40 (review: David Mirvish Gallery)

Reid, Dennis. *A Concise History of Canadian Painting* (Toronto 1973)

1974

Fenton, Terry. 'High Culture in Prairie Canada.' *Art News*, September 1974, 27-9

Fulford, Robert. 'Art on the Edge of Empire.' *Art News*, September 1974, 22-6

Kim, Whee. 'A Personal Definition of Pictorial Space.' *Arts Magazine*, November 1974, 74-8

Marshall, W. Neil. 'Style, Toronto and Younger Art.' *Studio International*, July/August 1974, 38-40

McCaughey, Patrick. 'Sydney Ball.' *Art International*, 20 October 1974, 50-2

McClean, John. 'Jack Bush: Recent Paintings.' *Studio International*, July/August 1974, 27-9

Nasgaard, Roald. 'Toronto: Jack Bush at David Mirvish.' *Arts Magazine*, June 1974, 70-1

1975

Greenwood, Michael. 'The Canadian Canvas.' *Artscanada*, March 1975, 1-16

Hale, Barrie. 'Still Knocking Them Out of the Park. Jack Bush at 66: a fully original master.' *The Canadian*, 27 December 1975, 10-13

Hudson, Andrew. 'Notes on Eight Toronto Painters.' *Art International*, October 1975, 23-5

Kaplan, Patricia. 'Jack Bush.' *Art News*, January 1975, 24 (review: André Emmerich Gallery)

Marshall, W. Neil. 'Jack Bush.' *Arts Magazine*, February 1975, 24 (review: André Emmerich Gallery)

1976

Dion, Thérèse. 'Ascension de trois artistes canadiens sur le marché de l'art: Jack Bush, Yves Gaucher, David Rabinowitch.' Mémoire de Maitrise des Arts (Histoire de l'art), Université de Montréal, December 1976

Toronto, Art Gallery of Ontario. *Jack Bush: A Retrospective*. Introduction by Terry Fenton. 'Reminiscences' by Jack Bush

1977

Burnett, David. 'Jack Bush at the National Gallery of Canada.' *Art in America*, July/August 1977, 102

Carpenter, Ken. 'The Inspiration of Jack Bush.' *Art International*, July/August 1977, 19-27

Heinrich, T.A. 'Jack Bush: A Retrospective.' *Artscanada*, March/April 1977, 1-10

'Jack Bush: Painter helped launch Canada's abstract school in late fifties.' Toronto, *Globe and Mail*, 25 January 1977. Obituary

Nasgaard, Roald. 'Jack Bush: Conservation et reduction.' *Vie des Arts*, printemps 1977, 32-8

Rosenbaum, L. *Art in America*, March 1977, 166. Obituary

Washington, DC, Hirshhorn Museum and Sculpture Garden, Smithsonian Institution. *14 Canadians: A Critic's Choice*. Introduction by Andrew Hudson

1978

Fenton, Terry and Karen Wilkin. *Modern Painting in Canada* (Edmonton 1978)

1979

Carpenter, Ken. 'New York: Jack Bush at the André Emmerich Gallery.' *Art Magazine*, May/June 1979, 90-2

Freedman, Adele. 'Film on Bush mirrors the Man.' Toronto, *Globe and Mail*, 17 May 1979

Oshawa, Ontario, Robert McLaughlin Gallery. *Painters Eleven in Retrospect*. Introduction by Joan Murray. Painters Eleven exhibition history by Jennifer C. Watson

Woods, Kay. *Artscanada*, December 1979/January 1980, 74 (review: Waddington Galleries, Toronto)

1980

Edinburgh, Talbot Rice Art Centre, University of Edinburgh, in association with the Edinburgh Festival. *Jack Bush: Paintings and Drawings 1955-1976*. Introduction by Duncan Macmillan. 'Reminiscences' by Jack Bush. Interview with Bush by Art Cuthbertson

Kramer, Hilton. 'A Garden for the Eye: The Paintings of Jack Bush.' *Artscanada*, December 1980/January 1981, 12-17

New York, Robert Elkon Gallery. *Jack Bush, a Selection: 1961-65*. Introduction by Clement Greenberg

Shipway, Alan. 'Jack Bush at the Talbot Rice Art Centre, Edinburgh.' *Art Scribe*, October 1980, 51

Toronto, Art Gallery of Ontario. *10 Canadian Artists in the 1970s*, an exhibition for European tour. Introduction by Roald Nasgaard. 'Reminiscences' by Jack Bush

1981

Dellamora, Richard. 'Jack Bush: A Film.' *Art Magazine*, September/October 1981, 30-2

Frank, E. 'Robert Elkon Gallery, New York.' *Art in America*, January 1981, 124

Murray, Joan. 'Jack Bush in Great Britain.' *Art Magazine*, February/March 1981, 27-30

Nemiroff, Diana. 'Les Plasticiens and The Painters Eleven', *Vanguard*, September 1981, 20-25

Wilkin, Karen. 'Ten Canadians and How a Controversy Grew'. *Art News*, February 1981, 104-107

1983

Fenton, Terry. 'A Selection of Paintings from Edmonton Collections', *Update*, May/June 1983, 8-12

Illustrations

PHOTO CREDITS
Jane Corkin p.6, p.84; Gilbert and John Milne p.8; Iris McCaig, p.29; Karol Ike p.34, p.48; Cora Kelley Ward p.60.